THE LAST CAMEL CHARGE

Other Books by Forrest Bryant Johnson

THE LAST CAMEL CHARGE

The Untold Story of America's Desert Military Experiment

FORREST BRYANT JOHNSON

BERKLEY CALIBER, NEW YORK

THE BERKLEY PUBLISHING GROUP
Published by the Penguin Group
Penguin Group (USA) Inc.
375 Hudson Street, New York, New York 10014, USA

Penguin Group (Canada), 90 Eglinton Avenue East, Suite 700, Toronto, Ontario M4P 2Y3, Canada (a division of Pearson Penguin Canada Inc.) • Penguin Books Ltd., 80 Strand, London WC2R 0RL, England • Penguin Group Ireland, 25 St. Stephen's Green, Dublin 2, Ireland (a division of Penguin Books Ltd.) • Penguin Group (Australia), 250 Camberwell Road, Camberwell, Victoria 3124, Australia (a division of Pearson Australia Group Pty. Ltd.) • Penguin Books India Pvt. Ltd., 11 Community Centre, Panchsheel Park, New Delhi—110 017, India • Penguin Group (NZ), 67 Apollo Drive, Rosedale, Auckland 0632, New Zealand (a division of Pearson New Zealand Ltd.) • Penguin Books (South Africa) (Pty.) Ltd., 24 Sturdee Avenue, Rosebank, Johannesburg 2196, South Africa

Penguin Books Ltd., Registered Offices: 80 Strand, London WC2R 0RL, England

This book is an original publication of the Berkley Publishing Group.

Copyright © 2012 by Forrest Bryant Johnson
Book design by Laura K. Corless

FIRST EDITION: April 2012

Library of Congress Cataloging-in-Publication Data

Johnson, F. B.
The last camel charge : the untold story of America's desert military experiment / Forrest Bryant Johnson.
p. cm.
ISBN 978-0-425-24569-9
1. United States. Army. Camel Corps—History. 2. Camels—Southwest, New—History—19th century. 3. Southwest, New—History—1848– I. Title.
UC350.J64 2012
357—dc23
2011038454

PRINTED IN THE UNITED STATES OF AMERICA

10 9 8 7 6 5 4 3 2 1

Edward Beale's Route (dotted line)

COURTESY OF MASTER SERGEANT ED HINES, USMC (RET.)

Utah Territory and the Mormons' proposed state.

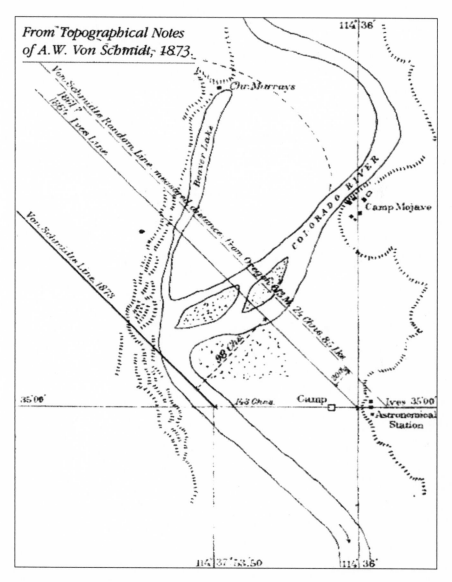

1873 map shows the location of Beaver Lake in what is now
Nevada. Beale's Trail (the Mojave Trail) is indicated by a dotted
line at the northern edge of the lake. From the "Topographical
Notes" of A. W. Von Schmidt.

Death Valley location

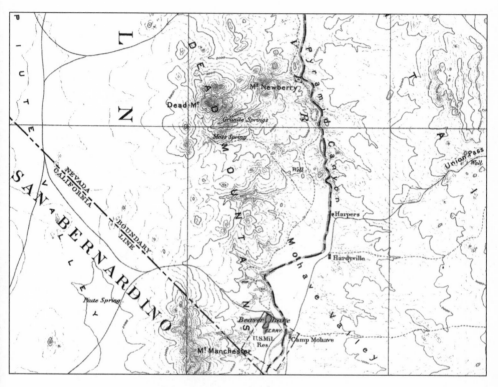

Beaver Lake. 1892 map of Camp Mojave. Beale's Trail indicated
by a line parallel to the Colorado River (Pyramid Canyon)
proceeding from Hardyville (now Bullhead City, Arizona, area),
crossing at Camp Mojave, passing above Beaver Lake.
Topography H. M. Wilson, 1892; from 1884 work by Henry
Gannen and the 1876 Powell Survey.

It takes much to bring down a charging camel!

Lieutenant Colonel T. E. Lawrence (of Arabia)

THE LAST CAMEL CHARGE

INTRODUCTION

The story began for me years ago on a hot August afternoon as I drove from Las Vegas to Laughlin, Nevada. South of the old mining town of Searchlight, I turned onto Highway 163, which corkscrews its way down a steep hill to the Colorado River. A lonely, weathered historical marker caught my attention and I pulled off the road to learn what could have occurred of importance in that barren part of the Mojave Desert.

A blast of hot, dry air greeted me as I stepped from the car. My eyes squinted in the brilliant sun that baked the black, rocky landscape around me.

The Camel Corps, the marker said. I read on, learning that a Lieutenant Edward F. Beale surveyed a wagon road through New Mexico, Arizona, and Nevada while testing the fitness of *camels*. They crossed the Colorado River near this spot in 1857.

Camels in Nevada? Edward Beale was a naval officer, a hero of the Mexican War. What was a navy man doing in the middle of the Mojave Desert? Where did he get the camels?

I spoke with a local historian who assured me that camels did pass

through the Southwest in the mid-1800s and he told of a battle between Indians and men riding camels at Beaver Lake in southern
Nevada.

Fascinated, I scanned a Nevada highway map but found no Beaver
Lake. Had it been a mirage, a figment of someone's imagination? A
navy officer leading an expedition through a desert, men riding camels
and fighting Indians, a lake that did not exist; I doubted the story.

Some years later, as I admired a friend's tattered 1873 map of Nevada, I made an interesting discovery. There was Beaver Lake! It appeared as an oblong spot on the map next to the Colorado River at the
southern tip of the state.

So, Edward Beale and the lake did exist. But what was the truth
about the camels?

To completely understand the camel story, it is necessary to connect a chain of historical events that form like a picture puzzle. Each
link is, in itself, a story of the involvement of brave, dedicated Americans from many ethnic backgrounds, working together in a harsh,
dangerous environment to accomplish a mission.

Soon a Civil War would split the country apart. But violence had
already infected parts of the United States. Whites were killing one
another in Kansas over the slavery issue, Indians and emigrants were
fighting in the West, and the United States and the Mormons in Utah
Territory were on the brink of total war.

To protect our citizens on the frontier, the army needed a new
weapon, something stronger than mules to carry supplies and faster
than horses for the cavalry.

For a few years, camels imported by the army played a vital role in
the history of the American West. Then, as if in a final charge, the
adventure came to an abrupt end.

CHAPTER 1

Old Douglas

Who is the slayer, who the victim? Speak!

Sophocles, Antigone *(442 BC)*

Vicksburg, Mississippi
The Civil War
May 1863

"They killed Old Douglas?" The frantic shout of a Confederate soldier on a smoke-shrouded hill pierced through the cracking sound of rifle shots.

Another soldier dead, a friend known by only one name. They could not call him "Private" or "Sergeant" or "sir" because he had not been given a rank. But to the Union sniper who shot him, Douglas was a rebel and deserved to die.

Did Douglas have a family? No one knew. He never spoke of family or home. He left no personal papers or possessions. But friends he did have, through the ranks from privates to colonels. And the Confederate army maintained his service record, which was sprinkled with notations of acts of bravery.

Douglas's history began during the Battle of Corinth a few months earlier. At least, that is when the men first met him. And that is when

General Ulysses S. Grant's Union Army began to drive the Confederates into a retreat from Tennessee to the river town of Vicksburg.

Now Grant had his former Mexican War colleague Lieutenant General John C. Pemberton and his rebel army trapped with their backs against the Mississippi River.

Union gunboats were patrolling the river, bombarding the city, while Grant's land forces pushed toward rebel fortifications.

Grant became impatient as the hours passed. His large reinforcement army was still days behind, so, on May 19, he launched an assault against rebel defense lines. That was a mistake. Testing those lines cost him heavy loss of lives. He reorganized and tried another attack on the twenty-second and again was driven back.

Grant needed a better plan. Storming rebel lines only cost lives. So he tried a new tactic. He would starve the city and its defending army into submission. The siege of Vicksburg began.

During this siege, the northern section of General Pemberton's defenses was held by the 43rd Mississippi Infantry Regiment, also known as the "Bloody 43rd." Their redoubt consisted of a series of trenches, bunkers, and a few forward pits for sharpshooters. This network followed along the base of a small hill and then linked with the defenses of another unit.

Despite all the protection, Union fire had been heavy, seemingly unending, and the 43rd's casualties mounted as the siege days crept by.

Replacements of all ages came from the city to fill the vacant ranks. Men from early teens and in their seventies fought side by side in a vain effort to drive the "Yankees" away.

Company A of the 43rd received Douglas as a replacement, assigned personally by Colonel William H. Moore. The big fellow must have been the colonel's friend, the men concluded, for he carried special orders instructing that he serve only as a noncombatant and never be exposed to enemy fire. Apparently, Douglas had earned that privilege.

In fact, Douglas wore no uniform when he arrived, and to add to the mystery, the transfer orders did not mention his rank or even a last name.

Colonel Moore was killed during the Battle of Corinth and with him died the details of Douglas's personal history.

But men from Company B claimed that Douglas once served with their unit and answered directly to Lieutenant William Hargrove. They reported that the lieutenant transferred Douglas to Colonel Moore. Then Hargrove disappeared during the Corinth battle, reportedly wounded and captured by Union soldiers.

At least papers attached to Douglas's transfer orders revealed something of his performance in combat. Douglas first served in the battle of Iuka a little south of Corinth near the Tennessee-Mississippi border. His unit citation read, "He stood bravely in the face of Union fire as his friends fell around him."

At the battle of the "Rail Roads" during the Confederate retreat, another certificate stated, "He faced the enemy bravely."

Soon the men of Company A learned that Douglas might be special, but he followed orders without hesitation. He was friendly, and even though somewhat "slow" and "simple-minded," he worked hard, always eager to help his new friends. If ordered to carry heavy band instruments for the unit or even cooking equipment, Douglas did so without complaint, earning the respect of everyone.

The men nicknamed him "Old Douglas," though no one knew his true age. Perhaps the affectionate name was a result of Douglas's gray whiskers. But there were many soldiers with gray whiskers. Few shaved, expecting death at any moment. And there wasn't enough water to shave with anyway.

A unit officer recorded in his diary, "Old Douglas was a quiet, peaceful fellow and a general favorite. A non-combatant who accomplished his work without rank or reward."[1]

On that hot, humid afternoon of June 27, 1863, Douglas stood silently, observing the battle from a grassy hill safely behind the lines, a little north of his unit's third redoubt.

In battle, death never discriminates; the young and old, the educated, the simple can fall until death's appetite is satisfied. At Vicksburg, death remained no stranger to soldiers, North or South. By June
27, the Confederates had lost more than 4,300 men, the Union almost
an equal number. And more would die that day.

It was 3 P.M. when a rebel soldier at the third redoubt repeated a
cry: "Douglas has been shot!"

The news traveled through the trenches like a brushfire. Then
someone yelled, "Murderers! Yankee murderers!"

Everyone had lost friends during the siege, but this death was different. The killers of their defenseless friend demanded retribution.

One squad of soldiers in the forward trench fastened bayonets and
prepared to charge Union positions. Officers raced among angry troops
restoring order. They knew that certain death waited for those who
entered the open area separating the warring armies.

Lieutenant Colonel Robert S. Bevier of the First Missouri Brigade
was standing behind the third redoubt, not far from the body of Douglas, when he received a report from a young captain. "We are calming
the men," the officer stated. "They are enraged at this useless cruelty!"

"Return to your unit," Colonel Bevier replied. "Tell them I share
their anger. I was standing on this hill. I saw Douglas fall, pierced by
an intentional discharge. The shot was no accident, no ricochet. Say to
your men, *there will be justice!*"

Colonel Bevier recorded the details of the event. His story continues.

"All who saw the murder were highly incensed. I was endeavoring
to discover through my fieldglass the perpetrator of the deed when I
saw a Federal officer standing in front of a patch of woods, so distant
that with the naked eye, only a dark line would be seen. He, too, was
using a large lorgnette. I waved my sword and then my handkerchief
to both of which he responded.

"Shortly I noticed a little puff of smoke by his side and could have
dodged the shot as we frequently did from long range, but the distance
was so great that I apprehended no danger and stood firm. The bullet

passed my head, however, and plumped into the bank at my back with a zip.

"This followed so close in time to the murder of Douglas and was treachery of the worse kind, almost equal to the violation of a truce."[2]

Colonel Bevier called for six of his best snipers. It was time for revenge. He directed their attention to the Union officer. The riflemen fired "simultaneously." They saw the enemy officer throw up his arms and fall to his knees.

Later the colonel learned that the man they shot, the murderer of Douglas, "was a major of an Iowa regiment." The colonel's report ends, "I refused to hear his name and was rejoiced to learn that he had been severely wounded."[3]

The death of Douglas had been avenged, and the battle continued.

Despite their gallant stand, the starving soldiers and civilians of Vicksburg could finally take no more. On July 4, 1863, General Pemberton surrendered after negotiations yielded a very reasonable arrangement.

General Grant offered lenient terms. Confederate soldiers were permitted to leave the city with their personal possessions and "paroled to return home." Officers were allowed to keep their "side arms" (pistol, sword, and knife) and staff and cavalry officers could retain "one horse each."

Confederates killed at Vicksburg have been remembered by loved ones who had names of the fallen engraved in stone markers.

Over the years, the Sons of Confederate Veterans collected data on units, including the 43rd, assuring each soldier a place in recorded history. But one name haunted historians because so little was known of the personal life: Douglas.

In 1893, thirty years after the fall of Vicksburg, J. W. Cook, a surviving member of Company A, wrote an article for the *Confederate Veteran Magazine*. It included this statement about a friend who could not speak for himself. "Douglas was faithful. His service merits record."[4]

Douglas had many friends but no family to erect a marker in his memory.

Recently, Wayne McMaster, historian and member of the Sons of Confederate Veterans of Mississippi, organized a committee and raised funds for a suitable memorial for Douglas.

Today, in Vicksburg's Cedar Hill Cemetery, at a section known as Soldier's Rest, rows of white granite stones silently mark Confederate graves. In one area reserved for members of Company A, 43rd Mississippi Infantry, a new stone serves as a lasting memorial for a simple soldier.

Engraved near the top of the stone is a Confederate flag and below, the only name in unit records: Douglas. A few words follow regarding his combat history, but no last name, place of birth, or rank is given. All that remains "unknown."

We do know something of his appearance. His profile was chiseled into the stone. It is reported to be a fair likeness. And now future generations will know . . . Old Douglas was a *camel*.

Why was a camel serving in the Confederate army during the Battle of Vicksburg? Where did he come from?

The answers were hidden in National Archives records. They tell of a strange U.S. Army experiment that began only a few years before the first shots of the Civil War were fired.

CHAPTER 2

The Mormons Move West

. . . for open defiance of the laws, the Mormons must be treated as enemies and must be exterminated or driven from the State . . .

Filburn Boggs, Governor of Missouri,
Extermination Order 44, October 27, 1838
(Rescinded 1976)

The fears of settlers at Haun's Mill materialized into horrible reality on October 30, 1838. These seventy-five families, living peacefully along the banks of Shoal Creek in Coldwell County, Missouri, worried that a militia from nearby counties might soon attack their community. They had good reason for concern; they were Mormons. At 4 P.M. that crisp autumn afternoon, 250 mounted militiamen suddenly rode into their village.

The Mormons had a plan in case of an attack. Women carrying small children ran into the nearby woods to hide, but they could not outdistance the men on horses. Many were thrown to the ground and raped.

Their men managed to retreat to a log cabin that served as a blacksmith shop. They found little safety there because the building had been constructed with logs spaced wide apart. Militiamen easily forced rifle barrels through the openings and fired on the defenders, and the cabin quickly became a killing zone.

In a few minutes, eighteen Mormons were dead, including two boys, ages nine and ten. A seventy-eight-year-old man handed over his rifle in an attempt to surrender. The militia shot him, then hacked his body into pieces with corn knives. Thirteen other Mormons were wounded.

The militia was not done. Many of the dead were mutilated, then their bodies were dropped into a well. Clothing was removed from the wounded and stolen (not an unusual practice in pioneer days for the victor to take the clothing of the victim). Horses, livestock, wagons, and home items were also stolen.[1]

The Haun's Mill massacre was over in less than an hour, the militia suffering a few wounded, none killed. Fifty-five militiamen involved in the killing were named by the survivors, including a county sheriff, a clerk, and members of the Missouri state legislature. None were ever brought to justice and it remains unknown if they were reacting to the Missouri Extermination Order Number 44 or had planned the attack on their own.

From the eastern states to Ohio and on into Missouri, the Church of Jesus Christ of Latter-Day Saints—the Mormons—suffered persecution, yet they continued to experience a remarkable increase in followers. This was a time when religions were forming quickly in the United States, and many, just as quickly, crumbled. Some were questioning the principles of traditional Christian religions and many sought a "true religion." Joseph Smith, the founder of the Mormon faith, promised that true religion. And the growth in numbers of the Mormon faith, their ability to function as an organization, frightened many non-Mormons who viewed them more as a "cult" than a true religion.

Wherever the Latter-Day Saints tried to find peace and an environment to practice their religion without outside interference, the situation soon became hostile. After the massacre at Haun's Mill, Joseph Smith knew it was time to relocate. He moved his church and followers to Commerce, Illinois, along the Mississippi River, and changed the town's name to Nauvoo (Hebrew, "to be beautiful").

It was 1839 and political parties in Illinois recognized the value of thousands of new voters. In 1840, Joseph Smith was granted broad powers, including the authority to create his own militia, which he named the Nauvoo Legion. By 1844, the legion's ranks included well-trained disciplined regiments of infantry and cavalry. They totaled 3,000 men at a time when the entire U.S. Army consisted of about 8,500.[2]

The legion was permitted to draw weapons from the United States, and though it was designed and authorized for the protection of the city of Nauvoo (the population was mostly Mormon), it could also be activated by the governor or the president.

Joseph Smith, mayor of Nauvoo, was also lieutenant general of the legion.

In 1843, the Mormons petitioned Congress, requesting that it declare Nauvoo and its surrounding area "independent territory"; then Smith announced he would run for president of the United States as a "third party." He organized a "council of 50," a secret organization having the authority to decide which national and state laws they needed to obey.

Soon popular opinion throughout the state turned against Smith and newspapers began to attack both him and his religion. In the spring of 1844, a dispute developed between Smith and several close associates, partly due to the doctrine promoting plural marriage. Smith's critics published a paper calling for reform in the church and announced that some members, including Smith, were practicing polygamy. Smith denied it but had the printing press destroyed.

Then the Carthage, Illinois, paper, the *Warsaw Signal*, went into action with an assault on Mormonism. Its editor, Thomas C. Sharp, declared in his paper, "War and Extermination is inevitable; Arise, One and All!"[3]

Fearing an attack from other counties, Joseph Smith mobilized the Nauvoo Legion and declared martial law. Carthage responded by calling up a small militia, and the governor threatened to raise a larger state militia unless Smith surrendered.

Joseph Smith and his brother Hyrum were placed in the Carthage jail, charged with "inciting a riot." Soon charges were increased to "treason against the State of Illinois."[4]

Smith sent a letter ordering the Nauvoo Legion to attack Carthage, but the acting commander refused to obey the order. Late in the day, on June 27, 1844, an armed mob stormed the jail and killed both Joseph and Hyrum Smith.

Brigham Young, who had returned from a mission in England, became the new Latter-Day Saint leader and the ranking officer of the Nauvoo Legion. Realizing that many sections of the American public were condemning his Saints because some were engaging in polygamy, he intended to follow through with the church's plans—move west, find an ideal place to create a utopian society, and begin their lives anew without interference.

Nauvoo came under attack periodically by men firing muskets and cannons, but all the Mormons managed to escape across the river during September 1846, into Iowa territory, where they established a camp for the winter.

The new territory the Mormons had in mind for their Zion was what is now Utah. Except for Native Americans, there were few people living there and it was unlikely any would compete for the land, because, at the time, all of it was owned by Mexico.

Young had already sent a representative to meet with President James K. Polk and asked for safe passage west. The timing turned out to be perfect for the Mormons and the USA. Congress had declared war on Mexico a few days before, and the Saints were needed to fight in that war.

President Polk offered the Mormons an opportunity to serve their country. The bulk of Young's people would be guaranteed the right to proceed to the Utah area, unmolested by the United States, providing he furnished soldiers. Accordingly, a Mormon Battalion consisting of more than five hundred men was formed. They had their own officers, but all would serve under the command of the U.S. Army. The Mormon Battalion men would be paid, and draw their weapons and other equipment from the U.S. Army.[5]

Brigham Young gladly accepted President Polk's offer. It was the first time the federal government had agreed to assist the Mormons and it gave the Saints an opportunity to prove their loyalty to the United States.

The battalion entered service officially on July 16, 1846, as part of the "Army of the West" under Colonel Stephen Kearny (later brigadier general).

As the majority of Mormons followed Young across country in wagons, hand-pulled carts, and on foot, the battalion arrived at Fort Leavenworth on August 30 and promptly moved out along the Santa Fe Trail to New Mexico Territory. They made it to Santa Fe in October and met their new commander, West Point graduate Lieutenant Colonel Philip St. George Cooke, who would march the battalion for the next four months over 1,100 miles through some of the most difficult terrain in the Southwest.[6]

While in New Mexico, Lieutenant Colonel Cooke enlisted a new guide to take them safely through the desert. He was a qualified explorer and mountain man known as Jean Baptiste Charbonneau.

Some of the more curious Saints became friends with Charbonneau and learned that this quite dark-complexioned frontiersman with long black hair spoke English, German, French, and Spanish and also spoke and understood several Native American dialects. He had been educated in Germany as a young adult, but his early years were spent in St. Louis, where he was raised by William Clark of the Lewis and Clark Expedition.

Jean Baptiste was the son of the Lewis and Clark French Canadian interpreter, Toussaint Charbonneau, and had traveled cross-county before, only much farther north. He didn't remember anything of that trip, however, for he was only an infant at the time, carried on the back of his Shoshone mother, Sacagawea.

Now a new generation of guides would lead an expedition west, this time to do battle with the Mexicans.

The Mormon Battalion approached Tucson on December 16, 1846, prepared for a fight with the Mexican garrison, but the soldiers had withdrawn and there was no battle.

After marching more than two thousand miles since leaving Iowa (one of the longest marches in military history), the battalion arrived in San Diego on January 29, 1847, only to learn that Mexico had surrendered all of southern California.

The battalion then entered into occupation duty, constructing a number of buildings, including Fort Moore. Equally important was the fact that they had opened a wagon road from Santa Fe to San Diego. When the battalion was finally released from "active duty," some of the Saints remained in California, some traveled along the Spanish Trail (aka Salt Lake Trail), past the Las Vegas Springs and on into Utah to join their families. Still others headed north in California and cut through various "passes" in the mountains to reach their Zion.

With the battalion troops back with the Mormon body, Brigham Young had an excellent cadre to train other men. While the Mormons hacked out an existence in the wilderness of Utah, the battalion members shared experiences and military knowledge with former members of the Nauvoo Legion.

Though they now could muster an army of many thousands, the Latter-Day Saints simply desired to be left alone and practice their religion. But, once again, they found themselves under the influence of the United States government. Their desired isolation would be short-lived. Thanks to the victory over Mexico, Utah, and most of the Southwest, were now under control of the United States.

By 1849, Mormons already inhabited a large section of the Southwest, so they proposed that most of it be incorporated into the United States as the state of Deseret. This would have included what is now Nevada, Utah, northern Arizona, southern California, and the western one-third of New Mexico and Colorado.

Congress had other ideas and formed the "Utah Territory" to include all of Utah, two-thirds of Nevada, and a small section of Colorado. President Millard Fillmore appointed Brigham Young as the first governor of the new territory, answering to the U.S. government.

In 1848 and 1849, thousands of emigrants traveled through Utah Territory to reach the gold fields in California. There was talk of a railroad from the East and even plans to link Salt Lake City to civilization by the wires of the Western Union. All this might be wonderful for commerce, but it would also open the doors for America to once again study Mormon activities.

At they entered the 1850s, Mormons were becoming more uncomfortable with outside interference, but they knew they could now defend themselves with the largest, most experienced militia in the country.

Soon they explored south, deep into the desert around and beyond what the Spanish called "Las Vegas Springs." And the more they traveled into that vast wilderness known today as the Mojave Desert, the more they were faced with one major problem . . . where to find water.

Unlike most of Utah, there were no streams or lakes in the desert. Survival depended upon finding natural springs with water suitable for both men and horses. Often the springs, which once produced cool water, held only dust and sand the next time they passed by.

To defend their southern desert borders, the Saints realized they needed better transportation, perhaps an animal as strong as a horse, but one that required less water on a journey. They knew of camels from their Bible studies. Perhaps camels were the answer. But there were no camels in the American desert . . . yet.

CHAPTER 3

A New American Hero

Today dawned on the most tattered, ill-fed detachment ever mustered under U.S. colors. Unless the three volunteers, Lt. Beale, Kit Carson and an Indian servant reach San Diego, and Stockton sends help, we are finished.

Lieutenant William Hemsley Emory, "Notes,"
San Pasqual Valley, December 7, 1846

NEAR SAN DIEGO, CALIFORNIA
DECEMBER 7–8, 1846

What remained of General Stephen W. Kearny's United States Army of the West retreated in a cold winter drizzle to a fog-draped hill near San Pasqual Valley and waited for the Mexican dragoons to deliver the final deathblow.

Of Kearny's 150-man army, twenty-one had been killed that day by enemy lancers. Seventeen men suffered from serious wounds, including the general and marine captain Archibald Gillespie.

Captain Gillespie had been deployed with a thirty-five-man detachment by Commodore Robert Stockton with the Pacific Squadron anchored at San Diego bay. The captain's orders were to warn General Kearny that at least one unit of Mexican dragoons was between his column and the coast.

Ignoring the warning, General Kearny ordered an attack. His men became separated in the fog; their rifles, with wet gunpowder, failed to fire, and his army, mounted mostly on mules, was no match for the Mexicans on horses.

Now their few horses were dead and the surviving mules were either injured or too sickly to carry soldiers. The gunpowder was still wet and the misty, cold rain unending.

The marines talked of a "last stand" fight. Kearny's men agreed. The Americans were beat but there would be no surrender. If rifles failed to fire, they planned to use them as clubs, and each man still had his saber.

Where was the Mormon Battalion they heard about? The battalion was marching across the southern Arizona desert toward the Colorado River. But they would not arrive for another six or seven weeks, too late to save Kearny at San Pasqual.

Near the base of that large hill where the Americans struggled to erect some effective defense, the Mexicans (often called Californios) reviewed the situation. Their army of one hundred lancers had lost only two men killed during the battle. All the wounded were expected to survive.

It seemed a perfect time to charge up the hill on their fast horses and finish off the Americans, but visibility remained poor and they had no way of determining the exact location of the enemy. Fearing they might ride into a trap, their commander decided the best tactic would be to surround the hill and starve the enemy into surrender.

Before the battle, Commodore Stockton had sent his personal secretary along with Captain Gillespie's marines to serve as an observer, with orders to report on the military situation outside of San Diego. Most of California was already under U.S. control, captured by Stockton's sailors and marines or John C. Frémont's California Battalion, consisting of pioneer settlers and American Indians. But there were still Californio militia units scattered about like the one General Kearny encountered.

Stockton's secretary was no marine, a fact that may have irritated Gillespie and his men. He was twenty-four-year-old navy lieutenant

Edward Fitzgerald Beale, who had proven to be an intelligent officer and good seaman during his several years aboard ship, but had no combat experience on land.

Beale, a man with tremendous energy, was never short of suggestions and continually craved adventure. He got his adventure with a taste of land combat, receiving a slight head wound in the process.[1]

Kearny, realizing they had but one option for survival, elected to send a volunteer to Commodore Stockton for reinforcements. Obviously, if three men were sent on the mission, one might succeed in avoiding the enemy.

San Diego was thirty miles away and they did not know how many Mexican military units were operating between their hill and the ocean.

There was one man, however, who knew exactly where to find Commodore Stockton: Lieutenant Edward Beale. But Beale had spent most of his adult life on a ship, not traveling through wilderness on foot. He volunteered anyway.

The other two men were experts in wilderness survival and accustomed to walking great distances: an American Indian and the already famous frontier guide Kit Carson.[2]

Fearing excess equipment might cause unwanted noise, the three men left canteens and weapons at the camp. Carson and Beale would later dispose of their boots.

Total darkness came early. The men cautiously slipped out of the perimeter and started down the hill toward San Diego.

Lieutenant William Hemsley Emory, Corps of Topographical Engineers, had been with General Kearny's army since they departed Fort Leavenworth.

His assignment was to create maps and keep records of the plants, animals, and Native Americans encountered along the march. He also maintained a diary, or "notes," as he called them, and recorded the following: "Today dawned on the most tattered, ill-fed detachment ever mustered under U.S. colors. Unless the three volunteers, Lt. Beale, Kit

Carson and an Indian servant reach San Diego, and Stockton sends help, we are finished."[3]

All three volunteers made it through Mexican lines and reported to Stockton, who wasted no time. He dispatched 120 sailors and 80 marines to relieve General Kearny and his men, saving them from possible disaster. Upon seeing the heavily armed American reinforcements, the Mexican dragoons quickly departed the valley and the entire U.S. force marched unmolested to San Diego.

The volunteers were nearly dead from exhaustion when they reached Stockton's ships. In fact, the Native American Indian died shortly after delivering his message.[4]

But they had succeeded in crossing thirty miles of cactus-studded desert in near-freezing weather with no food or water.

Kit Carson, the strongest of the group, was bruised, scratched, tired, and dehydrated, but he recovered quickly after a few days' rest.[5]

Lieutenant Edward Beale was in very poor physical condition. His arms, legs, and knees were cut, bruised, and bleeding. During his first brief meeting with Stockton, he confessed he had to crawl "part of the way" to avoid capture. He had a high fever and, after sipping a quantity of water, became delirious.

Stockton provided a private cabin with the "best accommodations" possible and a doctor checked on the young lieutenant's condition daily.

News traveled of the Beale-Carson mission through the military and civilians' quarters. California, a new territory (not yet official), had a new hero.

Beale managed to cheat death during the next five weeks and appeared to be making a good recovery. On February 9, 1847, Commodore Stockton ordered Kit Carson and Ed Beale to travel east to Washington with documents describing the U.S. victory in California. Several soldiers were assigned as an escort.

Stockton naturally wanted a navy man to deliver his reports in Washington, but appreciated the fact that he needed Carson's knowledge and experience.

During the four-month journey, Beale often relapsed into an almost helpless condition, suffering some days with high fever, requiring Carson to assist him in mounting and dismounting his horse.

Carson, a skilled hunter, killed a variety of wild game from which he prepared a broth and, when necessary, spoon-fed the lieutenant. Some days it was the only food Beale's stomach tolerated. But with that tender care from the rugged frontiersman, the patient grew stronger. Beale credited Kit Carson with saving his life during the trip and spoke often of Carson his entire life.

One night, somewhere along the trail before they reached Santa Fe, the two discussed the possibility of employing camels in the desert they crossed. Ed Beale, having traveled the world with the navy and studied both the Bible and the Quran, was somewhat familiar with the qualities of the camel, but he had never actually seen one. The talk was general in nature, based, perhaps, on their location and the poor performance of mules in the desert (and in combat) against the Mexican horses.

Beale and Carson reached Washington about June 1, 1847, and presented the Stockton letters (which included a complete report on the brave action of both men at the Battle of San Pasqual) to the secretary of war and the president.

The newspapers now had an abundance of exciting stories to report: the new war hero, Edward Beale, more on the exploits of the already popular Kit Carson, and, of course, the war and victory.

For the next two months, Beale rested at home, cared for by his widowed mother, and was visited by Carson before the explorer departed for his home in New Mexico Territory. Carson commented to mutual friends that he worried Beale might never completely recover.

But Beale did recover and began to enjoy "good whiskey" while participating in social events, making the most of his fame.

Edward Beale was a small, handsome man of Scotch Irish stock, plagued with a complex personality. Sometimes sensitive, often outspoken (almost blunt at times), but polite, charming, and witty in the presence of ladies or important political figures.

There was a concern about his frail appearance during that stay in Washington, but he dismissed the talk, reminding everyone that he had always been "underweight."

A dark side to Ed Beale existed, seldom witnessed by anyone other than family members and very close friends. Some blamed the navy and those years at sea, away from the city. Others believed he suffered terribly after the loss of his father during his teen years. And Beale, himself, commented in an early diary that he could drift into a mood, which he feared was similar to depression, then display an outburst of temper. But he also possessed the ability to regain his composure quickly and once again be a charmer, holding everyone's attention with stories of his journeys to faraway places and that new land called California.[6]

Ed Beale had entered the navy after his appointment to the naval school by family friend President Andrew Jackson. At age twenty, Beale sailed to Russia, Brazil, the West Indies, Europe, and South America, and at each port attempted to learn all that time permitted of local culture and history.

In 1845, he was assigned to the squadron of (then) Captain Robert F. Stockton and instantly became the commander's favorite. Beale soon was appointed to be Stockton's personal assistant and secretary. In two more years, they would sail together into history at San Diego during the U.S.–Mexican War.

After those recovering months in Washington, Beale's nervous energy seemed to return and he became restless to be on the move again. In early 1848, he sailed to Central America and crossed over to the Pacific side, arriving in Baja in July. There he learned that gold had recently been discovered near Sacramento. He was off to the gold fields to see for himself if the news was true.

Beale had no intention of becoming a prospector. He had other plans, recognizing the importance of the discovery for the nation and the world. He managed to procure a few large nuggets and started to Washington with the news. There would be a race, for the army had just dispatched a messenger, also bound for Washington.

In a serious effort to be the first with the news of the gold discovery, Ed Beale came up with a dangerous plan. He traveled south, then cut across northern Mexico disguised as a Mexican rancher, boarded a ship on the east coast, and sailed north. He arrived in Washington in late September 1848, weeks ahead of the army messenger.

A master actor and with a knack for gaining public attention, Edward Beale now had the perfect stage—gold. And his news: gold was free for anyone who was strong enough to go and search for it.

California was not yet a state and few had any idea of how to reach that "land of opportunity." Some joked, "Go west until you come to the ocean, then back up a little and start digging!"

Beale visited the president and later donated a sample of his gold to the U.S. Patent Office. Editors of newspapers in Washington and New York scrambled to interview the war hero and see his samples of gold. Soon headlines led the country, already wrapped in gold fever, to the thought of traveling west. And, with the help of newspapers, Ed Beale once again was a national hero.

Now an urgency developed for making California a state. Proposals were quickly prepared for the people of California to consider, and who would be better to deliver those documents than Edward Beale? Once again, Beale crossed the Southwest, bound for San Francisco. With that mission complete, he returned to Washington, arriving in May 1849.

On June 27, 1849, having used a little of his California gold to buy a ring, Lieutenant Edward F. Beale married his childhood sweetheart, Mary E. Edwards of Chester, Pennsylvania.

The honeymoon had to wait. The country needed Beale again. The day after the wedding, the Navy Department ordered him to prepare to sail to California and deliver "important military documents." At least this time he could travel by ship.

CHAPTER 4

The Mojave

In the beginning, God created the heavens and the earth.

Genesis 1:1

It was a violent beginning, a horrible chaos following the collision of earth and sky, but from this the Great Spirit Matavilya was born. Treachery came with earth's creation. Before the Great Spirit could accomplish anything, he was killed by his sister. His little brother, Mastambo, now had the responsibility of completing the universe.

Mastambo grew to be an adult and in the process became lonely, so he created people. With this came responsibility, for his people were hungry, thirsty, cold, and had no knowledge. The desert surrounding the people was master of everything. Mastambo pushed a willow stick into the earth and water came forth, and he colored it red so it complemented the desert with beauty. He made the water become a river and then he made the mountains on both sides from the mud of the river.

In the water he placed fish. He made birds and all the animals and told the fish to share water. He taught the people how to plant melon, corn, pumpkin, and the mesquite tree, from seeds in the pods of which they could make food. Now people were not hungry or thirsty, but they were cold, so Mastambo taught them how to make fire and build shelters to protect themselves from the desert's blazing sun. He gave the people fingers and showed them how to count, measure distances, and understand the four directions. He also gave them the wonderful gift of dreams and visions and thoughts.

Mastambo told the people that the red river was their center of existence and the universe flowed in front of them every day. The river and all that grew or lived along the waters belonged to the people.

Then Mastambo was no longer lonely. People talked to him and knew he would answer in his own way.

To people, everything had a name. River was, simply, river. Many generations passed and strangers came to the people's land. They called the red river by a different name, Colorado.

People were special to Mastambo. He had created them and gave them a name, Aha Macave (the people who live along the water). The strangers called them the Mojave.[1]

The Mojave practiced a farming method similar to other ancient cultures whose people lived in a river basin. They depended on the regular overflow of the Colorado River to irrigate crops, but they also mastered a complex engineering system of irrigation. All of this required a constant removal of weeds and brush to ensure good crop growth.

Fish were taken with traps and nets made mostly from willow branches and fibers of yacca stems, which they also used as thread for sewing animal skins and rope.

From the riverbanks they removed clay and, mixing it with crushed sandstone, formed pottery—bowls, pots, dishes, and ladles, which they often decorated with geometric designs.[2]

During most of the year, while the weather was warm, men went about in the nude or wearing a small waist cloth. The women wore skirts fashioned from bark, rabbit, and beaver skins. They developed a blue ink from cactus and used it to tattoo parts of the body.

Their language is linked linguistically with other tribes in Arizona, California, and northern Mexico.[3]

The Mojave traveled and quickly learned they were not alone on this earth. To the northeast the Yavapai (Hualapai) occupied what is now northern Arizona, to the west (now Nevada and California) lived the Chemehuevi and Piute (Pah-Ute), and to the south along the Colorado the Quechan (or Yuma) seemed to always be at war with other tribes, especially their neighbors, the Pima and Maricopa.

The Mojave were physically a tall, strong, fearless race who traveled unmolested on trails that took them hundreds of miles as they pursued their great love, trading for items they did not have along the river. Usually they were blessed with an abundance of food and carried melons and pumpkins as far west as the Pacific Ocean using a network of trails, surviving in the desert from one freshwater spring to the next. At the ocean they traded for their favorite item, seashells.

The Mojave needed weapons to hunt even small game and protect themselves from intruders. The river area provided everything. From the hardwood of the mesquite tree they fashioned two types of war clubs, one almost four feet long and the other (their preferred weapon) a twenty-inch-long club called a "potato masher" by the white men.

Bows were made from the desert willow, designed to be five to six feet in length. Arrows were feathered "arrow weed," the shaft usually thirty to thirty six inches. The arrow weed, found mostly in river bottoms of the Southwest, has stems that, when dry, are lightweight, gray in color, and naturally straight. They tipped the arrows not with stone or flint but with a detachable hardwood cut with barbs perpendicular to a sharpened tip. The weapons may have been primitive but were very effective in the hands of their large, powerful warriors.[4]

The Mojave were usually good-natured and happy; they had all they needed in their river valley, but the seventeenth century brought a series of events that would, at first, produce change, then drastically force the nation into modern times.

In 1604, an expedition in search of silver led by Don Juan de Oñate wandered into Mojave territory, but it wasn't until 1775 that a Spanish missionary, Fray Francisco Garcés, actually spent time with the River People. Fray Garcés was searching for a way west through the desert. The Mojave accommodated him and guided the fray along one of their trading routes. In his journal, Fray Garcés stated that the Mojave were "friendly, very healthy, and robust."[5]

In 1821, the southwest area (which would eventually belong to the United States) was transferred from Spain to Mexico. The new government permitted Americans to travel through their land, but trapping was against the law. The early American explorers, who were mostly trappers, ignored that law.

Spanish adventurers explored the Colorado River from its mouth at the Gulf of California, but the American trappers ventured in from the north, heading south to investigate business opportunities. And so it was for one of America's most famous early west explorers, Jedediah Strong Smith.

With a face horribly scarred from a grizzly-bear attack, Smith was perhaps the first white man to cross the future states of Nevada and Utah and the first American to explore the Pacific wilderness from the Spanish town of San Diego to the Columbia River.

A strong Christian, Smith often claimed that his Bible and rifle were his closest friends.[6]

Traveling cross-country in 1826 with a few companions, Smith passed through part of northern Utah, then turned south and, following the Colorado River, reached the Mojave nation in October. It was remembered as a productive meeting, the River People giving the white men food and shelter. Visiting the Mojave at the time were also two Tongva men from the Pacific coast. They had brought seashells to trade for pumpkins and corn. The Tongvas made their home between tribes of the Chumash in a basin now known as Los Angeles and were experienced travelers. Long ago they acquired the skill of navigating the ocean in seaworthy canoes capable of hauling twelve men.

This was an exciting time for the Mojave and Tongvas. Everyone was pleased with gifts from Smith's group and offered to guide them to the ocean along a trail used by the Mojave. The Mojave, of course, added a few men to the expedition.

But the storm of trouble seemed to blow in from the north. The next year, 1827, another party of trappers led by Kentucky-born adventurer James Ohio Pattie entered Mojave territory and, without permission, began to trap and skin beaver, leaving the carcasses on the riverbanks to rot in the sun.[7]

The Mojave were appalled. The beaver belonged to them. Not only was the meat wasted, the balance of nature in their world had been disrupted. They demanded that the white men pay for the destruction with a horse.

Pattie ignored the demand and he and his men continued trapping for another two days. Finally the River People could take no more and launched an attack. Pattie managed to escape across the river and started west. He left behind two dead companions and sixteen dead Mojave.[8]

James Pattie reached San Diego, where there was more trouble waiting. Mexican authorities arrested him and his friends and confiscated all their beaver pelts.

Following Pattie, trappers from the Canadian Hudson Bay Company invaded Mojave territory. They were driven off at a cost of twenty-six more warriors.

In 1828, Jedediah Smith, unaware of the previous year's troubles, returned to visit the Mojave nation with eighteen men, expecting to find another friendly reception. The River People no longer trusted white men and had developed a strategy to deal with intruders.

When the Smith party was halfway across the river, the warriors released a barrage of arrows. Ten of Smith's party were killed in minutes, but he and eight others managed to escape and reach safety at San Gabriel.[9]

During the next twenty years, word of the Mojave's warlike nature spread, their people described as often friendly, sometimes deadly, but always unpredictable.

At the same time the Mojave looked at the white men as intruders who had no respect for their culture and hospitality.[10]

The Mojave had been content to live in their river paradise given to them by Mastambo. Truly, the Mojave had no other place to go and no way to prepare for a future of change being forced on them by the intruders who came to steal and kill.

The Mojave would stand and fight to protect their world. They would win battles, but not the total war swooping down upon them.

CHAPTER 5

The Army Explores the West

It is the sandstorms that shape the stones of the desert.
It is the struggles of life that form a person's character.

Native American Proverb

In the early 1840s, explorers like Lieutenant John Charles Frémont thrilled easterners with reports of strange lands west of the Mississippi River, of towering snowcapped mountains and deserts with plants and animals they had never seen before.

On one expedition Frémont followed a river (now called the Mojave) near present-day Barstow, California, then turned onto the Spanish Trail, traveling it until arriving at an oasis called Las Vegas by the Spanish. (It is doubtful he dreamed that a city with a street named in his honor would grow there someday.) Frémont needed water, and the oasis furnished all he could drink and carry.

Lieutenant Frémont was in the West to explore, not claim territory. At the time all the land he traveled belonged to Mexico. But there were very few Mexicans living in this "wild frontier." In fact, in most places there was no one at all except Native American Indians.

Then, starting with disputes over the annexation of Texas, the United States declared war with the Republic of Mexico on April 25, 1846. In two years, it was over and the United States gained vast unmapped territory in the West, stretching two thousand miles from the

Mississippi to the Pacific Ocean. The efforts of men like Lieutenant Frémont were suddenly very important.

At the war's end, a treaty with Mexico required the United States to establish and maintain a series of army posts near the border to prevent Indians from attacking Mexican ranchers. It was soon clear that the soldiers would also be needed to protect American travelers.

Both infantry and dragoons (mounted riflemen, later called cavalry) manned those forts. Garrison life was miserable in the arid climate of the desert wilderness with its extreme temperature ranges of 120 degrees in summer months and below freezing during winter.

Newspaper articles in the East about explorers such as Frémont, Kit Carson, James Pattie, and Jedediah Smith stimulated imaginations, but still, very little was known by the general public of the "great American Desert."

With the discovery of gold in California in 1848 and Lieutenant Edward Beale's "proof," the so-called civilized part of America was engulfed with gold fever and the great Gold Rush began.

Some believed that the best trail to California would be the same route followed by the Mormons crossing the frontier in the north. But many feared reprisals for the persecution the Latter-Day Saints endured in the Midwest a few years before.

A four-month sail around Cape Horn of South America was dangerous, uncomfortable, and very expensive.

Many elected to disembark from a ship at Panama, cross the isthmus and board another vessel on the Pacific Ocean side, and then continue on to California. This adventure required three months, sometimes more.[1]

Others thought of traveling by horse, mule, or ox-drawn wagon directly west on the thirty-fifth parallel. No trail existed along this route and nothing was known about the availability of water and food for animals, nor was there any information on the friendliness of Indians.

The "southern route" became the one of choice. General Cooke had marched his Mormon Battalion through this part of the wilderness.

Prospectors, adventurers, and emigrants traveled to Santa Fe, New Mexico Territory, on west to Tucson, to the Gila River, then south to a Colorado River crossing at the future site of Yuma. Only 180 miles of desert remained to reach San Diego.

In a year, thousands of treasure seekers traveled that route and were relieved to find that the army had erected a fort on the bottomlands near where the Gila River emptied into the Colorado River. The fort and its soldiers were there to control the warlike Yuma Indians, but it soon became a key resting area for travelers. The soldiers even operated a ferry to cross the Colorado.

In March 1851, the fort was moved to a higher elevation on the west bank (California side) and officially named "Camp Yuma." Then, in June, the army began to withdraw and abandoned Yuma. In December, the fort was completely empty. The cost of supplying the men, mules, and horses had become impractical, and it made no difference if supplies were moved across the desert from San Diego or sent by sea into the Gulf of California and then up the Colorado River.

The military now faced a serious dilemma. By treaty with Mexico, they were required to keep the post open, and with thousands of Americans traveling the trail, soldiers must be there to protect them.

It seemed logical to the army to travel the most direct route through the desert from San Diego, but for one mule-team wagon loaded with supplies for the soldiers, two additional wagons were required to carry water and food for the mules.

The military simply had to find a more efficient means of transportation across the desert, not only for Camp Yuma but all the frontier outposts.

With the army gone from Camp Yuma, the Indians seized the opportunity to attack travelers within one hundred miles of the post. But the Indians were not the only danger. White and Mexican outlaws took control of the area and robbed and killed travelers. By the first of March 1852, the army returned, restored order, and the "Camp" officially became "Fort" Yuma. But the wild days of 1851 had become a famous part of the violent history of the American West.

The government in Washington recognized that communication and transportation needed to be developed between the East, California, and the entire western territory. A few primitive maps existed, but no reliable charts. Was it possible to navigate by river from the center of New Mexico to the Gulf of California? No one knew.

Before 1852, citizens in the East had been spoiled by the availability of rivers for transportation and the movement of supplies. Did a new network of similar rivers exist in the Great American Desert?

With the discovery of gold in California, pressure increased on the government to find a suitable way to travel cross-country. Then, in 1849–1850, as California became a state, rumors persisted that there would be trouble with the Mormons in Utah Territory. Perhaps the talk began with some knowledge of the Mormons' strong military, but at the time few outside of Utah knew exactly their military strength.

In 1850, government expeditions most logically fell upon the military. The War Department selected a forty-year-old West Point graduate, Captain Lorenzo Sitgreaves of the Army Corps of Engineers, to lead the first official scientific expedition west through the wilderness to the Colorado River. His assignment: explore and map the rivers in the West and determine their navigability.[2]

Captain Sitgreaves, a hero of the Black Hawk Wars and Creek nation battles, had a reputation for being a cautious officer with a clear understanding of how to deal with Native Americans. He realized that they could be very friendly, but quickly shift to a dangerous mood. Regardless, he had a strong policy of treating native people with respect.

During the Mexican War, Sitgreaves had been promoted to captain for "extreme bravery" in combat, but his experiences extended beyond war. He was sent into the wilderness of what is now Wisconsin early in his career to build roads and survey the border with Canada.

Now, in 1851, Captain Sitgreaves prepared for another dangerous assignment: the expedition into the virtually unknown wilderness of the Southwest.

In September, Captain Sitgreaves's group consisted of a small but impressive list of scientists, topographers, artists, naturalists, a medical doctor, and, of course, support personnel of mule drivers and laborers. For protection, a military escort of fifty men joined the expedition at the little village of Zuni in western New Mexico Territory. Along with their mule pack train, a large number of sheep was included for food.

They traveled southwest along the Zuni River and then northwest following the Little Colorado River. Here, their fifty-year-old, experienced guide, Antoine Leroux, suggested it was not necessary to follow the river any farther because it flowed into a deep canyon and then emptied into the "great canyon" (now called the Grand Canyon).

The expedition gave up on river travel and headed due west, deeper into the wilderness, unaware that they were entering an area suffering from the worst drought in years. Many water holes were dry, and grass, necessary for mules and sheep, was in short supply.

Somehow, mostly by sheer determination, they continued west until reaching the Colorado River at a point a little south of modern-day Bull Head City, Arizona.

Completely exhausted, after days with food and water on ration supply, the expedition moved south along the river and was suddenly greeted by the Mojave people.

The reception was friendly; the River People laughed and talked, trying to communicate with the white visitors. The Mojave produced pumpkins, beans, corn, and wheat and wanted to trade for whatever Sitgreaves was willing to give up. They were thrilled to learn the captain had many wonderful things: beads, blankets, and a variety of trinkets.

For a while everything seemed perfect—the Mojave happy with the trade and the expedition enjoying food and water.

Sitgreaves recorded in his journal that the Mojave were a race of friendly people, the men mostly well over six feet in height and all with "athletic figures."[3]

Soon the expedition members became restless and concerned. Some expressed fear that an attack by the Mojave was imminent. Had they staggered into a situation that was developing into an ambush?

When the soldiers ejected the Mojave from their camp, the Indians responded by releasing a number of arrows, one striking the expedition's doctor in the leg. Though the wound was not serious, the act of aggression was enough for the expedition to quickly break camp and start down the Colorado toward their destination, Camp Yuma.

It would seem that fifty armed soldiers plus an equal number of civilians with rifles could have easily defended themselves against warriors armed with primitive weapons. But it was not Captain Sitgreaves's desire to enter into combat with the Mojave. His men were still weak from their journey and he did not wish to lose a single soldier in a needless battle. A successful mission was paramount.

Sitgreaves and his men marched south, following the river for a week. All were near starving and were forced to eat their mules to survive.

Then they came to another "Mojave" settlement and were told by one of its residents who spoke Spanish that they still had an eight-day walk to Camp Yuma.

Here again, the "Mojave" were friendly and excited to do some trading. Beads and other trinkets were exchanged for food, and after a short rest the expedition started for Camp Yuma.

They had moved only a short distance when someone noticed that a soldier, suffering from an illness, had lagged behind. In moments, fifty to sixty warriors attacked the man, killing him with arrows and clubs. They then launched an attack on the main body of the expedition with arrows.

That was a mistake. The soldiers, hungry and exhausted, were still professional military men. They formed a line and began firing their rifles directly into the charging Indians, killing four and wounding several others. The warriors broke off the attack, gathered their dead, and carried them toward the north. Sitgreaves and his men continued on south and stumbled into Camp Yuma a few days later.[4]

After a long rest, the captain and his men traveled through the California Imperial Desert, finally reaching San Diego.

Captain Lorenzo Sitgreaves had accomplished his mission, though the information he gathered was not what the government, especially the War Department, wanted to hear.

The expedition did produce excellent maps of the routes, and explored and recorded detailed observations of the geology, plants, and animals they encountered.

The captain's report revealed that the Zuni and Little Colorado rivers were not navigable and completely useless for transporting troops or supplies. However, he believed the Colorado River was navigable, at least from Camp Yuma to the Mojave villages. He did not know what to expect beyond the villages where Mormon Territory began.

With this information on the Colorado, the War Department seemed convinced that the United States could be defended in the area providing the army held Fort Yuma, and to do that, they still needed to find a better way to supply the post.

Then there was the subject of the Mojave. Most members of the expedition believed, with good reason, that the River People could not be trusted, reporting that the Mojave were "unpredictable."

The Mojave had their own opinions. To their way of thinking, the white men were rude and inconsiderate for not allowing more time for trading. The intruders, they insisted, had suffered because of their bad behavior.[5]

Without the possibility of river transportation, those supporting a rail system to California felt a greater urgency to continue their pursuit. But before a railroad could be built, they needed more information regarding the route and then a road must be built to move workers and supplies.

CHAPTER 6

California's Growing Pains

Father is gone. We will live with the whites no longer!

Yo Semite Chief, August 1852

By May 1849, news of the gold discovery in California had flooded into the frontier towns of Missouri and snatched the attention of twenty-three-year-old wagon maker Samuel Addison Bishop like a "clap of thunder."

Some of Bishop's friends in Callaway County were already preparing for the journey through the "Great American Desert," as the territory west of Missouri was called. Soon they were on their way to seek fortunes, and none thought of returning a failure. They moved out, it seemed, with the excitement of a Sunday picnic, some riding mules or horses, some in wagons pulled by oxen, and a few, with no other options, walking.

Samuel Bishop would join their train. He had pooled what little money he accumulated from years of hard labor with that of a few close friends. Together they invested in a wagon, oxen, and a few cattle to supply food along the way.

Bishop hugged his parents in a tearful good-bye, not fully realizing at the moment that he would never see them again. He was leaving home, as were thousands of others in Missouri, but he had never really thought of that place as home. The first ten years of his life were spent on a farm in Albemarle County, Virginia. His father had been a farmer, as was his father before him, and that life of working with the earth, growing and harvesting, would remain in his memory forever.

Sam Bishop attended school, the best the frontier could offer in those days. But, as with most farm boys, his parents needed him to help with the chores. Nonetheless, he learned to read and write and discovered he had a natural ability for solving mathematical problems. Perhaps that talent drew him at an early age into the "mechanical world." He learned to work with gears and the ratios required to accomplish a certain job; and in making gears, he learned the art of blacksmithing. Then building and architecture produced a little income, and by the age of twenty he constructed a mill with gears of his own design to move the grinding stone. But building wagons and their wheels provided a more steady income. America, more than ever before, was on the move and wagons were a good business to be in. On April 15, 1849, he left all that behind and headed for that golden treasure waiting in California.

Bishop and friends followed the Santa Fe Trail and then went on to Tucson, down the Gila River, then finally, after an uneventful three-month journey, arrived at Yuma along the Colorado River. There at Yuma local frontiersmen warned that little or no grass remained along the California trail through the desert. Earlier trains passing through had depleted what little grass had been available.

While his friends debated the wisdom of continuing with their oxen, Sam Bishop made a desperate decision. He disposed of his investment in the wagon team, packed thirty days of provisions plus a blanket, a pick, and a shovel, and set out alone on foot.

He survived the hike through the desert and arrived in the village of Los Angeles on October 8, 1849, six months after leaving Missouri. He rested for several days, regained his strength, then began the walk to the Mariposa mining district, where, if rumors were true, gold could be found.

Bishop reached his destination in early 1850 and set up a camp along the Merced River. At that point, he had walked a little over seven hundred miles since leaving his friends at Yuma.

Thousands of hopeful gold prospectors, some migrating north through California after crossing the Colorado at Yuma, others moving west along the Oregon Trail then south to the gold fields, settled in the Mariposa area. By the time Bishop had his campsite functional, some twenty thousand prospectors were already hard at work seeking riches in the soil. In another year that number would double.

By the end of 1850, the population of non–Native Americans consisted mostly of men from other parts of the United States. However, there was truly an international mix, immigrants from Mexico, South America, Australia, Europe, and China, and a growing number of African Americans: some "free men," a few escaped slaves.

Before long, Anglos began to fight with one another over mining claims, equipment, the price of supplies, even the weather. With the stress of treasure hunting and the swelling of the international and culture mixture, tempers flared, logic often disappeared, and more violence erupted. Sam Bishop had a reputation for being a peaceful, polite, soft-spoken "southerner" and managed to avoid fights and dangerous arguments by working alone on an engineering project. He had designed and constructed a series of small dams and canals to control the river water so it moved slowly through his claim.[1]

After five months of backbreaking labor and experiments with water flow, Bishop found very little gold. Then fate stepped in and put him completely out of business. September rains came in torrents, swelling the streams and rivers in the valley, and swept away his elaborate system. He managed to save from the flood his original pick and shovel.

Discouraged but still determined, Bishop moved closer to the mining town of Mariposa, which had a population of four thousand and was still growing. Here he set up a primitive camp and started digging again.

One day, while visiting Mariposa, Sam Bishop met two men who would soon greatly influence his future and lead him into a new world of war and business.

James Burney, his first contact, had the frustrating, almost impossible, task of maintaining peace in Mariposa. As sheriff, Burney made a serious effort to eliminate the shootings, knifings, and general brawling among the prospectors that had existed since the start of the Gold Rush in 1849. But as American whites pushed immigrants from other countries off their claims, the true owners of the land, the Native Americans, entered the fight.

Some Indians agreed to work the claims for whites, content with the "beautiful" items and food they were paid. Indians who would not give up their land to prospectors suffered when their villages were raided by armed mobs.

By late 1851, the gold fields around Mariposa were saturated with a population of more than one hundred thousand (not counting Native Americans). That number would reach two hundred thousand briefly by December 1852, as a new wave of prospectors arrived from eastern states.

Bishop's move to Mariposa "just in time" for the flood that ruined his prospecting efforts may have saved his life. As waters receded and prospectors returned, Indians began to attack white people along the Merced River. The Native Americans had finally been pushed too far and were ready to fight back.

The governor of the "new state" of California authorized Sheriff Burney to muster a militia of two hundred men to protect the population of Mariposa County and suggested that the sheriff lead the unit. Burney had enough to worry about with whites fighting whites and recommended a famous mountain-man-turned-wealthy-miner-and-trading-post-owner, James D. Savage, who held the rank of major since California's war with Mexico a few years earlier.

Samuel Bishop, unsuccessful with gold prospecting, became one of the first to enlist as a volunteer in the militia. He was assigned to Company C and given the rank of sergeant in the "California Battalion."

Now, at age twenty-six, Bishop received his first military training and a taste of combat as the "Mariposa Wars" began. In a series of small battles, the battalion drove the Indians back into the mountains and out of the river valleys. Cavalry charges provided an experience for Bishop, the practical knowledge of which would serve him well during a critical moment of his life in the future.[2]

That long walk from Yuma to central California and two years of strenuous work had transformed, in a positive way, the man from Virginia. Short, muscular, and barrel-chested, Sam Bishop had developed into a powerful but not particularly handsome man. But an important part of him had remained unaffected by all he endured. There existed a calm, patient manner about him that drew the respect of those he met. And when he spoke, there was something about his deep voice and southern drawl that expressed authority and captured attention. His narrow-slit eyes seemed to lock on, revealing confidence and inner strength, but they also transmitted an impression of peace, leaving one with the thought that his entire face might break into a brilliant smile at any second.

Men, the rugged, brawling first generation of California's American emigrants, liked Sam Bishop, and some began to follow him with devotion, trusting him as a friend in a difficult place at a most dangerous time.[3]

Major James D. Savage was perhaps the second and most influential individual in Bishop's early life in California and would lead the young Virginian into spending a short time in the military and a longer one in the world of business. It would be, as is often the case in unusual circumstances, a very unlikely friendship: Bishop, much the southern gentleman with only recent knowledge of the wilderness, and Savage, the mountain man turned entrepreneur.

Born in Cayuga County, New York, in 1817, James Savage moved to Illinois at age twenty-one. There, he married, but like so many Americans of the time, he was restless and craved adventure. In 1846, two years before the Gold Rush, he convinced his wife, Elisa, that they should move to California. They joined an emigrant train, but during that difficult journey through the wilderness, Elisa and their young daughter died.

The train reached Sutter's Fort in late October 1846, and Savage, depressed and bitter over the loss of his family, joined with Frémont to fight for California independence. After the Mexican War, he returned to Fort Sutter and was working at the mill in January 1848 when gold was discovered.[4]

Savage became a prospector along streams in the area and employed local Indians to do the digging, paying them with blankets, trinkets, knives, and other useful things. He soon opened a store, becoming an "Indian trader" selling a variety of items to prospectors and Indians who paid in gold. In weeks, Savage became extremely wealthy.

By late 1849, as more people prospered, there was even greater opportunity for business. Savage expanded, opening more stores employing Indians.

Much of his time was spent in developing "reservations," areas where the Native Americans could live unmolested by the miners. Savage had already learned several Indian dialects and become well respected among those people. He married at least five young women from different tribes to strengthen friendship with all the local Native Americans.[5]

But in the months to come, fights, often deadly, persisted between whites and Indians, and despite Savage's efforts to settle disputes peacefully, there would be more bloodshed.

In a new area occupied mostly by Yo-Semites, Savage seemed unable to establish friendly relations, and one of his stores came under attack. Employees were killed and the raiders escaped with his merchandise.[6]

Savage, a few whites, and some of his "friendly Indians" followed the raiding party up the Merced River but, fearing an ambush, they stopped the pursuit in a narrow canyon. They had entered Cascade Canyon and may have been the first white men to see that part of Yo-Semite Valley.

Soon other stores owned by Savage were raided, but the one that probably ignited the Mariposa War was at the trading post where clerks were murdered and all his Indian wives carried off.

On January 13, 1851, with the authority of both the governor and James Burney, sheriff of Mariposa County, Major James Savage became commander of the Mariposa Battalion. He was described as "courageous, fearless and a handsome man with bright blue eyes and flowing blonde hair," and one thing was certain: no one knew or understood the local Native Americans better than Savage.[7]

The battalion followed the retreating Indians in a deep snow into a valley across from what is now called El Capitan on March 27, 1851. During a skirmish, most of the Indians escaped, but a few surrendered and returned with Savage's unit to Mariposa.

As peace seemed to return to the mining area, Savage constructed new trading shops, employing Native Americans and, with continued success, entered the cattle business late in 1851. Then he introduced his friend Sam Bishop to the business world.

Bishop started in the trading shops, then phased into cattle ranching. Savage made all the business decisions and Bishop studied his moves, often taking notes for future reference.

During this educational phase of his life, Bishop, like Savage, developed an understanding and respect for the Native Americans and a deep concern for their struggle to survive with the whites in the area.

But his friend James Savage began to have problems with some of his own people. One does not succeed in so many fields in such a turbulent time without creating enemies and experiencing jealousy over accomplishments. The fact that Major Savage continued to help the Native Americans did not sit well either with some powerful men in the county. Basically, a few of the miners wanted *all* the land to search for gold, including those sections set aside as "reservations" for the Native Americans. Savage was determined to protect the Indians' rights to land and continued to be very outspoken and critical of a few men in the county, especially a local judge, Major Walter H. Harvey. Once, Major Harvey called Major Savage a "liar" and a "damned scoundrel," to which Savage responded with a few names for Harvey.[8]

The arguments quickly escalated beyond name-calling. Sometime in July 1852, Major Harvey led a band of men on to the King River Indian Reservation and slaughtered seven unarmed Indians.

Major Savage, upon learning of the incident, decided not to settle the matter himself, but let the government step in. He demanded an investigation be conducted by state and federal officials.[9]

On August 16, 1852, Major Savage and Judge Harvey were on the way to the "hearing" when they confronted each other. Harvey refused to retract the names he had called Major Savage. James Savage struck Harvey on the jaw with his fist, knocking him down (some say Savage struck the judge twice).[10]

Before Savage could strike another blow, Judge Harvey drew his Colt Navy Revolver and shot Savage through the heart. Savage fell and the judge fired three more shots into his body. Major James D. Savage was dead at age thirty-five.

At a brief trial, Judge Harvey had the charges dismissed. Even though he shot an unarmed man four times, the presiding judge decided that the action had been in "self defense."[11]

The murder of Major Savage would have a profound effect on the Native Americans at the local reservations and in the counties where they considered him a friend and business partner.

The whites feared that the Indians would begin raiding and murdering again. But peace, though uneasy, would continue in that part of California for the next two years.

Savage had struggled to protect the Native Americans in the area. He was their one hope for justice, especially in land disputes.

The words of one of the Yo-Semite chiefs traveled from mining camps to the small towns and even reached San Francisco. "Father is gone. We will live with the whites no longer!"

After the death of James Savage, Californians appreciated the fact that the U.S. government must have a program to assist, protect, and, perhaps, even educate the Native Americans in California.

Indeed, the government was in the process of doing just that by appointing a national hero, Lieutenant Edward Beale, to be in charge of "Indian affairs" for California. He would assume these duties in that new state in less than a year.

Meanwhile, Dr. Lewis Leach, a close friend and business partner of James Savage, took over the stores, ranch, and business affairs of the major's empire. This included the mining operations along the Fresno River. He named the new enterprise Leach and Company, and appointed twenty-seven-year-old Samuel A. Bishop his new partner.

Bishop continued in Major Savage's footsteps by doing what he could to protect the Native Americans while everyone waited for the director of Indian Affairs to arrive from Washington.

CHAPTER 7

Trouble in Utah

I love the government and constitution of the United States but I do not love the damned rascals that administer the government.

Governor Brigham Young,
Utah Territory, 1850s

National hero Lieutenant Edward F. Beale had many irons in the fire in the early 1850s. He would need all his nervous energy and persistence to keep on a successful track. With the excitement of the Gold Rush, which he had helped create, still ringing in his ears and before he could enjoy a honeymoon with his bride, the War Department ordered him to return to California.

His old commanding officer, Commodore Robert Stockton, and millionaire investor William H. Aspenwall had acquired large sections of land in southern California, and at Stockton's recommendation, Beale was hired as the "manager" of the property.

Then on March 3, 1853, President Millard Fillmore, impressed with Beale's adventures and accomplishments, appointed him superintendent of Indian affairs for California. Congress approved the huge sum of $250,000 to improve the living conditions of Native Americans in the new state. Just how the funds were to be used would be up to Beale. Before he could experiment with that budget, the government had another project for him.

The Sitgreaves and Whipple expeditions would provide enormous data regarding the feasibility of a railroad along the thirty-fifth parallel, but not everyone in Washington supported the idea of that route. Senators from northern states insisted that more be learned about the feasibility of a route along the thirty-eighth parallel.

The main proponent of that idea was the powerful Missouri senator Thomas Hart Benton. Originally from Tennessee, Benton had long been a strong advocate of expansion into the West. He was once a close friend of Andrew Jackson, serving on his military staff during the War of 1812.

In many ways, the personalities of Benton and Jackson were similar. In 1817, Benton found himself faced with a duel. Known to be an expert marksman, Benton faced his opponent, Charles Lucas, at a distance of only nine feet. They both fired their pistols and Lucas died from a shot near his heart. Jackson had fought in more than one duel and retained a fearless reputation in dueling.[1]

It was a tight group in Washington during the 1850s. The Beale family and Andrew Jackson had been close friends and now Ed Beale established himself as a fine American hero. Benton knew both families, so naturally he wanted Beale, a man of vast wilderness experience, to conduct a preliminary survey along the thirty-eighth parallel. Lieutenant Beale would be going to California anyway, to begin his duties as supervisor of Indian affairs.

Ed Beale persuaded his cousin, journalist and writer-artist Gwinn Harris Heap, to accompany him on the railroad survey expedition. The two, along with twelve other men, departed Washington on May 6, 1853, and crossed through southern Colorado and southern Utah on horses and mules on what was recorded by Heap as a "relatively uneventful" journey. They arrived in Los Angeles on August 22, 1853.[2]

Ed Beale began work without a rest from the expedition in his new position. He planned to bring his bride, Mary, to California in another year.

Beale and Heap's expedition passed peacefully through southern Utah during July 1853. After that, things took a tragic turn for future visitors in that territory.

The appointment of LDS leader Brigham Young as governor of the territory by President Millard Fillmore came as a relief to the Mormons, but the relationship between the Saints and Washington began to break down.

The Mormons believed that they were correct to elect their own leaders, regardless of church positions. But many Americans saw this as a violation of principles and looked at Young and his team as tyrants and immoral for their practice of polygamy.

Federal judges and key territorial positions began to be filled by the president with Senate approval. Some of the appointees fit in well in the Latter-Day Saints society, yet many others, usually those with anti-Mormon feelings, of course, did not.

As early as 1851, a number of those federal appointees left Utah and returned east, claiming the Mormons were near rebellion against the United States. William W. Drummond, a Utah Territory justice, accused the Mormons of murder and suggested the army be sent to enforce federal laws and regulations. Drummond reported that the Mormons were immoral, although he himself had left his wife and brought another woman with him to Utah.[3]

In 1852, Utah's delegate to Congress, Dr. John M. Bernhisel, suggested a committee be sent to his territory to see if any of the negative reports were true. Most easterners had already formed strong opinions against the Mormons. During a very "moral" time in America, most considered the practice of polygamy an outrage and some were demanding the government find a way to stamp out the practice.

Meanwhile, in Washington, senators continued to disagree on the western route for a railroad. Beale's report supported the feasibility of the thirty-eighth parallel, but Lieutenant Whipple had not yet completed his expedition to the Colorado River along the thirty-fifth parallel.

With pressure from Senator Benton, the army prepared another survey along the thirty-eighth to follow closely in Ed Beale's footsteps. This one would be a true survey and commanded by forty-year-old New Hampshire native Captain John Williams Gunnison, who graduated second in his class at West Point. Gunnison, like his fellow officers following the thirty-fifth parallel, was in the Corps of Topographical Engineers. His combat experience fighting Indians had been in Florida, but now he and his team would be facing a miserable winter in Utah.

Gunnison's survey party left St. Louis in June 1853 with Lieutenant E. G. Beckwith second in command. They crossed the Rocky Mountains and entered Utah Territory in early October.

Soon the weather turned cold and an "early winter" with "raw" wind and snow flurries greeted the party as they worked their way west. Disagreements developed regarding the location of a winter camp and the importance of warnings passed on by Mormons telling of Indian plans to attack the group.

At Lake Sevier, Gunnison divided his party into two teams temporarily to speed up the mapping of the area.

The captain and eleven men continued a short distance, and on the bitter cold morning of October 26, 1853, their detachment was ambushed by "Pahvants" (Pah-Utes). In the massacre, Captain Gunnison and seven of his men, including artist and topographer Richard H. Kern and botanist F. Creuzfeldt, were killed.

The survivors of the attack managed to make it back to the main camp and Lieutenant Beckwith with his men rode to the rescue, but they arrived too late. They found their captain and the others stripped of their clothing and their bodies mutilated.

In the investigations and trials that followed, some Utes were accused of the murders but found innocent. Rumors circulated that the Indians had acted under direct orders from Brigham Young. Reportedly, he and other LDS leaders were worried that a railroad entering their territory would bring too many "outsiders." No proof of these claims existed.

But other rumors circulated, saying that "white men" had assisted the Indians in the massacre. This was backed by the fact that Indians in the area lacked the firepower to wipe out the captain, an experienced Indian fighter, and his men so quickly.

The dispute continued for another three or four years until, with the help of a report from federal judge William Drummond, all fingers of guilt pointed toward the Mormons for Gunnison's murder.

The country exploded in outrage, ignited by a letter from Drummond to Captain Gunnison's widow describing in gory details the circumstances of the massacre. The letter appeared in the *New York Times* on May 1, 1857.[4]

In the letter, Judge Drummond stated that the Indians acted under "orders from Brigham Young and the church"; "the whole affair," he wrote, "was a deep and maturely laid plan to murder the whole party of engineers or surveyors and charge the murders upon the Indians."[5]

Drummond revealed that "only four shots were fired by Indians and that all the rest were fired by Mormons" and "by order and direction of the Mormons, the Indians sprang out of ambush and went across the river to scalp and otherwise maltreat the men in their agonies of death."[6]

With the death of Captain Gunnison and his companions, the project to survey the thirty-eighth parallel came to a halt.

While the talk of war resounded in the East, the Mormons prepared to face all problems, including the best plans for defending their territory.

Brigham Young sent a scouting party south through the desert, along the Old Spanish Trail. They paused and rested a day or two at a small stream called the Muddy River, replenished their water supply, and then traveled through the part of the desert where they knew there would be no water source for seventy-five to eighty miles; nothing after that stream but rock, sand, sagebrush, yucca, creosote, and chola cactus. No trees grew along the desert trail that had claimed the lives of many Spanish explorers less than a hundred years earlier. The destination of Young's party was a wide valley, a creek, and an oasis. Here, it all began with water, the only water in the valley, water rising from aquifers into springs that supplied a creek that flowed for several miles then disappeared in the desert. For thousands of years, this oasis supported animals and plants that thrived with its life-giving nourishment. Native Americans over those years visited and hunted here, enjoying the shade of willow and cottonwood trees that lined the springs and creek.

It was the Indians who had directed the early Spanish explorers to the oasis and the Spanish who gave the place a name—Las Vegas— "the meadows."

The Spanish continued traveling along their trail, moving supplies by horse and donkey from their settlements in San Diego to Santa Fe, New Mexico, until shortly after the U.S.–Mexican War. Then mountain men, gold prospectors, and now the Mormons followed the trail from Utah to parts of southern California.

Brigham Young's scouts reported back to Salt Lake City. The Las Vegas spring was, indeed, a perfect place to build a fort. It could provide a safe resting point for Mormon travelers while protecting their southern boundary. Young recognized another purpose. They might also convert the local Native Americans to Christianity and the Mormon faith.

So, in June 1855, as the usual hot summer set upon the desert floor, Brigham Young deployed William Bringhurst and twenty-nine fellow "missionaries" to the Las Vegas spring to begin construction of a small fort.

The structure would be 150 feet square, made of adobe and timber cut from the trees near the creek. The walls, also adobe, were fourteen feet tall and included "watch towers" at the northwest and southeast corners.

Although labeled a fort, the Las Vegas structure was never really intended as a military installation. In fact, Brigham Young was so impressed with the success of his men in cultivating crops, building irrigation systems, and developing good relations with the Native Americans that he ordered a second group of missionaries, including women and children, to the Las Vegas Springs.

The key purpose of the missionaries was to work with the Native Americans, instructing them in farming and, of course, preaching to them the gospel. The Mormons succeeded in this and baptized a number of the local people, mostly Pah-Utes.

When time permitted, the men explored beyond the immediate desert valley, traveling into the mountains twenty-five miles west of their "fort" and east to the Colorado River. In those mountains they discovered lead and undertook limited mining.

Transportation through the desert now became a major problem, as it had been for the U.S. military to the south.[7]

CHAPTER 8

The Army Crosses the Colorado

You shall cross the barren desert but you shall not die of
thirst.

Gospel hymn by Bob Dufford

After guiding Captain Lorenzo Sitgreaves's expedition in 1851 and
surviving the Mojave attack, Canadian-born Antoine Leroux considered retiring and becoming a sheep rancher near Taos, New Mexico.
But the thirst for adventure bothers a man like Leroux, so when the
U.S. Army requested him to lead another expedition, he accepted,
happy to serve his adopted country and thrilled with the opportunity
to enter the wilderness once again.

After careful study of Captain Sitgreaves's report, the War Department accepted the disappointing fact that transportation by water
in the West was impossible, and disputes on the location of a railroad
continued in Congress. Some favored a northern route; others demanded it pass through the south. Of course, every major city in the
East wanted rails to pass through their town, showing little concern
for the route west after it left "civilization."

All routes would need to be studied scientifically, so in 1853 Congress passed the Pacific Railroad Survey Bill, appropriating $150,000
for the project. This was a sizable amount of money at the time, but
increasing worries about the Mormons in Utah had eastern citizens

demanding a solution to the "problem" even if the involvement of the army was required. The railroad project suddenly took on both civilian and military importance.

One proposed route gained favor—the thirty-fifth parallel from the Mississippi River to the Pacific Ocean. This route split the country almost in the middle and was below Mormon territory, not through it.

With funds and agreement (somewhat) on the route, the project was turned over to the War Department for the army to carry out the research. West Point graduate, thirty-four-year-old Lieutenant Amiel Weeks Whipple, a topographical engineer, was chosen to lead a large expedition to find a practical route for a transcontinental railroad along the thirty-fifth. The lieutenant had earned a reputation at the War Department as a true engineer with a curious mind. To his friends he was a serious, deeply religious man who had recently converted to Catholicism.

In 1853, the War Department still had very little knowledge of the Native Americans Whipple might encounter. Sitgreaves's report on his experiences with the Mojave left many officers perplexed. How should Whipple prepare, for friendly or aggressive people?

The lieutenant's philosophy was to treat all Indians as human beings and with respect. And he packed a good supply of items to trade with the Native Americans he encountered: colored beads, tobacco, blankets, and strips of red cloth.

This new expedition would be better equipped than the one assembled for Captain Sitgreaves. Whipple had the advantage of the captain's maps and notes and a trail to follow. He would find, though, that two years of rain, wind, and snow had erased much of the trail in some places.

Lieutenant Whipple's expedition rolled out of Fort Smith, Arkansas, on July 14, 1853, with a team of seventy workers, engineers, and scientists, 240 mules, a large flock of sheep, twenty wagons (each requiring six mules to pull), and an army escort of seventy soldiers.[1]

The scientific staff was very impressive, consisting of astronomers, geologists, naturalists, artists, botanists, and surveyors. Second Lieutenant Joseph Christmas Ives served as chief topographical engineer, assisted by Second Lieutenant David Sloan Stanley.

In New Mexico, they were joined by Leroux. The group reached what someday would be the border of Arizona and New Mexico on November 28, 1853.

Unlike Sitgreaves, who crossed the area during the hot, dry summer months, Whipple faced a different challenge. Winter set in with heavy rain, then snow and ice storms.

In spite of the difficulties, side trips were necessary to search for trees suitable for railroad ties, trestles over depressions, and good wood to provide heat for steam engines.

They would need to locate water in quantities to support work crews, their animals, and the railroad men, and to feed the locomotives. Also needed was stone suitable for road building and to support tracks and trains.

The expedition proceeded west along the thirty-fifth parallel, passing south of the San Francisco Mountains at the site of present day Flagstaff, Arizona.

Rather than following Sitgreaves's trail, Whipple headed south and proceeded directly to the Colorado River.

When they reached the river, the Mojave, fully aware of the slow-moving train, were waiting for them. It was February 23, 1854. The expedition had been traveling for seven months since leaving Fort Smith, a distance of more then 1,200 miles.

The first encounter with the River People was friendly, with families presenting wheat, flour, pumpkins, and gourds, anxious to begin the trade for which Whipple was well prepared.

A different atmosphere reigned during Whipple's visit. The Mojave found these new white men friendly and apparently eager to trade. (Their leader had coached them well, preparing his men for what to expect and how to behave, while remaining alert for danger.)

Also unlike the Sitgreaves visit two years earlier, there was no drought in the desert. The men, though exhausted, were well fed. The Mojave believed that Whipple had an honest face and a comfortable manner about him. This was the "first white man they could trust," a subject much discussed among the chiefs.[2]

Whipple explained that they wished to establish a road from the east that would bring more of his kind of people, who desired to come in peace and trade. Naturally, this sounded wonderful to the Mojave at the time.

After several days of trading and relaxing, Whipple's pleasant personality (and entertaining gifts) brought its reward. On March 2, 1854, as the expedition prepared to continue its journey west, the Mojave not only helped them cross the Colorado, but also assigned several warriors to lead them along the River People's secret trade route through the desert to the Spanish Trail. There, the warriors pointed the way to the Pacific Ocean.[3]

Whipple's expedition provided valuable information about the thirty-fifth route and that, added to Sitgreaves's findings, indicated a railroad along the parallel was, indeed, feasible.[4]

America was growing at a thrilling pace during the 1850s and citizens naturally craved news of her progress. From the populated eastern states to the scattered communities in California and the lonely army outposts along the frontier, there was a great hunger for news, especially reports on the adventures of heroes.

In 1852, Western Union wires buzzed with information in the East, but the news they carried was limited and without drama. These were the days for newspapers to gain attention and great power as reports flooded in by letters, interviews, and agents sent into the wild frontier of Kansas, Texas, and Missouri.

Slavery and abolition were key topics, intertwined with politics. But there were no sports figures or movie stars to occupy space in the papers, though coverage was provided for stage actors and musical performers.

The vast distances over which news had to travel presented the major problem. Trailblazing through the wilderness for explorers and the military held another purpose—the distribution of news.

It was a perfect time for heroes in America. Since its conception, the country has needed heroes to inspire the people. Heroes were real people to admire, not fictional characters, though the papers often portrayed them and their exploits with great exaggeration.

The population was given the heroes and plenty of front-page space on which to read of their accomplishments. It was positive news, not attacks on the heroes' personal and family life, that people wanted, information about what the men did to become heroes. If there had been no heroes and thrilling stories of their exploits, America would have grown at a slow, dull pace.

When news about the adventures of Kit Carson and Edward Beale, and about the accomplishments of Captain Sitgreaves and Lieutenant Whipple, reached the eyes of readers, the admiration they felt was often like a flame, igniting their desire to accomplish a feat of their own. And the place to test themselves was America's new wild frontier.

It took a certain type of individual to abandon their community and seek adventure, perhaps a fortune, in the wilderness. But this was the spirit of Americans; this is what drove the country toward success.

Some would survive the adventure and return home, others began a new life in a new place, and many were never heard from again.

Counted with the many explorers and trailblazers glorified by the newspapers during the early 1850s was Francis Xavier Aubry (sometimes spelled Aubrey or Auberry).

This French Canadian was born in 1824 along the St. Lawrence River in western Quebec, but because of financial hardships, his family relocated to St. Louis, Missouri. Before the age of twenty-one, Francis, as his American friends called him, moved to Independence and started a business hauling wagon freight to Santa Fe, New Mexico Territory, the hub of business for the frontier.

Aubry's reputation for making fast, successful trips along the Santa Fe Trail, a distance of over 780 miles through the "great plains," began, perhaps, with an article in the *St. Louis Republican* in 1848. The newspaper detailed his trips, making mention that horses and mules often died by being pushed to exhaustion.

He was also known to go for days without food or rest in order to complete his business, sometimes tying himself in the saddle to keep from falling off if he fell asleep.[5]

The public thrilled at news of Aubry's accomplishments and questioned what motivated a man to push himself beyond normal human endurance. Some believed his below-average physical characteristics were to blame. He was only five foot two inches tall, with tiny hands and feet. But Aubry simply took pride in his success.

In February 1852, the *St. Louis Republican* again praised Aubry, calling him "the most daring traveler on the prairies" after he escorted twelve supply wagons and a group of men through eighteen inches of snow in subzero weather from Santa Fe to Independence.[6]

Possessing tremendous energy, Aubry could not remain in any place for long. While Captain Sitgreaves was completing his expedition to the Colorado for the U.S. government, F. X. Aubry conducted one of his own. He departed Santa Fe with a large flock of sheep, bound for California, following the trail through Yuma into southern California. He returned by a different route, crossing the Colorado somewhere north of present-day Bullhead City, Arizona, and safely north of the Mojave villages. Then he followed the thirty-fifth parallel, returning to Santa Fe.

The trip, from a business point of view, was successful. Californians needed sheep, Aubry made a nice profit, and though he covered some very rugged desert, it had not been much of a challenge for one who had already experienced so many difficult journeys.

Shortly before Aubry departed for California with another flock of sheep, he was interviewed by his friend Major Richard Hanson Weightman, the publisher of an Albuquerque newspaper. The resulting article about Aubry, perhaps intended as a satire, was not very complimentary to Aubry.

Aubry successfully completed that trip, again enjoying a profit, and returned by the same route north of the Mojave as before.

Upon learning of Major Weightman's article, Aubry, known to

have a temper, was furious. He considered the account to be an attack on his diminutive size and his reputation. He did not understand or appreciate the major's humor.

Aubry confronted Major Weightman in a local saloon about the article and an argument ensued. Weightman and companions tried to calm Aubry by explaining that the piece had been written as a joke, but they were unable to convince him.

Things escalated and the major tossed a glass of whiskey (some say it was tequila) in Aubry's face "to calm him down." It had the opposite effect.

Aubry pulled his Colt revolver. During a brief scuffle, he fired one shot, the bullet smashing into the saloon's ceiling.

The major quickly drew his Bowie knife and stabbed Aubry in the chest. F. X. Aubry, "the most daring traveler of the prairies," died a short time later, at the age of twenty-nine.

History would not forget F. X. Aubry. A shortcut along the famous Santa Fe Trail, an army post, and a Kansas town carry his name. And the maps and notes he created during his travels were of great value to future explorers, and the trail he blazed while crossing the Colorado River north of the Mojave became an important route.

CHAPTER 9

Weapons of the 1850s

God created man; Sam Colt made them equal.

1850s Frontier Expression

To survive in the wilderness during the 1850s, one needed the best weapons available for hunting and protection against those who might try to do harm.

In the western territories, the large wild animals capable of attacking travelers were wolves, bears, and the mountain lion (often called puma, cougar, or catamount).[1]

Before the 1850s, men carried a single-shot rifle and maybe a pistol or two, also firing only one shot each. Once those were fired, he had little or no time to reload (depending on the situation) and survival often depended on his ability to fight with a knife.

Upon encountering a hostile Native American Indian, white travelers were at a disadvantage. The southwest Indians usually carried a knife, maybe a war club or spear, and could shoot several arrows from a bow before their enemy reloaded his single-shot rifle. In addition, they knew their territory long before the intruder arrived.

Since the early days of American history, men in the wilderness carried knives, usually large knives, which they needed for a variety of purposes. Mostly, the blade was used as a tool, but when necessary, it became a weapon. Most of the early knives were carried in sheaths and closely resembled those that a modern-day butcher needs for his trade.

The evolution of knife-making technology and fighting techniques took a giant leap in 1827 because of a fight that occurred near Natchez on a sandbar along the edge of the Mississippi River.[2]

A pistol duel, common at the time, had just ended with no one hurt and the two gentlemen restoring their honor and settling differences by shaking hands.

But that ending apparently was not what sixteen supporting spectators wanted to see. They all had previous grievances. First, a fistfight with shoving and name-calling erupted. Suddenly a rifle shot was fired, the ball striking a man wearing a large sheath knife in the leg. He was not the intended victim, but another man, seeing the wounded man fall, rushed at him with a sword cane and stabbed him in the chest. His sternum deflected the blade.

The wounded man stood, jerked the sword from his chest, drew his knife, and quickly killed the one who stabbed him.

During the next ten minutes, the fight developed into a true American brawl, going down in the pages of history as "the Mississippi Sand Bar Fight."

The man with the knife continued to protect himself but was wounded once more by a pistol shot to the arm. Using his strange-looking knife in a style no one had ever seen before, he managed to kill two more of his assailants and wound several men before the others fled.

Newspapers throughout the South carried eyewitness accounts of what they labeled "the Great Sand Bar Duel." When papers in the North picked up the story, it simply was reported as "the Sand Bar Fight."

A new American hero was created by the news media. A boy, wounded and outnumbered, fought his enemies alone with only one weapon, a large knife.

So began the legend of James "Jim" Bowie.

Actually, the knife used by Jim Bowie at the sandbar, a gift from his brother Rezin, was not the final design for which he became so famous.

The sandbar knife was reported to be slightly less then ten inches long, about one-fourth of an inch thick, and only one and a half inches wide. But because of the news coverage of the fight, Jim Bowie and his knife became world famous. Cutlers in Sheffield, England, began to mass-produce a similar design, and blacksmiths east of the Mississippi River were having difficulties filling orders.

In 1830, Bowie employed Arkansas blacksmith James Black to produce a new design based somewhat on the original. The Black-made knife became the true "Bowie knife."

Black's knives were famous for being tough but flexible. Some believed he had learned to produce true Damascus steel; others speculated that he incorporated a certain percent of iron from a meteorite. Whatever the truth, Black died with his secret, and no one has produced a knife exactly the same since his death.

One special characteristic of Bowie's knife was the "clip point," a point that is at the tip of the blade but lower than the spine. This yields a sharp stabbing point. Above the tip is a "false edge" that may or may not be sharpened.

This type of design removes some metal weight but facilitates penetration.

At the back of the blade near the handle, a strip of soft metal, usually copper or brass, served as a hand guard.

Bowie relocated to Texas with his knife, and his reputation traveled along with him. There he was constantly challenged by those who desired to "test" his fighting skills. One famous story is about three men hired to kill him who were foolish enough to select knives as their assassination weapon.

Bowie killed all three in less then two minutes.

But there was one fight in which his knife could not save him. Jim Bowie died fighting for Texas freedom at the Alamo in 1836 at the age of forty.

Within a few years, every frontiersman traveling through the Southwest wore some type of Bowie knife. It had become standard survival equipment in the wilderness. Over the years, thousands of knives have been manufactured and marketed as Bowie knives.[3, 4]

Major changes in firearms development were under way in the mid-1800s, partially due to demand during the Mexican War, but mostly the result of the innovating minds of Americans at work.

Sixteen-year-old Samuel Colt, for example, was to learn the seaman's trade, but his observations of the ship's wheel during his first voyage inspired him to invent a weapon that would change history.

It was 1832, and Colt was puzzling over an interesting fact about that wheel. No matter which way it turned, each spoke came directly in line with a clutch, holding it in position. Was it possible to design a cylinder for a pistol that could operate in a similar fashion? He carved a wooden model of a pistol with a revolving cylinder, improvised a mechanism that held it in place, and a hammer that, when pulled back, rotated the cylinder. He called his invention a "revolver."

Though several inventors came up with similar designs, most, with the exception of a flintlock pistol in Europe, were based on a revolving barrel. Sam Colt's design was one with a stationary barrel and revolving cylinder, fired by percussion caps.

Colt started a small factory in Paterson, New Jersey, and in 1836 obtained his first patent for a "Paterson Pistol." He also promoted the idea of an assembly line producing interchangeable parts with serial numbers.

With single-shot pistols on the market before 1836, a man under attack had but one shot. His survival then depended on his ability with a knife. Sam Colt changed all that.

Before the perfection of metal cartridges, the early Colt revolvers were "percussion" or "cap and ball," as the old-timers called them. The chambers of the cylinder were loaded with a measured amount of "black" gunpowder, then a lead ball topped off with a grease-soaked patch, packed tightly with the self-contained "ramrod." At the rear of the cylinder were "nipples," one for each chamber, on which a soft metal cap was placed.

The early (prior to the Civil War) pistols were "single action." That is, each time the hammer was cocked, the cylinder rotated. When the trigger was pulled, the hammer fell upon the cap, which contained a small explosive charge, and a flame ignited the gunpowder.

Colt suffered a number of financial setbacks, until an order arrived from Texas Ranger captain Samuel Hamilton Walker. The production model, partially designed by Walker, put Colt firmly in the revolver business.

Walker was already a national hero, famous for his bravery in combat during the Texas fight for independence.

In 1847, a new, more powerful revolver was needed to give the American soldiers an advantage over the enemy in the Mexican War. The Walker Colt would be the first revolver actually purchased by the United States Army.

The Walker pistol .44-caliber was fourteen inches long and so heavy that Sam Colt once conceded, "It would take a Texan to shoot it!"

The pistol became legendary and a financial success for Colt, but Captain Walker was killed by a Mexican lance at the Battle of Huamantla in October 1847.

After the Mexican War, Sam Colt went on to design two of the most successful revolvers in American history. The first was a small, .31-caliber weapon sometimes called a "pocket model," and it gained popularity during the early Gold Rush days in 1848–1849.

The next was the "Colt revolving belt pistol of Naval Caliber," most commonly known as the Colt 1851 Navy, Naval Revolver, or Colt Navy.

In .36 caliber, the Navy, like its predecessors, was percussion fired and single action (the hammer must be cocked each time it is to be fired, causing the cylinder to rotate), but it was lighter and designed to be carried in a holster on a belt.

The lead ball of the .36-caliber weighed about eighty-six grams and, traveling at a velocity of one thousand feet per second, had the power of a modern-day .380 pistol cartridge.[5]

The model became so popular that its use was continued from 1851 through the Civil War, and it remained in production until 1873 when revolvers began using metal cartridges. An estimated 250,000 were produced in the United States and another 20,000 were manufactured in London under Colt's patent.

The Navy got its name from the cylinder of early models, which were engraved with a scene of ships battling: Colt's way of honoring the Texas navy's victory over Mexican ships in May 1843.

The revolver was actually purchased by civilians and army (land forces) and became the major weapon in the Southwest through the 1850s. Soon the famous line was coined, "God created men, Sam Colt made them equal."

By the mid-1850s, Colt's revolvers had become known as "equalizers" with a little help from pistols engraved with the words "Fear no man, regardless of his size. Call on me and I will equalize."

A testimonial written in the journal of famous explorer Francis Xavier Aubry on August 15, 1853, explains that he and his party came under attack by a superior force of Indians near present-day Prescott, Arizona. Aubry states, "We shot them down so fast with Colt's revolvers that we soon put them to flight. We owe our lives to these firearms."

While Sam Colt's invention revolutionized pistols, shoulder weapons (rifles) had a few years to go before they became "repeaters."

Emigrants crossing the Southwest and flooding into California during the Gold Rush days were still depending on the single-shot, muzzle-loaded, percussion (cap) rifle.

There were many independent gun makers producing the type known as the Kentucky or Pennsylvania rifle, which was extremely accurate with its long, slim barrel that allowed frontiersmen to hit a man-size target at three hundred yards.

Samuel and Jacob Hawkins introduced a shorter, heavier rifle in larger caliber, ranging from .50 to .58. Soon other makers copied the design and all similar rifles were called "Hawkins."

The real advantage of the rifle was that it could be loaded with more gunpowder (actually required to propel a large-caliber ball) and it was capable of killing a buffalo or even a grizzly bear. For this reason, the Hawkins became popular with "mountain men."

The first important change in shoulder-fired weapons came in 1848 when a new design with a "falling block" was introduced by Christian Sharps. This rifle, also called a "breech block," had a self-cocking design that enabled the shooter to load through the breech at the rear of the barrel (near the stock) rather than through the muzzle. This improved firing and reloading speed.

The rifle weighed about eight pounds and fired a .50-caliber projectile at 1,200 feet per second at an effective range of 500 to 600 yards.

The U.S. military quickly ordered fifteen thousand Sharps rifles in 1851 and again in 1853.

Sharps also designed a smaller, lighter model called a "carbine," which was perfect for mounted riflemen, then known as dragoons.

In addition to the Sharps's fast-firing and -reloading capabilities (eight to ten shots per minute), the military was impressed with the extreme accuracy at six hundred yards. For this reason, Christian Sharps would be remembered through history. At least his name would. Today we call good marksmen "sharpshooters."

As is often the case with the introduction of new weapons, the army units most needing the Sharps rifles would not receive them until late 1858.

CHAPTER 10

The Bishop and Beale Company

The Indians are driven from their homes and deprived
of their hunting grounds and fishing waters at the dis-
cretion of the Whites.

Edward F. Beale,

Presentation to the Indian Affairs Committee,

Washington, 1853

First it was the trappers, then the gold prospectors, digging away the
land and rerouting the streams. Now the intruders wanted the land for
themselves, all the land.

The Native American Indians in the interior of California were
rapidly losing their land, beginning with the 1849 Gold Rush. Soon
they would have no more.

In the Fresno River area, Samuel Bishop attempted to follow the
concept of treating the Indians fairly and protecting their rights, as his
friend Major James Savage had done.

This was at least true on the reservations that had been established
for their safety. Then came the suspicion that gold might exist on Indian land, so efforts began to relocate these people once again.

Men like Sam Bishop who truly cared for the Indians hoped that
"outside" help, once promised by the federal government, might be "on
the way." The situation with Indians in California had, at last, the attention of Congress in Washington. Several treaty proposals pertaining to the Indians had been presented to Congress, but the California

delegation blocked the progress, claiming each suggestion included too much land (land that might contain gold) to be given to the Indians.

Lieutenant Edward F. Beale had recently returned to Washington from California with ideas that could resolve the disputes. The suggestions were studied by Arkansas senator William Sebastian, chairman of the Indian Affairs Committee. Edward Beale, American hero, was appointed superintendent of Indian affairs for California. Beale arrived in Los Angeles after his "uneventful" survey trip along the thirty-eighth parallel and received another appointment, this one from California's governor, John Bigler. Edward Beale, lieutenant in the U.S. Navy, was now also brigadier general of the California Militia. From that time on, the news media and just about everyone in California called him "General Beale."[1]

The title gave Beale authority to negotiate in the state with both whites and Indians. Now he had federal and state support for his programs.

General Beale then went to work with his first project, reform in the highly volatile area of Fresno and San Joaquin Valley in the heart of the Gold Rush country.

Now fate was about to ensure a meeting of two characters who would have influence on both California and U.S. history. It was time for Edward F. Beale, general, lieutenant, and superintendent, to meet Samuel A. Bishop, former prospector, rancher, Indian trader, and one of the few white men whom the Indians respected in the San Joaquin Valley.

Bishop was just the man Beale needed to help set in motion his master plan, which included the relocation of local Indians.

Essentially, Beale and Bishop communicated well from the beginning. Bishop was hired to supervise the movement of Indians out of the gold country as soon as possible.

The area selected for the Indians' new home would be Tejon Canyon and Tejon Pass along the southern tip of the San Joaquin Valley at the western edge of a desert now called the Mojave. The new reservation was near the modern-day town of Lebec, about thirty miles south of Bakersfield and sixty miles north of Los Angeles.

Beale planned to call the reservation San Sebastian.

Most of the Indians who once admired Major Savage loved and respected Sam Bishop, who had always treated them with kindness. They were willing to follow Bishop to their new home, hoping to find peace away from the madness and violence in the gold country.

The story of who actually owned the land in the Tejon Valley where the San Sebastian Reservation was to be located is complicated. In 1843, the Mexican government made grants for land that became three ranches, one being El Tejon. But after the Mexican War, some in California believed all that land now belonged to the U.S. government. In a legal argument, Beale proposed that since the land was unoccupied, it could be purchased by companies or individuals. Conveniently, Bishop came in and purchased much of the land, including the El Tejon Ranch property (where the reservation would be located).

In December 1853, many of the northern (Fresno) Indians arrived at the reservation. By then, the "Bishop and Beale Company" had established itself as a growing organization. The partnership planned to "raise livestock and buy and sell land" (though they seemed only to be buying, not selling).

By mid-1854, General Beale reported that 2,500 Indians were living peacefully on the reservation and 7,500 more were expected by year's end.[2]

Sam Bishop made friends with Alex Godey, a former army scout and guide, and planned to use the frontiersman to assist in doing business at a military base about to be constructed near the reservation. The army would need beef and farm goods and Bishop and associates (Beale and the Indians) could supply the need.

Meanwhile, Beale's plans at the reservation were taking shape faster than even he imagined. He really planned for a series of reservations, protected by a military post next to the area. Each reservation was to be "self-supporting" through farming and other trades. He requested $500,000 to implement the plan. He received $250,000.

With the help of Sam Bishop, they procured equipment and supplies for the reservation. Soon farming tools, cattle, and sheep arrived and a staff went to work teaching the Indians agriculture. Hundreds of acres of land were planted with wheat, barley, and corn. Tejon Creek was rerouted with an irrigation system for gardens, vineyards, and orchards.

Nearby mountain wilderness provided wild game to hunt. Trees were cut in the Upper Tejon Valley and the Indians learned to make lumber for storage sheds and houses.

Beale had based his concept for Indian reservations on the old Spanish mission programs that were designed to help the California Indians become "civilized" and self-supporting while introducing Christianity. The missions seemed to have worked on the coast but were something entirely new to tribes in central California. Beale, with all his energy applied, had the concept working once again, but he was realistic. If the Indians remained in the gold country, they would suffer continual loss of land and life. At the time the reservation was the best thing for them.

By mid-1854, Beale's project had experienced success. The second phase went into effect. This included additional education for the Indians.

In July 1854, Lieutenant Alfred Latimer camped at the reservation with a detachment of dragoons, but the area had no water or forage for their horses and no timber to build permanent structures.

The military camp relocated to the end of Grapevine Canyon, about seventeen miles southwest of the reservation. Here they had everything needed to build a post.

On August 10, 1854, the First Dragoons arrived and began construction of a complex that, upon completion, included more than forty buildings. A small town quickly developed next to the project from which the army drew the necessary laborers.

Someone suggested the new fort be named for Peter Le Beck, whose name was found carved in a large oak tree. The inscription read, *Peter Le Beck—killed by a bear—October 17, 1837.* But nothing could be learned of Le Beck—where he came from or what brought him there or even who buried him and left the inscription.

Since the area already carried the name Tejon (from the Spanish meaning "Badger"), that seemed appropriate; thus, Fort Tejon.

The "fort" was designed more as a garrison than a fortress since no one expected it ever to be attacked. The buildings at Fort Tejon were mostly rectangular, constructed of wood and adobe. Some were single level, others had two floors. Roofs were gabled and shingled with either pine or redwood, and all structures had stone foundations.

Colors used on window frames and doors ranged from white to "burnt cream" to Prussian blue, and inside walls were plastered.

In all, Fort Tejon was a handsome garrison situated in an almost perfect location at 3,500 feet elevation, with a semiarid climate, nestled between beautiful rolling hills and wooded mountains.

Summer temperatures ranged from mideighties to midnineties; winters often dropped to temperatures below freezing. For this reason, most buildings had large fireplaces.

An abundance of wildlife could be found in the surrounding hills: songbirds, woodpeckers, deer, rabbit, bobcats, badgers, coyotes, and gray foxes.

Even though Fort Tejon appeared to be a military paradise, the usual problems frustrated the men stationed there. Some felt the long, dry season with no rain made homesickness, loneliness, and boredom even more difficult to tolerate.

But the men did draw patrol duty. They were there to protect the Indians, but they also had the responsibility of helping "keep the peace" in the Owens and San Gabriel valleys. Often the dragoons chased after Indian raiding parties who attacked the reservation Indians (in an attempt to steal cattle). These raiders were mostly Paiute, Chemehuevi, and sometimes the Mojave who crossed the vast desert, even during summers when temperatures were over 110 degrees.

While the army was busy building their garrison, the Bishop and Beale Company had several business projects, including selling meat, grain, fresh fruits, and vegetables, some from their ranch and some raised on the reservation.

Sam Bishop became the "legal" expert in the Fort Tejon area, having been appointed justice of the peace, notary public, and judge of the plains.

The fort and its adjoining little town formed the hub between the central valley and the southern areas of California. It would remain a key military installation until the beginning of the Civil War, when its dragoons were relocated to guard Los Angeles.

General Beale, as might be expected, had political enemies. His rank and fame both in California and Washington, his business enterprises, and the Sebastian reservation opened him to criticism and attack, even in the news media (which had always promoted him in the past). Fueled by jealousy, a few of those enemies suggested that Beale had set aside too much land for Indians, land that might hold gold.

But at the end of the first year, Beale enjoyed an abundant harvest, especially in wheat. Smaller ranch owners complained of "unfair" competition once the Indian crops hit the market. This did little damage to his business or reputation, but the huge sum of money Washington sent to Beale's reservation attracted enemies, and they closed in like sharks. A few even dared to accuse Beale of "embezzlement of government funds."

True or not, the publicity and questions regarding business activities became too much, and Beale was removed from office, replaced by the far less flamboyant Colonel Thomas J. Henley. Indian responsibility in California was then split between Colonel Henley and Colonel James R. Vineyard, who became "resident agent" at the Sebastian Reservation.

But the Bishop and Beale Company did not suffer and was far from broke. In fact, it continued to prosper. The two men had the large ranch, raising cattle and selling beef to the army, villagers, and prospectors. They became so busy that Sam Bishop remodeled an old estate on their property, moved in, and set up his offices for ranch management and a variety of legal businesses.

The next year, 1855, Beale purchased the adjoining large tract of land known as Rancho La Liebre. Then Samuel Bishop decided it was time to start a family. He married a Los Angeles beauty, fifteen-year-old Francis Ella Young, and the newlyweds settled in at the remodeled ranch house.[3]

One day, after a brief honeymoon, Bishop received a message from the commander of Fort Tejon, delivered by a dragoon. Apparently, the commander was in need of a justice of the peace.

Bishop promptly reported to Captain John W. T. Gardiner, who, as a prolific writer of descriptive letters and lengthy reports to his headquarters, recorded his observations of that first meeting (in a letter to his parents).

The delightful description of rancher Samuel A. Bishop by Captain Gardiner in 1856 reads, in part:

> "I have here a Justice of the Peace on my hands, who I sent for on some public business. I have given him an intelligent soldier for a clerk and he, the Justice, is preparing himself by reading a thick volume of California laws.
>
> "His appearance is not very judicial. He is in shirt sleeves, with a hat considerably the worse for wear, a huge pair of Mexican spurs, with buckskin leggings and, of course, what no Californian travels without, a revolver in his belt."[4]

Sam Bishop remained busy between ranching and legal practice. In less than three years, his name would become famous throughout California for an event that had no connection to any business project.

Regardless of the problems encountered with the reservation program and those created by enemies, Ed Beale had proven to Washington that the system would work.

As 1856 drew to a close, the War Department was busy evaluating a strange new idea, a project never before attempted in the United States. Even the new president agreed that Ed Beale was the perfect man to get the project under way.

CHAPTER 11

Camels to America?

> That the sum of $30,000 be, and the same is hereby appropriated, to be expended under the direction of the War Department, in the purchase and importation of camels and dromedaries to be employed for military purposes.
>
> *U.S. 33rd Congress, 2nd Session,*
> *Section 04, Chapter 169, 1856*

Josiah Harlan captivated the secretary of war with fascinating stories about his times in Kabul. The news media reported that Harlan had been the "first American in Afghanistan," stating that he led a liberating army of four thousand infantry and cavalry to victory over slave-trading warlords in that barren country.

For his victory (and some fancy political dealings), forty-year-old Harlan, the son of a Pennsylvania Quaker, was given the title "Prince of Ghor."[1]

Harlan really wanted to be a king, if not of Afghanistan then at least of a province, like Ghor. But, unfortunately for the new prince, the British army had their own dreams and marched into Afghanistan. British officers were, of course, surprised to find an American in Kabul, especially one with so much power and influence. The prince was one thing the British did not need in their territory, so they "suggested" he leave, without his army. Harlan eventually made it back to America and his army retreated into the mountains with plans to deal with the Englishmen later.

Josiah Harlan, like so many early American adventurers, was a self-educated man, but he was also brilliant and very lucky. He had mastered the languages of Latin, Greek, and French and passed a British exam to be a military surgeon in India, all before the age of twenty-two.

His heroes were historic military conquerors, especially Alexander the Great. In fact, if the British had not interfered, Prince Harlan may have succeeded in the conquest of Afghanistan, where Alexander and many others had failed.

Some in Washington believed that Harlan was nothing more than an adventurer and mercenary. Perhaps he truly was a prince, but of a place most Americans had never heard of.

Secretary of War Jefferson Davis shrugged off negative people. He had a proposal before Congress requesting funds to purchase and test a new weapon desperately needed by the army in the Southwest, and the Prince had some very important information related to that proposal.

There was a part of Prince Harlan's story that fascinated Secretary Davis and a handful of top army officers. Harlan claimed that his army, which marched on Kabul, had four thousand troops, including fourteen hundred cavalry. One thousand of those rode horses but four hundred of the riflemen were mounted on *camels*!

The timing of Harlan's appearance in Washington was perfect. The entire population along the East Coast knew of the War Department's interest in procuring camels, thanks to the news media and local (Washington) gossip.

But now, the Prince of Ghor, an American, was in Washington. He was not only familiar with camels; he had actually commanded four hundred of them in combat.

The War Department learned that camels performed admirably in battle, not only carrying heavy loads great distances with little or no water, but remaining calm and easy to control in combat in spite of rifle and cannon fire.

Harlan's request, in exchange for information, was the right to import Afghan camels to the U.S.A. with himself, of course, being the procuring officer.

No need to worry about the British, Harlan explained. Their army, along with dependants, had attempted to withdraw from Afghanistan and all sixteen thousand soldiers, women, and children were slaughtered by Afghan tribesmen. And, Harlan was still a prince, willing to renew old contacts.

Secretary Davis expressed his appreciation for Harlan's knowledge but he believed that importing camels from Afghanistan would be too costly. The War Department had already made plans to obtain the animals from another location, easier to reach by sea.

Throughout the 1800s, America continued to produce extraordinary, charismatic individuals so necessary in the growth of a young, aggressive nation. And these men often proved to be extremely versatile.

In an effort to be involved with providing camels for the army, or to compete in what some believed to soon be a thriving camel market in the U.S., Charles Wilkins Webber, a writer from Russellville, Kentucky, joined with three other men, procured a charter from the New York Legislature, and formed "the American Camel Company" in 1855.

Webber, once a frontier adventurer, had served with the Texas Rangers, then studied medicine, then entered the Presbyterian ministry before moving to New York. He authored numerous articles and novels, some based on his experiences with the Rangers. At times, he used the pen name Charles Winterfield, for unknown reasons.

He claimed to have befriended wildlife artist John James Audubon, who, according to Webber, suggested the idea of using camels as a "beast of burden" in the Southwest. True or not, Charles Webber, by the middle of 1855, was convinced that America needed camels for transportation. He announced in newspapers that if the army was not interested in his project, perhaps the Mormons would be. That suggestion brought on considerable comment from the public. But his project came to a sudden end.

Webber dropped from sight and reappeared in Central America. Apparently the new call for adventure was much more interesting than importing camels.

Webber moved to Nicaragua and joined the famous revolutionary William Walker in his struggle to conquer that country.

William Walker, a medical doctor and attorney, had gained fame by his conquest of Baja California (Republic of Mexico), where he set himself up as president of what he called the "Republic of Lower California." Receiving no military support from the United States, he was finally driven out by the Mexicans.

Walker seemed to enjoy the title and power of president and set his next target as Nicaragua. He raised an army of about one hundred Americans, mostly from Kentucky and Tennessee, and proceeded to establish a new "state" for the United States.

After several battles and political dealings William Walker was appointed "president" of Nicaragua. He declared English to be the official language, legalized slavery, and began to seek admission for his country as a state of the United States.[2]

President Franklin Pierce, impressed with Walker's accomplishments, "recognized" his regime as the legitimate government of Nicaragua on May 20, 1856.

But Walker's devoted follower, Charles Wilkins Webber, did not live to see this great day. Charles Webber had been killed in the Battle of Rivas on April 11. He died at age thirty-seven, never completing his dream of an American Camel Company.

It is difficult to determine who should receive credit for being the first to suggest using camels in the American Southwest. Some argue that Kit Carson and Edward Beale deserve recognition for the discussion they had on the subject when crossing the desert after the Battle of San Pasqual.

Most agree that the thought of using camels originated in 1836 with a West Point graduate, George Hampton Crossman, while he served as a second lieutenant with Zachary Taylor during the Seminole War in Florida.

Lieutenant Crossman believed that camels could substitute for horses and mules, transporting military supplies, and for the next fifteen years he studied the subject carefully.[3]

Ten years after the Seminole War, during the Mexican War, officers close to (now) Major Crossman listened to his ideas and wanted to promote the camel theory further.

After the Mexican War, Major Crossman, serving in the Quartermaster Corps in Washington, became friends with Major Henry Constantine Wayne and soon converted his new friend to his idea. They both were now convinced that camels were a practical solution to the army's transportation problems in the American desert.[4]

Wayne became very enthusiastic about the concept and began to meet with senators, receiving the best reception from the Kentucky-born senator from Mississippi, Jefferson Davis. A key individual in the promotion process, Senator Davis was chairman of the Senate Committee on Military Affairs.

Davis had served in the Mexican War and was especially interested in providing the army with a better way of chasing Indians in the West. Horses and mules required water frequently and were often outdistanced by the clever Native Americans, who managed to remain elusive in the mountains and even in open desert terrain.

The concept began to roll rapidly when Wayne made a formal recommendation to the War Department. Davis attempted to win an appropriation in 1851. His speeches in Congress included details on the expected capabilities of camels and their great speed, making them ideal for the dragoons.

But, since there were no camels in America in the 1850s, they had to be imported and that would cost a sizable amount of money.

With the news media involved, suddenly the public became interested.

Journalist Gwinn Harris Heap (Edward Beale's cousin) published a journal of his trip along the thirty-eighth parallel. It is not known how much influence, if any, Beale had in the matter, but Heap stated that he believed camels to be the answer to the military's transportation problem in the West.

In 1854, George Perkins Marsh, a former congressman from Vermont and noted diplomat and environmentalist, gave a series of lectures at the Smithsonian Institution and discussed how camels were used in Turkey. Marsh had served as minister to Turkey under Zachary Taylor. He continued to push for the U.S. government to study the feasibility of the camels in our desert.[5]

Then George Glidden, a famous American Egyptologist, offered his expert opinions, writing a memo to Congress supporting the camel project.

Author and scientist John Russell Bartlett had just returned from working along the U.S. Southwest boundary. He was certain that camels should be used in that region.[6]

In general, Congress was impressed with all the suggestions from some of the most brilliant men of the century. They were "neutral," not politicians or members of the military. But the government seemed preoccupied with the slavery issue and the Mormon situation.

The big break for Crossman and Wayne came in 1853 when Jefferson Davis was appointed secretary of war. Davis had done all the necessary research on camels and, having once been a member of Congress, fully appreciated the thinking of his colleagues. He knew how to work within the system.

Like everyone else in Washington, Davis also understood the need for a railroad to link east and west.

At the end of 1854, Secretary Davis made a passionate presentation to Congress in which he went into great detail about the western territories, the lack of navigable streams or roads, and how horses and mules were inadequate due to the lack of water and grass in the region. He stressed how California was defenseless in the event of a foreign attack unless better transportation existed between east and west.

And then, on to his favorite subject, he pointed to increased Indian attacks on emigrants traveling west and how easily the Native Americans made their escape, avoiding capture and punishment.

The one subject he did not touch upon was the worry about the Mormons and what moves they might try in the West in the near future.

Davis did not need to mention the Mormons. Everyone in Congress had concerns as to just what the LDS members might do next.

Secretary Davis requested money to import and test camels. In December 1854, Congress refused the request. Then, just after the first of the year, things changed. Rumors reached Washington saying the Mormons were preparing for war if the United States did not give in to their demands.

Actually, other than to be left alone, the Mormons had made no demands. But rumors persisted, telling of a huge army being raised by Mormons in Utah.

And then Secretary of War Jefferson Davis won his long struggle to procure and test camels for the army.

An amount of thirty thousand dollars was granted to the War Department for their camel project. The bill would become law on March 3, 1855. Davis had to prepare to proceed at once to obtain the animals from the Levant (the area now known as Israel, Jordan, Lebanon, Syria, and Palestinian Territories), though that plan would change.

Prince Josiah Harlan had, perhaps more then anyone, influenced Davis with his stories of a camel cavalry. Unfortunately for Harlan, the answer was still "no, thank you" for camels coming from Afghanistan.

The congressional bill made it clear that the camel experiment would be for the military. It read in part: "Statutes at Large. 33rd Congress, 2nd Session. Chapter CLXIX, page #635, Section #04 And be it further enacted; that the sum of $30,000 be, and the same is hereby appropriated to be expended under the direction of the War Department, in the purchase and importation of camels and Dromedaries to be employed for military purposes."

A leader was needed for the first mission to the Orient to locate camels. The position was first offered to Major Crossman as a reward for his twenty-year effort on the project.

Crossman declined, recommending his younger (forty-year-old) friend who had helped move the program along, Major Henry Constantine Wayne.

At long last, camels would soon be coming to America.

CHAPTER 12

What Is a Camel?

Why do they not reflect on the camels and how they are created?

The Quran 88:17

In 1856, as the War Department in Washington prepared to send a party to the Middle East to purchase camels, most people who had been following the story for at least two years faced reality. They knew nothing of the animal the army claimed they desperately needed.

The origin of the English word *camel* is often debated. It may have derived from the Greek *kamelos*, or Hebrew, *gamal*, or Arabic *jamal*.

Camels were domesticated more than a thousand years ago and served men as companions and work animals before the writings of the Bible or Quran. Early men had learned that the animal was patient and docile when properly trained, but dangerous when mistreated.

We think of camels as large, long-legged, cud-chewing animals with one or two humps on their back, used for travel in desert areas. We have also been educated to believe that camels can go a long time without drinking water; very important, of course, in desert lands. But understanding the origin and qualities of the animal involves much more.

Actually, camels are no strangers to North America. They originated and survived here millions of years ago, becoming extinct after a glacial period about 15,000 BC. By that time many had migrated to Asia. Others made their way into South America, evolving into distant relatives known as alpacas and llamas.

In the 1850s, camels were concentrated in the Gobi Desert. Two varieties dominated: the Bactrian, with two humps, and the one-hump species, the dromedary or "Arabian" camel.

The dromedary (one-hump Arabian camel) is taller than the Bactrian and usually is bred in two variations, one for hauling baggage and one for riding and racing. Mixtures of the two exist and even the baggage type can run extremely fast if relieved of his burden.

They range in color from faun and brown to black with a small percentage being white.

The Bactrian (two humps) is smaller and stronger, with the ability to carry up to a thousand pounds, where the dromedary has a load capacity of four to six hundred pounds. But with these weights they both can cover thirty miles in one day, depending of course on the terrain.

The camels' height varies with the Bactrian, usually about seven feet tall at the top of his humps, while the dromedary is often eight to nine feet at the tip of the hump. The average U.S. Army mule of the 1850s carried a load of about two hundred pounds, often a little more.

In a magazine article published November 19, 1859, Edward Beale was quoted as saying, "I have tried effectively, the comparison value of mules and camels as pack animals. The mule carries a burden of 200 pounds, the camel packed with 400 pounds besides a rider, armed with rifle, revolver, and ammunition and his bedding load over the pack to sit on."[1]

Lieutenant Beale knew how to excite readers by feeding carefully chosen information to the news media, which stimulated the reader's imagination and drew his attention to the lieutenant's exploits. A rider armed with "rifle and revolver," for example, painted a picture in one's mind of Beale and his team moving through the Wild West, ready for action.

In the 1850s, the name dromedary applied to any swift camel, and it will be that one-hump variety of animal on which this story will mostly focus.

Speed was a factor that caught the attention of the army, though the capacity of hauling heavy loads long distances originally had priority. With only a rider and his weapons, a camel can run ten miles an hour for up to eighteen hours and hold a speed of twenty-five miles an hour for a full hour, beyond the capabilities of mules and horses. And then, as an added benefit for dragoons (cavalry), the camel can run forty-five miles an hour in short bursts, up to about three miles, outperforming any riding animal in the Americas.

Another quality that intrigued the U.S. Army was the ability of camels to travel days without water. In the Southwest, where water is in short supply (or nonexistent in many areas), water had become a major concern for the military attempting to travel between outposts. But it was unknown at the time in the United States just how far or how long a camel could go without water.

To the traveling Arab, the camel is *ata Allah*, "God's gift." For the bedouin, who owns no land, camels are a measure of wealth. Land, to him, has no value. It is only something others fight over. But the camel can take these nomads to food and water and away from danger.

The camel is, indeed, a gift and necessity for those trying to live and work in or next to a desert. The entire structure of the camel is a wonder, especially considering its physiological adaptation.

In recent years, man has advanced the study of this interesting animal to understand just how it accomplishes what it must do to survive in harsh conditions.

The camel's hump is not exactly a storage place for water but a mass of fatty tissue from which moisture and energy are absorbed, metabolized, and extracted by the body as needed. The animal can lose one-fourth of its total weight without adversely affecting its energy level. A human can tolerate only a 10 percent loss.

If given the opportunity, the camel will drink water every three to five days, then, depending on weather and land conditions, he may take in fifteen or twenty gallons. In mild weather (temperatures less than 95 degrees) and/or where he has had a nice supply of juicy greens to eat, he has been known to exist more than a month without drinking water. Most mammals, under exertion, lose moisture by perspiring, which keeps the body temperature within a certain range. Survival depends on this. Humans, for example, function best when the body stays within one degree of 98.6 degrees. At higher temperatures we perspire faster and lose more moisture. The camel sweats during exercise in very high heat, but he has a special mechanism to help absorb heat during the hot part of the day, which he then releases during rest. His body can tolerate temperature ranges of 93 degrees to 103 degrees.

Camels possess four stomachs. Food is passed from one to another then back to the mouth to be rechewed (the cud). Every drop of moisture is extricated from the food, and with very efficient kidneys, urine often passes as a thick "syrup." Likewise, feces are extremely dry. Even their red blood cells have a shape different from other mammals, which allows the blood to flow freely in a dehydrated condition. Their body seems to sweat only in temperatures well over 106 degrees. Their thick coat aids in reflecting sunlight and their long legs support the body high above the hot ground.

As the camel breathes, water vapor exhaled into the nostrils is trapped and returned to the body, and during a dust- or sandstorm, the nostrils "seal" and the eyes are protected by long lashes and a series of "lids."

The camel's mobile lips and long neck aid in gathering food in difficult places without using the tongue (which could cause loss of valuable moisture). He can manipulate two flaps of his lips like fingers (camels have been known to untie a line or rope attached to a post with their lips).

And when it comes to food choice, the entire desert is his smorgasbord. He will eat most anything growing, including bushes and branches with thorns. Horses and mules will eat grass, preferring corn and oats. Camels will eat those as well.

His front teeth are razor sharp, which helps in biting through things a horse or mule cannot. Two large incisors and two canines with twelve molars on top and six incisors and two canines and ten molars on the lower jaw give the animal great crushing power and serious weapons if it must fight. For defense, the camel relies on kicking, biting, and his speed, but he also uses these if he becomes the aggressor.[2]

Young camels, called calves, like the young of most animals, are curious and playful. In 1859, a Boston newspaper quoted Edward Beale's experience: "The young are wonderful pets in camp but very mischievous, poking their nose into every pot and pan about the camp. Their great aim in life seems to be to ape the manners and habits of their sires—kneeling down and growling and complaining precisely as the old ones do when the train is packed."[3]

The foot of the camel is much different from that of the horse. Camels have two toes on each foot and each toe has a hoof at the front. The heel is a soft pad of fat enclosed in thick skin. On sand or soft soil the foot is like a snowshoe, supporting the heavy (550- to 1,500-pound) animal from sinking.

This foot, however, was to cause a problem in some parts of the American Southwest, where sharp stones often lodged between the toes, resulting in the animal becoming lame.

The knees and chest of the camel are coated by thick, leatherlike pads, protecting him as he kneels or crawls.

The female usually delivers only one calf, which can actually run when only a few hours old. The calf is weaned at one year, but will stay close to his mother for several years unless, of course, they are forced apart.

The average life span is forty years, but some camels have been known to live sixty to seventy years. "Topsy" survived in the Los Angeles Zoo until 1935. He was born about 1855. If this story is true, he was eighty when he died.

The intelligence of the camel is something the Western world has not found a way to accurately measure. It is believed, however, that the camel is much "smarter" than the horse, though it is not clear by what standards this was determined.

Horses and mules have alert instincts and can react much faster than men if frightened or shocked by an unwanted event. The camel is less likely to be "spooked," or react, the same way as a horse does. The camel seems to pause and analyze a situation for danger before reacting. He is confident (perhaps overconfident) in his ability to either fight, if necessary, or outrun the problem.

In the mid-1800s, most Americans may have never seen a camel, but they knew a little about them, thanks to the Bible and a few books written by those who traveled to Egypt and the Mideastern countries.

There were no zoos in the United States in 1856 and the circus, with its unusual animals, though introduced in the late 1700s, performed only in the eastern states. P. T. Barnum would not begin his shows until the 1870s, followed by Ringling in the 1880s, well after the Civil War.

As far as "Beasts of Burden" were concerned, Western civilizations knew of the horse, mule, donkey, and ox. To the American, these were work animals, created to make man's life easier. The horse was something special, an animal owned with pride.

The horse held a special place in Americans' hearts; there were none on the continent until the Spanish introduced them into the Southwest and Europeans brought them to the new colonies on the East Coast. Like the camel, the horse had been extinct in North America for thousands of years.

Horses were for riding, betting on, "showing," and for pulling a sleigh, plow, or carriage.

In the American's mind, fancy ladies, elegant men, leaders, and the military rode horses. Men exploring the wilderness of the new country depended on the horse. If an explorer's animal died, he knew his chances for survival were slim. Man cannot outrun a mountain lion or a band of determined Indian warriors, but on his horse he at least has a chance.

Horses are beautiful to look at, smart, fast, and hardworking, and in the settlement of America, the carving of a country from the wilderness, they earned the respect of all citizens, as they had for centuries in the "old world."

But in 1856, despite all the admiration and respect for the horse, the U.S. government led by the War Department believed something better was needed for transportation in the Southwest.

The men who would evaluate the efficiency of the camel were facing an equally difficult task of educating others into accepting the animal as a new beast of burden. Simply based on the camel's appearance, this would not be easy.

Men who "drove" or handled work animals were accustomed to using whatever force was necessary to get the animal to perform, especially true with "stubborn" mules. Compassion for work animals existed but so did brutality.

In the 1850s, there were no organizations to curb "cruelty to animals," no SPCA or Humane Society. But some men developed a strong relationship with their mule, donkey, or horse, recognizing their value for survival, and some few even possessed a natural affinity for all creatures.

With the army, the horse and mule were military (U.S. government) property. Since the inception of armies, especially in America, the mistreatment or destruction of military property was a very serious crime. After all, the public paid for the equipment and the army was expected to protect it. This applied to animals as well as rifles or other hardware. And camels would soon be added to the list of U.S. Army property.

CHAPTER 13

Shopping for Camels

The camels your government sent to us are worthless and diseased. It is fraudulent and a discourtesy to the United States of America which I will not tolerate!

David Dixon Porter, Lieutenant, U.S. Navy,
Letter to the Viceroy of Egypt, 1855

The little wooden sailing ship officially known as the USS *Supply* carried only four cannons, each capable of firing a twenty-four-pound ball. The ten-year-old, 141-foot-long vessel, obviously no ship of war, had seen duty, as her name implied, hauling supplies, mostly munitions, repair equipment, and essentials needed by the larger ships in a fleet.

With all her sails on three masts full and with a nice wind, she cruised at five knots (about 5.8 miles per hour), but she managed to keep up with Commodore Perry's fleet of seven ships as he entered Japan's waters the second time on March 8, 1854.

Now, in 1855, America needed the *Supply* once more. She was docked at the New York Navy Yard, being fitted for a new assignment, which at first seemed to her thirty-seven-man crew far less glorious than forcing Japan to open its doors to international trade.

By orders of James C. Doblin, secretary of the navy, the *Supply* was receiving a face-lift to ready her for that new mission: hauling camels from somewhere in the Mediterranean area back to the United States.

Her new commander would be Lieutenant David Dixon Porter, son of the War of 1812 hero David Porter and himself a hero during the Mexican War.

Porter's first job was to redesign the *Supply* to accommodate safely and comfortably a number of camels. Not only did Porter draw up the changes on paper, he personally supervised the construction. The changes included a stable between the ship's two decks and a structure sixty feet long, twelve feet wide, and ten feet high on the upper deck complete with large portholes fitted with glass windows and heavy shutters. Planning for the event of heavy storms (when portholes must remain closed), he provided a large hatch, eleven feet long and seven feet wide on top, so the animals could enjoy fresh air in all kinds of weather.

Lieutenant Porter had done his homework, reading all he could find (or was provided by the War Department) about camels, but this was the first time anyone in the Western world had designed a ship to transport the animals.

Porter was joined by Major Henry Constantine Wayne, commander of the entire camel-purchasing expedition, for a final inspection of the ship. Wayne was not only satisfied but amazed with the naval officer's ingenuity. They departed, planning to link up later.

The *Supply* sailed for the Mediterranean on June 5, 1855, with Lieutenant Porter in command. He had a very important passenger on board, writer and diplomat Gwinn Harris Heap, the same fellow who accompanied his cousin Lieutenant Edward Beale on their survey march along the thirty-eighth parallel to California two years earlier.

Heap, a longtime supporter of the use of camels in the Southwest, had served as vice consul to Tunisia in North Africa and lived in its capital, Tunis, for a while (his father had served as consul at Tunis from 1839 through 1840).

Gwinn Harris was, indeed, a man of many accomplishments, and he would prove valuable in the days to come, especially with his knowledge and understanding of Mideastern culture and languages.[1]

Perhaps the camel-buying program of 1855 cannot be compared to the landing of a man on the moon 114 years later, but the logistical and technological (not to mention diplomatic) complications that had to be faced before the completion of the project were, for the times, as staggering to one's imagination.

Members of the War Department had done considerable research while waiting for Congress to approve funds for the program. Now all of their planning was about to yield positive results.

Once the thirty thousand dollars was granted the program got under way. They knew where to search for the camels—somewhere in the Middle East. The exact location would be determined upon arrival.

They had planned, thanks to Porter, how to transport the animals. And they knew where to deliver the camels—to the army, at a port along the southern Texas coast.

Major Wayne was to remain the program commander even after the camels were unloaded in Texas, but for a while, most everything would be up to Heap. He had to locate the animals and arrange their purchase.

As the *Supply* made its way across the ocean, the War Department had other things to worry about. Tensions between the United States and the Mormon rulers of the Utah Territory were increasing. The army needed a good plan if it was called upon to march on Utah and enforce the laws of the country. Some military officers would welcome orders to move into Utah.

They felt bitterness for the death of Captain John Gunnison in that territory, and the thought of revenge had nothing to do with religion. Meanwhile the army had plenty of problems with Native American Indians, especially in Texas, where raids by Apache, Comanche, and Kiowa on farms, ranches, and villages were terrifying settlers. On March 4, 1855, Congress approved the organization of four new regiments, one of which, the Second Cavalry, would be specifically in service on the Texas frontier, the area where the camels were to be delivered.

Seven hundred and fifty cavalrymen under the command of Colonel Albert Sidney Johnston departed Jefferson Barracks near St. Louis on October 27, 1855, and arrived at their new post at Fort Mason, Texas, in January 1856.

The regiment moved with eight hundred horses and twenty-nine wagons loaded with supplies. Each trooper carried the latest weapons, the 1851 Colt Navy percussion revolver, the dragoon saber, and the Springfield carbine.

The Fort Mason headquarters would become one in a chain situated one day's horseback ride apart. It was part of a system to protect emigrants and settlers or to chase Indians, whenever practical.

Fort Mason was a sprawling complex of twenty-five buildings constructed of natural stone and in a perfect location to provide protection to a smaller post not far away, along the Verde River. This fort would eventually be named Camp Verde (located just south of present-day Kerrville, Texas).

Construction of Camp Verde began in July 1855, and within a year, the camp took on a peculiar design. A large, almost one-hundred-yard-square area was surrounded by a twelve-foot-tall adobe wall. Stalls, complete with a roof and feeding troughs, indicated that the post might expect to house a large number of animals. The troops guessed, logically, mules or horses.

Finally the buildings for officers neared completion, but still there seemed to be no one who knew the purpose of the walled-in yard. The area was large enough to be a parade ground, but if that was true, why the wall?

Camp Verde was a beautiful post, situated between two streams and near the Guadeloupe River. Green pasturelands surrounded the entire area, making it an ideal location for any grazing animal. The Second Cavalry continually patrolled between the forts in the "chain," including, of course, Fort Mason and the unit's main headquarters at San Antonio.

The War Department in Washington felt comfortable with their plan for the camels' new home—Camp Verde. At this post the camels should be safe from Indians, who were always trying to find a way to steal the army's animals.

The army and the navy were going to a lot of trouble at taxpayer expense to bring the camels to Texas. No one in the War Department wanted to face the embarrassment if one of the valuable animals were stolen.

Into the spring of 1856, the peculiar stalls and "parade ground" of Camp Verde were still empty. As usual, army rumors bounced about. Then, from somewhere, a new story circulated that went beyond the earlier ones. It may have been a joke and it brought a lot of laughter. *Camels* were coming to Camp Verde, the rumor declared. How ridiculous! Even the lowest-ranking private knew that there were no camels in Texas.

On his trip to the Middle East, Major Henry C. Wayne carried letters of introduction from the U.S. secretary of war and a variety of articles for study to further his knowledge of camels.

He arrived in England and met with officials at the zoological gardens to discuss the British use of camels in war, then he continued on to Paris to consult with the French officers who had employed camels in Algeria.

Wayne recorded extensive notes of the meetings along with his personal observations and opinions. His journal would be presented to the secretary of war upon his return.[2]

Then Wayne sailed to La Spezia, Italy, where he had planned to join Lieutenant Porter.

After delivering supplies to the American fleet, Porter was now free to conduct his own research on camels while awaiting the arrival of Wayne. He traveled to view camels at the farm of the grand duke of Tuscany, then returned to the ship, where he found Wayne interviewing the crew.

The two officers discussed an idea. They decided it would be wise to study the behavior of camels on board the ship before attempting the long trip home to America with a full load. They set sail for Tunis, arriving in August 1855. There they met the other member of their team, Gwinn Harris Heap, who had sailed on ahead from La Spezia to begin the buying expedition. Heap had already negotiated with the

Mohammed Bey, who presented as a gift to the United States two camels. Wayne purchased one additional animal, which became the "veteran" of the herd, sailing on the *Supply* for more than ten thousand miles and landing in Texas many months later in excellent health. (The two "gift" camels were determined to be diseased and sold by Wayne, later, in Turkey.)

The *Supply* sailed to Smyrna and then to Turkey, arriving in early October. Leaving the ship for a while, the Americans met with British military officers to review the use of camels in the ongoing Crimean War. What they learned boosted their enthusiasm. The English regarded the performance of camels as beasts of burden and as cavalry animals superior to horses in the desert areas.

But because of the Crimean War, camels were in short supply throughout the area.

The Americans discussed the possibilities of journeying on to Persia (Iran), but it was now December and trails were impassable due to snow and ice. The sultan offered to send searchers into the interior in hopes of locating camels, but Wayne and Porter became impatient and, with their one Tunis camel, sailed for Egypt, arriving in late December 1855.

At Alexandria, Egypt, the Americans separated. They sent Heap back to Smyrna to work with the sultan to locate camels—somewhere in that area. Major Wayne went to Cairo to obtain permission to carry at least twenty camels out of the country—if they could locate any worth taking.

Lieutenant Porter remained in Alexandria, spending most of his time writing lengthy reports for the secretary of war containing details about what they had learned thus far in their search and a complete list of expenses.

Imagine how difficult the situation was for the American officers. There was no communication with the United States, very few (often no) Americans lived in the places they visited who could provide information, no GPS, no computers, and very unreliable maps. They were not prepared for the camel-buying problems they encountered because they had no knowledge of the ongoing war that was causing the short-age of the animals.

And things were not going to improve in Egypt. The first problem came as Major Wayne discovered that the viceroy had issued a procla-mation forbidding any animal, in particular camels, to leave the coun-try. Egypt had been drained of those animals (which were sent off to the Crimean War).

The viceroy expressed interest in the proposed American experi-ment and decided to give six camels as a "gift." This gesture seemed a way to get rid of the visitors while showing pseudo friendship.

Forty-five-year-old Major Henry Constantine Wayne was a gen-tleman from Savannah, Georgia. He had earned his rank the hard way—in the Mexican War. He was known to be an extremely polite officer, but the trip had been a trying and tiring one for him. His patience was now thin due to lengthy negotiations, all of which re-quired the presence of a translator (with the help of the local Ameri-can consul).

Likewise, Lieutenant David D. Porter became irritable and ner-vous. He and his colleagues had been away from home for eight months, traveled thousands of miles in unfamiliar waters, and encoun-tered strange cultures and people.

The bravery of those Americans in the *Supply* must be admired, especially considering the situation they were in. The audacity of their government to send them into the Mediterranean area while the com-plex Crimean War remained in high gear and the determination of Porter and Wayne to complete this mission are somewhat difficult to comprehend today.

When the *Supply* arrived in the area, the conflict among Russia, France, England, and the Ottoman Empire (Turkey) plus a few other states, which had started in October 1853, seemed nowhere near com-pletion. Sevastopol had fallen and disputes over the "Holy Lands" added new fuel to the war's fires.

But despite this, the War Department in Washington obviously had its own agenda. War or no war, they had to have the camels for evaluation.

At the port of Alexandria, Lieutenant Porter and Major Wayne were becoming irritated and concerned with the delays. The Egyptian government continued to avoid the request for camels. What transpired next between the American officers and representatives of that government almost developed into a serious conflict, one that the *Supply* and her crew were in no position to win should things reach the point of a military confrontation.

The viceroy announced that he would give, as a gift from Egypt, six camels for the United States, but when the animals arrived, the American officers were shocked and outraged. Not only were the camels old and in poor condition; they appeared to be diseased. If the viceroy wanted to provoke the Americans, he and his staff succeeded. History did not record whether the viceroy intended his "gift" as a joke, a test of the Americans' sense of humor, or, as they took it, as an insult.

The eighty-year-old United States might have been young at the time, but its citizens, certainly members of the military, were proud.

Major Wayne and Lieutenant Porter planned to send a letter to the viceroy reminding him that Americans had defeated England, the most powerful military in the world, not once but twice, on land and at sea. Americans had defeated Mexico only a few years earlier, and opened the doors of Japan after hundreds of years of isolation. Now U.S. ships sailed every ocean in the world.

And, if the viceroy needed to be reminded of an incident near his own country, marine lieutenant Presley Neville O'Bannon led a bayonet charge and with a handful of U.S. Marines captured the fortress at Tripoli only fifty years earlier. Then the American flag flew for the first time over foreign soil.

Lieutenant Porter did not have Lieutenant O'Bannon with him, nor did he command a unit of Marines. There were not enough men on board the *Supply* to threaten any country, but he did have one powerful weapon: the power of the pen and diplomatic bluff.

On January 13, 1856, Lieutenant Porter penned an indignant letter to the viceroy of Egypt, which read in part:

> *The camels your government sent to us are worthless and diseased. It is fraudulent and a discourtesy to the United States of America which I will not tolerate. We have too good a country, my dear sir, to allow anyone to deprecate it by such offerings.*
>
> *U.S.S. Ship Supply*
> *(signed) David D. Porter,*
> *Lieutenant, Commanding*

It had all been a terrible mistake, the viceroy's minister explained to the Americans a few days later. He reported that "a servant" was responsible for the "mix-up" and would be punished. And with the apology came six healthy camels.[3]

The *Supply*, now with nine camels on board, sailed for Smyrna on January 22, 1856. But where was Gwinn Harris Heap? Had he arrived at Smyrna and made contact with the sultan, as planned? Did he have camels so they could all return home? Or, with the war still raging in the Mediterranean area, was he even still alive?[4]

CHAPTER 14

The USS *Supply* Sails Home

Allah has 100 names. Man knows 99 of those names, but only the camel knows the 100th name.

Old Arab Proverb

Twenty-six-year-old Hadji Ali completed his military enlistment with the French army in Algiers and journeyed home to Smyrna (Izmir), Turkey. During those years with the French, Ali acquired a number of skills, but, of course, had no way of knowing the importance they would have on his future. At the time they seemed simply another part of day-by-day survival. Ali had been trained in Algeria in the art of purchasing and caring for camels for the French army. During that time, he also managed to learn a little French and English, and as an alert young man who was full of curiosity, he paid close attention to discussions he overheard around army headquarters. He said nothing, understood little, but what he remembered of military logic prepared him for an unexpected journey and adventure.

Mostly, he enjoyed his work with camels. He believed them intelligent, patient, and reliable animals and treated them as friends, since he had no others.

Now he was searching for his mother in Smyrna. He wanted her to see what a strong man he had become and speak to her in Greek to prove, regardless of all his travels and experiences, that he had not forgotten her native language. His mother, a Greek, had been abducted as a teenager by an Arab, sold to a Syrian, and carried off to Smyrna as a slave-wife. When Ali was born, his mother gave him the Greek name Filippou Teodora, and during his childhood, his father permitted him to be orthodox Christian. Teodora converted to Islam as a young teen and completed the pilgrimage (the hadj or hadji) to Mecca and assumed the name Hadji Ali.[1]

Ali was normally a cheerful young man, but after weeks of searching for his mother, he began to slip into a depression and his usual bright smile faded. Much had changed in Turkey during his absence, as the result of the Crimean War. He could not locate his mother or even any information about her.

Somehow he managed to find his cousin Mico Teodora, who knew nothing of the mother's disappearance but did have an unusual story to tell. Mico had encountered an American who was buying camels. Even more unusual, the man spoke Arabic and said he would be hiring men with experience in handling camels, but they must be available to travel to the United States. Mico led Ali to the American, who introduced himself as Gwinn Harris Heap.

Ali, always a man yearning for adventure and believing he no longer had a reason to remain in Smyrna, told Heap of his "extensive" experience with camels and his desire to visit and work in America, a place he actually knew nothing about.

Heap, in his journal, described Ali: "this swarthy little Arab with sharp dark eyes proved so helpful in teaching us about camels that we made him an offer to return with us to America."[2]

Cousin Mico was also ready to travel with Ali.

On January 30, 1856, the *Supply* arrived at Smyrna. The officers and crew were relieved to find Gwinn Harris Heap not only alive and well but very organized, having completed his assignment beyond their expectations. With the help of Ali, Mico, and six other men he hired, they had camels, saddles, blankets, bells, and an assortment of other gear for the camels all waiting to be boarded on the ship.

Now it was time for Lieutenant Porter to once again work his engineering magic and load the camels. At first glance, this would be no easy task. However, Porter had already designed a system and put the crew and new men to work assembling it as he watched over every detail.

First, they constructed a bargelike boat, twenty feet by seven feet, with a flat bottom so it would slide on the beach. Then a "camel car," built of wood, supported by iron strapping, and with a door at each end, was mounted perfectly on the "boat."

One at a time, camels were coaxed, pushed, or pulled into the car, which rolled on tracks down the beach and onto the boat, which was then "poled" out to the *Supply*.[3]

Finally, their voyage home began on February 15, 1856, with a total of thirty-three camels including one calf and a huge "tuilu" (the offspring of a bactrian and a dromedary). This animal was well over seven feet in height and ten feet long. A special hole had to be cut in the upper deck to accommodate his hump.

The little *Supply* met tremendous gales in the Mediterranean and even worse weather as it sailed across the Atlantic. But Porter had designed special harnesses of wide, strong canvas strips that held the camels secure in a kneeling or resting position. Because of the severe weather, the animals had to remain in that position a few days at a time, but this did not interfere with their ability to eat and drink comfortably.

Lieutenant Porter enforced his rules and treated the camels as if they were his own pets, often spending time with them in an effort to learn all he could of their habits.

One camel died giving birth and so did a few of the young who were born shortly after departure. Saddened by the deaths, Porter became even stricter with his rules, having the men pay special attention to the animals' feeding and the cleanliness of their quarters.

The camels, by Porter's thinking, were government property and his companions. He required one man to be on duty at all times watching over the animals. They were to be fed and watered each day at 3 P.M. Females and young were fed a second time at 7 A.M. They were brushed every day for thirty minutes and their feet and legs washed with soap and water. Hay was added under their knees and haunches when they lay down and stalls were cleaned daily.

Each camel was fed a gallon of oats, ten pounds of hay, and a gallon of water daily. Salt was given once a week. Although their normal diet had included tree leaves and desert "shrubs," they got along well on the ship diet. They even developed a taste for "white wash," which they scraped from the walls with their sharp teeth. (Fortunately, the coating had no ill effects on the animals.)[4]

Two calves survived and, after a few weeks, were given the run of the "camel deck," where their behavior and friskiness amused the crew. Even during the worst weather, the young ones had steady legs and continued to play about while sailors held on to anything they could find for support.

Finally, after weeks of rough weather, the little ship reached Kingston, Jamaica, and made a brief stop so the sailors could enjoy a day or two "shore leave." During that time, visitors were permitted to come on board to view the strange cargo. Soon the *Supply* was sailing for Texas.

On April 29, 1856, after more than seventy days at sea, the ship reached "Pass Cavalla," off Indianola, Texas, which had been serving as a major port since 1846. Here, the camels were to be unloaded, but the sea was so rough that Lieutenant Porter decided on a safer alternate plan. After all they had been through, he did not wish to lose a single camel during unloading.[5]

Porter sailed the *Supply* to the southwestern mouth of the Mississippi River. There, in calm waters, he transferred his camels to a small steamship, the *Fashion*. The camels were now in the care of Major Wayne. They landed three miles from Indianola at "Powder Point" on May 14, 1856.

Thirty-four camels, a gain of one during the voyage, all in excellent condition, were unloaded safely. For the first time in many thousands of years, camels were on American soil in the Southwest.

A number of "Arab men"—some reports say seven, others eight, all hired by Heap—disembarked. The correct spelling of some of their names has been lost in history, and the nationality of most has, likewise, been debated, but most are believed to have been of Greek descent.[6]

On the *Supply,* American sailors made little, if any, attempt to pronounce the "Arab" men's names correctly. They gave everyone nicknames, which were easier to remember.

Records indicate the "Arab" men hired to care for the camels were as follows:

Hadji Ali renamed Hi Jolly
Yiorgos Caralambo—Greek George
Mimico Teodora—Mico
Hadjiatie Yannaco—Long Tom
Anastasio Coralli—unknown
Michelo Georgios—unknown
Yanni Illato—unknown
Giorgios Costi—unknown[7]

Of these, and a few more "Arab" handlers (drivers or herders) who arrived almost a year later, only two would survive in western American history and become legends—Greek George and Hi Jolly. And, of these, Hi Jolly's name was destined to be remembered in western lore as a camel driver and frontier scout. Some records suggest that Hi Jolly arrived with a second shipment of camels that reached Texas in February 1857. Gwinn Harris Heap and Major Henry Wayne contracted with Hadji Ali (Hi Jolly). Since Wayne remained in Texas with the first shipment of camels and did not travel with the second expedition, we must conclude that Hi Jolly actually arrived with the *first* shipment.

The "Arabs" who accepted the offer made by Wayne and Heap could remain in the United States and work for the army with the camels. Or, if they chose not to remain, they were "discharged," paid a "bonus," and given free transportation on the next navy ship leaving for Smyrna. Some took one look at Texas and elected to go home.

A few worked for a while then disappeared, at least so far as recorded history is concerned. Hi Jolly's cousin Mico, for example, vanished, though legend says that Mico Creek in Texas is named for him. Others say that Mico Creek in Mico, Texas, is named for the Medina Irrigation Company, established in the area in 1913.

Major Henry Wayne remained with the camels at Indianola and began to make preparations to move them north to San Antonio, then to Camp Verde.

Lieutenant Porter and Gwinn Heap, meanwhile, sailed aboard the *Supply* to New York.

The efficiency of the camel-buying expedition was, by today's standards, almost unbelievable. The men completed their mission under budget, spending less than ten thousand dollars. Porter presented his "Camel Deck" journal, the complete record of his journey, including his "disagreement" with the Egyptian government, to Jeff Davis, the secretary of war, and then delivered the wonderful news that more than twenty thousand dollars of unspent, allocated funds were ready to be returned.

A very pleased secretary of war had some news of his own. Lieutenant Porter was ordered to take ten thousand dollars of that unspent money, prepare the *Supply*, and sail once more to Smyrna. There, Gwinn Heap would be waiting with more camels and another team of "Arab" drivers to care for the animals.

Porter and the *Supply* arrived at Smyrna in early November 1856, loaded Heap and the camels (by the same process as before), and sailed home on November 14.

On this voyage, the *Supply* encountered even worse weather than before, which was partially to blame for the death of three of the camels. They arrived at Indianola on February 10, 1857, with forty-one animals in excellent condition.

Five camels in Major Wayne's herd had died of various causes during Porter's absence. But now the United States Army had seventy healthy animals. The camel experiment in the Southwest was ready to begin.

CHAPTER 15

The Camels' New Home

The camels are coming!

Road Warning Cry,

Texas, June 1856

Major Henry Constantine Wayne had always been a foot soldier, not a sailor. In May 1856, after nearly a year at sea, he was finally back on solid ground and shared his joy with the camels who were now free of their canvas harnesses.

Lieutenant Porter recorded his observation of the camels expressing their appreciation for liberty: "On being landed and feeling once again the solid earth beneath them, they became excited to an almost uncontrollable degree, rearing, kicking, crying out, breaking halters, tearing up pickets, and by other favorite tricks demonstrated their enjoyment of the liberty of the soil."

Texans gathered to observe this unusual show and seemed to be impressed with the animals' wildness. Porter added a bit of humor in his journal: "Perhaps the love of amusements may render the importation of camels in Texas popular if their utility does not recommend them."[1]

Lieutenant Porter and G. H. Heap, their mission complete, departed on the *Supply* for New York. From there, Hemp visited family in Pennsylvania while Porter journeyed to the office of the secretary of war, Jefferson Davis, in Washington and presented his journal. That report, now part of the "Camel File" in the National Archives, includes drawings by Heap showing the loading and securing of the camels as well as a lengthy narrative and copies of letters pertaining to his dispute with the Egyptian government over the "present" of sickly camels.

Davis preferred to send an army officer on the second camel-buying trip. Major Wayne insisted by letter that it was necessary for him to remain with the camels and see them to their new home. He also planned to train army personnel to eventually take over the project in Texas. The major's plans were logical. He proposed that Major Crossman, once again, be given the honor of making the trip. And, once again, Crossman turned down the opportunity.

Meanwhile, Major Wayne faced the task of moving the camels away from the coast toward San Antonio. But first, a situation presented itself for Wayne to become a showman. This was strictly out of character, but he had to come to the defense of *his* camels because of public "opinion."

Many of the local citizens who gathered near the docks to see the camels began to laugh, pointing fingers at the animals and shouting "rude" comments about their legs, humps, and the general appearance of the strange creatures they had never seen before.

Wayne, like a proud father who had just been insulted by individuals with lesser intelligence, moved through the crowd, suggesting, here and there, that they would be impressed when they learned how the army would use the animals.

Many fell silent. A major in the United States Army, who obviously, by his age, had fought for their independence from Mexico, deserved respect and attention.

The major had one camel, "a large male," brought to the center of the crowd, where he planned a demonstration. He ordered the camel to kneel. Then he had two bales of hay weighing about 314 pounds each attached to the camel's luggage saddle. Then he added two more hay bales, bringing the total weight to almost 1,300 pounds.

On command, the camel rose slowly and, with no apparent strain on effort, let the major lead him around the dock.

No mule or horse could carry so much weight. Every Texan knew that fact. The crowd began to cheer and applaud. They all seemed to agree. The animals might look weird, but the army had proven an interesting point.

The *Indianola Bulletin* and *Victorian Advocate* ran stories about the camels' strength and potential use. Within weeks, papers across the South and all the way to New York carried the story, and Major Wayne reported the event to the secretary of war in detail.[2]

Soon after this, the camels, the "Arab" drovers (drivers), and a few civilians hired by Wayne began the long march to San Antonio. At first they moved slowly so the calves, including one born at sea and named "Uncle Sam," and their mothers could keep up with the herd.

No doubt Hi Jolly and Greek George played key roles during the movement. They at least gave the appearance of having a serious interest in their work, and since no one other than Wayne had any prior knowledge of the animals, the "Arabs" seemed in complete control.

As they began to leave Indianola they encountered their first problem, one that would haunt the camel experiment for years to come. Often, when horses or mules first caught scent of the "smelly" camels, they became uneasy, prancing about with eyes wide. The smell was something new, and after the first glance at camels, fear quickly led to panic. A panicked horse is dangerous and can inflict damage to property or people.

Not all the horses were alarmed by the camels. Those that were usually calmed down in a few moments, especially when they observed men controlling the new animals. This must have indicated that camels were not predators to be feared. Nonetheless, caution had to be exercised when entering a public place.

On June 4, Wayne's convoy moved on to Port Laraca, then to Victoria and Cuero. Wayne reported that the camels were still very frisky and excited with their freedom, and people were also excited. At every village, crowds lined the roads to stare at the strange animals parading by and see history, of some kind, in the making.

To clear the road of spectators and warn those with horses that their animals might be "spooked" by the sight and smell of the new arrivals, a rider moved ahead of the convoy shouting, "The camels are coming! The camels are coming!"

On June 17, at Grayson, twelve miles from San Antonio, Major Wayne called a halt and, leaving his "clerk and veterinarian" Albert Ray in charge, rode on to the city. There he met with Colonel A. C. Myers, who made arrangements with the town council for camels and crew to camp along the river at San Pedro Springs, where there was an abundance of grass and water.

Wayne's little "army" actually consisted of no soldiers or members of the military. At this point, he did not command a military unit, certainly not a corps, as has been suggested. There were only a few civilians hired to temporarily assist the "Arabs" in moving the herd and controlling the village observers.

They marched on to the small village of Medina.

Over the next few weeks, Major Wayne's reports to Secretary of War Davis were lengthy and contained numerous suggestions on how the army might proceed with the camel program. Wayne believed, and rightfully so, that he was qualified to make these recommendations. He suggested that the camels he had and the ones expected from Lieutenant Porter's second trip be allowed to multiply for a year or two in order to build a larger, stronger herd, one that was accustomed to its new life. This was, he felt, important for the creation of a cavalry unit, one built with camels.

Wayne suggested that the camels be tested under different conditions and exercised regularly until they became fully acclimated. To accomplish all this, he thought an army unit should begin training: its members could later serve as a cadre to educate soldiers from other units in the correct use and care of camels.

From a military viewpoint, Wayne's ideas were sound. Time was necessary for men and animals to understand one another, and for the men to learn the camels' capabilities and determine where their services could best be used.

If the War Department followed Wayne's suggestions, the camel experiment might have had more positive results. But those in Washington saw things differently. A number of factors played a part in high-ranking opinions and decisions on the experiment.

First, Major Wayne answered through the military "chain of command" directly to the quartermaster general's office (where he and Major Crossman shared offices and ideas when the camel program began). The ranking or superior officer over the quartermaster was, of course, Secretary of War Davis, who, as a former army officer with combat experience, had taken an interest in the camel program.

Lieutenant Porter returned the unused portion of the thirty-thousand-dollar grant for camel procurement. That was a positive point for the military in the eyes of Congress. But it was almost the middle of an election year when Major Wayne's suggestions came raining into the War Department. Secretary Davis might be gone if there was a change in the administration. Duties and priorities among high-ranking military officers might be reorganized under a new secretary of war.

The issue of slavery continued to bring unrest across the country. Indian attacks on emigrants on the way to California continued. And then there was that unending worry about the Mormons, which had politicians and the military uneasy. The military command in California reported that the Mormons were increasing their purchases of weapons to carry to Utah, and Mormon "scouts" were exploring the Colorado River in increasing numbers.

A letter to Major Wayne dated July 14, 1856, from Quartermaster General Thomas S. Jesup, stated strongly, "The establishment of a breeding herd [of camels] did not enter into the plans of the Department."

To be sure Wayne understood, General Jesup stated in another letter dated July 30, 1856, "The first and important point to be determined is their [the camels'] fitness for our military service."[3]

The rejections of Wayne's ideas were coming from his immediate superior, not Secretary Davis. Major Wayne was a good soldier. Regardless of personal disappointment he would, of course, follow orders.

Perhaps Wayne had become a little spoiled during the beginning of the program. He traveled under orders from Secretary Davis. His reports, like Porter's, were directed to Davis, and the praise for his work and actions came from Davis. Now the military system was back in place.

But Wayne knew more about the camels than anyone in the United States. He had become fascinated with the animals and seriously believed in the idea of training soldiers with the camels to form a cadre. And, he knew it was possible to test the animals at the same time. The camels might be army property, bought with taxpayer money, but he considered the animals "friends" and he wanted U.S. citizens to get their money's worth. When a camel became ill or was wounded in a fight with another camel, it troubled him greatly.

Wayne ordered autopsies if a camel died, and sent extensive details on the results to Secretary Davis.[4]

On August 12, Wayne completed his inspection of Camp Verde and reported to Davis, "The position is, in every respect, favorable for our camels." Indeed, the camp's location, with small streams, trees, and grass, was perfect.

The camp's commander, Captain Innes N. Palmer of the Second Cavalry, took an immediate and sincere interest in the camels, recognizing their potential value to the cavalry. Fortunately for Major Wayne, the thirty-three-year-old Palmer would remain post commander through 1858.

In early September, the first test of the camels' capabilities came when six of them were sent with packs from Camp Verde sixty miles to San Antonio. It became a race between the camels and three wagons, each pulled by six mules. The mission was to return with oats and other supplies.

The camels went directly through the hill country, where the wagons could not pass, picked up loads of 608 pounds each, and returned to camp in fifty-four hours.

The three mule wagons did succeed in carrying 1,834 pounds each but required ninety-six hours to return, being restricted to a road and requiring frequent stops to rest and drink water.

Captain Palmer was amazed with the results, and Major Wayne was ecstatic. He reported that the six camels had carried as much as two mule-drawn wagons, for the space of forty-three hours, almost two days faster than the mules.

On November 5, he reported another test, during which twelve camels happened to be in San Antonio for supplies when a heavy rain began. The animals were already packed with 325 pounds each. They made the trip to Camp Verde in rain and mud in only fifty-four hours.

It would have been "impossible for mules to pull wagons through deep mud," Wayne proudly reported to Secretary Davis.

By the first of December, Wayne, recognizing his days at Camp Verde might be coming to a finish, began to work closely with Captain Palmer, providing him with as much information as possible on the camels, including all the details of the buying expedition. To Wayne's relief, the captain continued to show interest in the program.

The results of the presidential election reached Camp Verde in early December. James Buchanan was the new president and rumors circulated that John B. Floyd would replace Jefferson Davis as secretary of war.

Davis had one last issue to resolve with the camel program. He wanted a face-to-face meeting with Major Wayne to thank him for his devotion and obtain a full report on the "experiment," as it was now being called. He ordered Wayne to proceed to Washington as soon as was practical.

On December 4, 1856, Major Wayne sent a letter to Secretary

Davis in which he suggested a "Regimental Commander take-over" the camel experiment, an officer who had command of enlisted men, noncommissioned officers, and officers. (Wayne still had no such command authority.) He recommended Captain Palmer as the most qualified to assume the command, and that his own clerk, Albert Ray, be promoted to remain on duty to care for the camels. The War Department accepted Wayne's suggestions. Palmer and Ray would continue in their positions.

Lieutenant Porter was expected at New Orleans with the second shipment of camels about January 20, 1857. Naturally, Wayne wanted to be there to meet him. But the arrival conflicted with Davis's plans. Wayne had to be in Washington, so he sent Albert Ray and the acting quartermaster of the army area, Captain W. K. Von Bokklen, to Indianola to meet the *Supply* and receive the new camels.[5]

This was another disappointment for Wayne, but he had his orders. The military seldom, for its own reasons, considers personal feelings.

The landing of the *Supply* was reported to have taken place on February 10, 1857. Lieutenant Porter turned over forty-one camels, all in good condition, to Ray and Captain Von Bokklen and they were marched in an uneventful movement to Camp Verde.

The *Supply* continued on to New York with Porter and Heap.

In four years, the United States would need Lieutenant Porter's services again, this time to preserve the Union of the country he so dearly loved.

Jefferson Davis left the War Department in March 1857, comforted, at least, by one thought. His replacement, John B. Floyd, would continue to be a strong supporter of the camel experiment. In a few years, Davis became president of the Confederate States of America.

Major Wayne, Gwinn Heap, and Lieutenant Porter performed their duties brilliantly, proud to serve their young country. But with the dawn of 1857, their services with the camel experiment were no longer needed. Other men would now take the experiment into its next phase.

For a while Major Wayne held a desk job in Washington, then

resigned his commission when Abraham Lincoln became president. He returned to his native state of Georgia.

Major George Crossman, however, remained with the army and was promoted to the rank of colonel.

And, for a while, the camels enjoyed a peaceful life at Camp Verde. Their service in the U.S. Army was only beginning.

CHAPTER 16

Lieutenant Beale's Strange Assignment

There is something in me and, no doubt in many of us
that longs, ungovernably for the wild and savage in
nature.

John W. Bingaman, Yosemite Ranger,
My Last Patrol *(1961)*

In mid-January 1857, the former superintendent of Indian affairs, Lieutenant Edward Beale, received a message from Washington. The country once again needed his services. Within two weeks Beale and his family were ready to leave their home in San Francisco and start the long journey east. His trusted friend and business partner, Samuel Bishop, would continue to run their ranch and handle all negotiations for the company during the absence.

Meanwhile, members of the War Department in Washington were seeing Mormons in their morning coffee, or so it seemed.

The abundance of reports concerning the Latter-Day Saints circulating in the department suggested a full confrontation could be expected in the West at any time. Fear had reached almost panic proportions with some civilians as news of Mormon scouting parties, sometimes called "spies," drifted in from San Bernardino and Fort Yuma.

The army was, of course, concerned about the Mormon interest in the lower Colorado River. If they were to attack and capture Fort

Yuma, the Mormons indeed would control all river traffic from the Gulf north.

But was it really the intention of the Mormons to take possession of the Colorado, or were they simply exploring while attempting to convert Native Americans to their faith?

The American army chose to believe the worse scenario. After all, being prepared for invasion, even from Utah, was part of their purpose.

It all seems extreme as we look back on it today, but at the time the fears and mistrust between Mormon and non-Mormon were very real. With slow communications in the 1850s, all worries or concerns had time to grow, and even logical-thinking people could be caught up in a wave of suspicion. There simply was no speedy method to verify information, and when news arrived, it had weeks, often months, to become distorted.

In 1857, the army had good reason to be uneasy with the Mormon situation in the West. The army was spread thin in the various forts or "outposts," the transportation of supplies was poor, and communication was often worse. Morale at those lonely posts remained low and combat units were exhausted from battles and the pursuit of Indians whose favorite pastime seemed to be attacking westbound emigrants. Bluntly put, the United States Army was in no condition in early 1857 to begin a major engagement with any other military.

But the U.S. government had reached a major decision regarding which route would become the first wagon road, then a rail line—the thirty-fifth parallel from Fort Leavenworth, Kansas, west to the Colorado River, then on to Fort Tejon, Los Angeles, and the Pacific Ocean.

Captain Sitgreaves and Lieutenant Whipple had completed the initial work, mapping territory and recording a tremendous amount of important data along the thirty-fifth. Now it would be up to the new administration of President James Buchanan to see the construction of the road completed.

Though slavery had been a serious issue during the 1856 presidential campaign, something else was now forced to the front, demanding action: what to do about polygamy and its practice by the Mormons in Utah.

Shortly after taking his oath of office in March, President Buchanan, with the help of close associates in Washington and eastern newspapers, began an anti-Mormon crusade. It was a well-calculated move to distract citizens from the haunting slavery issue. For a while the plan worked.

Would Washington politicians actually create a situation, or take advantage of an existing one, and build upon prejudices and suspicions in order to direct Americans' attention away from a serious issue to which there was no quick and easy solution? The answer was, yes! And for Buchanan, the project became an easy one.[1]

The slavery problem was already causing bloodshed in Kansas, and Buchanan needed something to draw people's attention away from it. Polygamy had been a practice attacked by most Americans for many years. What could be better than a little war against a people whose religion had provoked anger across the United States for almost two decades?

Americans needed to be reminded that the Mormons not only practiced polygamy; they had defied the laws of the United States and even expressed interest in electing their own government officials from among their religious leadership. The lesser of the problems facing Buchanan, the Latter-Day Saints, was an easy way out.

With almost perfect timing, Judge W. W. Drummond's letter to the widow of Captain John W. Gunnison regarding the captain's and his men's murder at the hands of Indians and Mormons was reprinted in all its gory detail in eastern newspapers, beginning with the *New York Times* on May 1, 1857.

The judge's letter ended with a "wish" to Widow Gunnison "that you may live to see the day when the foul stain of Mormon oppression and tyranny shall be effectively checked in this, our happy country . . ."[2]

Though the murders took place in Utah Territory in 1853, the appearance of the letter in 1857 set off a national outcry for justice and demands that the government take action. How, the public inquired, could the murder of U.S. soldiers go unpunished?

To add fuel to the fire, other disgruntled federal employees who had been stationed in Utah Territory resigned their positions, returned east, and discussed their distaste for polygamy. Some of these men had been prejudiced against the Mormons before their assignments, yet some were not. Some officials returned and reported that they had good relationships with the Latter-Day Saints.

Many of the Mormons believed polygamy was a practice reinstituted by God as in the days of the Bible's Old Testament. It was, therefore, a religious sacrament but was not practiced by more than 50 percent of the Mormon population at the time.

Nonetheless, even the onetime supporter of the Latter-Day Saints Senator Stephen A. Douglas denounced Mormonism and polygamy in early June 1857, stating in a public address, "Mormons are alien enemies . . . a loathsome, disgusting ulcer."[3]

To those who demanded that the Mormons be forced to follow U.S. law, President Buchanan already had an answer. Secretary of War Floyd and General in Chief (Chief of Staff) Winfield Scott had been ordered to mobilize available troops and create a new branch of the military called the Military Department of Utah. Troops began to assemble at Fort Leavenworth, Kansas.

On April 22, 1857, as the mobilization was under way in Kansas, Lieutenant Edward Beale reported to the office of Secretary of War John B. Floyd. President Buchanan, a family friend of the Beales, had requested the American hero be appointed superintendent of a government survey and superintendent of the construction of a "military wagon road from New Mexico Territory to California."[4]

Edward Beale's name had been fresh in Americans' minds for years, aided with bits of information in eastern papers on his current activities. People wanted to know what Beale was doing, and their curiosity would be piqued when they learned of his new assignments.

Beale had wisely avoided public debates or comments on the Mormons or slavery, though he strongly opposed slavery. (Later he took a strong public stand, suggesting that "Black Americans" be allowed to vote.)

Here was a man who may have become a great politician, but such an occupation would be much too confining for him. Beale believed in truth and the freedom to seek adventure whenever he felt the need—which seems to have been often.

Supervising the construction of a "military" wagon road may not, at first, have sounded very adventuresome to someone like Ed Beale, but he understood the need and value of such a trail. And success would surely do no harm to his image in the minds of Americans. At age thirty-five, Edward Beale was ready for that next adventure.

He listened carefully as Secretary Floyd revealed the details of the road project. There would be ten wagons, pulled by mules loaned by the army, and, of course, an army escort, because they would be passing through Indian territory.

Beale's crew of men had to be be composed of civilians. Other than the small escort of twenty-five soldiers, there would be no other active members of the military on the convoy. However, Floyd had no objection if Beale included a few "former" officers like himself who were among his personal friends.

Floyd did not guarantee what type of reception Beale could expect from the Native Americans along the route because so little was known about the tribes. But, of course, Floyd encouraged Beale to order the team to be as friendly as possible. Some of the wagons would contain a good supply of "gifts" and items to trade when the opportunity presented itself.

Beale had worked closely with the Native Americans in California and led the successful thirty-eighth parallel expedition. He knew the native people's behavior was unpredictable, but he had no concern in this regard, confident he could handle any situation.

Floyd also explained in detail the current situation with the army and the Mormons, but it was the next announcement that appeared, at least on the surface, to take Beale by surprise.

Beale was to evaluate a new army "weapon," quite unlike anything ever tested in America before. In fact, this phase of the project,
Floyd emphasized, was considered by the War Department to be
"most critical."

At first Beale's face was expressionless. Then he quickly inquired,
"What is the nature of this weapon?"

"Camels," Secretary Floyd replied calmly. And then before Beale
could respond, Floyd continued with more details.

Floyd's words for a few moments drifted over Beale's head. Beale
was furious, but he held his temper. Building a road a thousand miles
or more through woods, desert, mountains, in Indian country, then
crossing the Colorado River, was difficult enough to comprehend. The
responsibility for equipment and the lives of men was yet another serious worry.

And now the army was ordering him to take camels, an animal
totally unfamiliar with the territory, and have their performance eval-
uated by men who had never seen the beasts before! It not only seemed
impossible, it could be an extremely dangerous undertaking.

While Beale thought of problems, Floyd continued to outline what
he expected the wagon expedition to accomplish. The camels were at
Camp Verde near San Antonio, Floyd explained.

Then, as Floyd grew silent, expecting a response, Beale said, "Why
don't I build the road and the army test their camels?" Beale knew the
answer, but he felt compelled to ask the obvious question.

Floyd outlined how serious the military situation had become both
from the manpower and the transportation standpoints.

Beale knew soldiers were scattered about the Southwest, but he
had heard little until now about the number of men who were needed
to control the population in Kansas. But the key issue had become the
possible war with the Mormons. President Buchanan had ordered the
War Department to prepare for a major engagement in the Utah Territory, but Floyd could not predict accurately how many troops would
be involved or, for that matter, just what Buchanan expected to accomplish with his "engagement."

Colonel Albert Sidney Johnston was already assigned overall command of the troops assembling at Fort Leavenworth.

Lieutenant Joseph Christmas Ives had been ordered to proceed to the Colorado River and determine if steamships could deliver troops and supplies from Fort Yuma into Mormon territory. A fifty-four-foot, iron-hulled stern-wheeler named the *Explorer* that had been built in Philadelphia was disassembled and shipped to the mouth of the Colorado, where Ives was already struggling to reassemble it. The ship even had a howitzer mounted on its bow.

Lieutenant Ives's orders were to have his ship ready by midsummer, a difficult assignment considering that his laborers were not experienced navy personnel but Mexican and Native Americans who lived in the area.

While Ives was busy at the mouth of the Colorado, army units in California were placed on "alert" and prepared to march east into Mormon territory.

The War Department plans called for Colonel Johnston's army to move west from Fort Leavenworth in August with the key purpose of replacing Governor Brigham Young with a new man to be selected by the president.

If the efforts to replace Young failed and a "shooting war" developed, the U.S. Army had to be ready to attack Utah Territory from the east, up the Colorado River from the south, and from California in the west.

So it was now obvious. While the army concentrated on Indian wars, Kansas, and the Mormons, someone had to construct the thirty-fifth parallel wagon road and evaluate the army's camels.

Beale was given permission to select his own crew of civilian workers and assured that the camels would be escorted by "experienced Arab camel drivers."

Once Beale accepted the position, he set about building the nucleus of his expedition team. He chose a few young men; some were family relations and several former navy associates whose capabilities he trusted. There was no time to waste. He and his men must proceed to Texas, then ensure that their movement west along the thirty-fifth coincided with Colonel Johnston's troops marching toward Utah and Lieutenant Ives's steamship expedition up the Colorado River.

While Beale prepared to leave Washington for Texas and the army organized its troops and plans, another situation developed far away in Arkansas, which would bring Mormon emotions to a boiling point.

The death of fifty-year-old Parley P. Pratt, a leader in the Latter-Day Saint movement and a member of the high "Quorum of the Twelve Apostles," would enrage all LDS members. Pratt, also a writer and missionary, practiced plural marriage. A dispute developed between Hector McLean and Pratt, motivated, in part, by the subject of polygamy.

McLean's wife had moved with their children to Utah and, in 1855, underwent a "celestial marriage" to Pratt, becoming his twelfth wife, though Mrs. McLean was not legally divorced from McLean at the time.

Hector McLean pressed criminal charges in the Midwest, accusing Pratt of assisting in the kidnapping of his and his wife's children. A trial was held in what is now Oklahoma. Pratt was charged with stealing the children's clothing, since there were no laws recognizing the taking of children by a parent as a kidnapping crime.

Pratt was acquitted for lack of evidence, but this sealed his fate. An angry Hector McLean, with a few friends, tracked Pratt into Arkansas and, on May 13, 1857, shot and stabbed the missionary along a lonely dirt road. Pratt died about two hours later from loss of blood.

Pratt's death, considered a religious martyrdom by many Mormons, only added to the bad feelings across the country. Some believed Pratt was immoral for having so many wives. Mormons claimed that McLean was a common murderer who acted as a jealous husband, unable to cope with the fact that his wife had elected to live with another man.[5]

The death of Pratt was a blow to the Latter-Day Saints, many of whom openly blamed the people of Arkansas for the crime.

Some months later, that blame would spark another horrible crime, this time in Utah.

At Camp Verde, Texas, Captain Innes N. Palmer of the Second Cavalry awaited the arrival of Edward Beale.

It must have been a puzzle for the captain. Why did the War Department choose a *naval* officer to conduct the cross-country experiment with *army* camels for the *army*?

But Palmer was a good officer and there is no record of him ever questioning Beale's assignment.

The captain had his orders. He commanded, at least for a while, the little post, Camp Verde, and was responsible for the condition and safety of the new "weapon," the camels. Like Major Wayne, Palmer had developed a fondness for the animals (though his passion was not entirely shared by all the soldiers at the post).

The "Arab" camel handlers had not convinced him that they were the experts they claimed to be. But they made an effort and even attempted to educate some of the enlisted men about the behavior of the animals.

Lieutenant Beale was expected to arrive in June, select a number of camels for the experiment, and then begin one of the most unusual adventures in western American history.

CHAPTER 17

Beale Selects Camels

*A feeling of insignificance and worthlessness I felt when
I gazed over the wide expanse of land.*

May Humphreys Stacey, Journal, 1857

Secretary of War John Floyd found little time to rest during his first few months in office; the Mormon threat from Utah, Southwest Indians attacking emigrants (and outrunning the army), and Lieutenant Beale on his way to build a wagon road while testing army camels kept him more than busy.

There was mounting concern in Washington that the wagon road might not be built fast enough and the camels, if proven to be truly essential for the army, might be too few in number for any major military engagement.

Then there was the bloodletting in Kansas, which showed no sign of subsiding even with the presence of army troops who were busy trying to keep pro- and antislavery supporters from annihilating one another.

If problems in Kansas were not resolved soon and if the Mormon situation turned into all-out war, the U.S. Army had to face hard facts. They lacked troops to deal with so many demands at one time.

The "Border War" or "Bloody Kansas," as the series of violent events between 1854 and 1858 had become known, had already escalated out of army control in early 1857.

The issue of slavery remained a serious matter. The United States had to admit new states into the Union as either "free" or "slave." Missouri, a slave state, was bordered by the free states of Iowa and Illinois. Should Kansas enter the Union as a free state, Missouri would be surrounded and outvoted in Washington.

Kansas had been settled mostly by emigrants from the South. Though many of these people never owned slaves, they were sympathetic to the system.

Antislavery organizations in the North, especially the New England Emigrant Aid Company, raised funds to relocate several thousand settlers to Kansas. By summer of 1855, over 1,200 New Englanders, armed with the newly developed and highly accurate Sharps rifle, arrived in the state and were prepared to fight anyone who confessed to being pro-slavery.

Rumors spread in the South that "30,000 Yankees" had moved to Kansas, so thousands of armed southerners known as "Border ruffians" flowed in to help shift the voting power so that a congressional representative who was in favor of slavery would be elected.

In October 1855, John Brown, a noted abolitionist, arrived in Kansas to further the fight against slavery. In May 1856, Brown and his followers attacked a pro-slavery settlement at Pottawatomie Creek and hacked a number of men to death with swords. Following this, small family battles blazed throughout the territory.

Five weeks later, federal troops began to break up gatherings in an attempt to "maintain peace." The "right" to assemble disappeared.

In June 1857, as Lieutenant Beale embarked on his expedition, the bloodshed in Kansas was far from over.

President Buchanan dreamed that a "Mormon crisis" would draw the public's attention away from Kansas and slavery. But in June 1857, a number of events in the West held the attention of Buchanan's public.

The news of Beale's expedition was out and the people waited for word of their hero's success. Then the news of Latter-Day Saint apostle Parley P. Pratt's murder in Arkansas spread through Utah and every Mormon community in the West.

Pratt's death, according to Mormon leaders, came while he was "serving a mission." There was very little mention that Pratt had taken another man's wife and that it was this, not an assault on the Mormon faith, that led to his murder.[1]

Soldiers scheduled to march out of Fort Leavenworth for Utah arrived in Kansas and were busy preparing for a mid-July departure. They originally were led by Colonel William G. Harney, but in June, the War Department changed its plans. Harney and his Second Dragoons must remain in Kansas to deal with problems there.[2]

Fifty-five-year-old Colonel Edmund Alexander replaced Harney, but Secretary Floyd's favorite, Colonel Albert Sidney Johnston, would soon assume total command of the Utah force.

An interesting fact frustrated the field commanders. Washington had not issued instructions as to just what the army was expected to do once the soldiers reached Utah. Were they to attack and invade Utah? If so, what was the objective?

At Fort Defiance in New Mexico Territory, officers were advised to be prepared to furnish an army escort for a civilian road-building crew, commanded by navy officer Edward Beale. The fort was a busy place for a while. Not only would Beale's expedition be visiting, but Colonel Alexander's first units should arrive about the same time. Then both Beale and the colonel's troops were to march out, about the same date. The War Department's plan was logical. Army units marching northwest toward Utah Territory might draw more attention from the Mormons than Beale's wagon road crew moving due west. With this idea Beale should be safe, at least from Mormon attack, and the camel experiment could remain (somewhat) a secret.

Soon troops at Fort Defiance became curious about the news that the road-building crew had camels. No one at the garrison had even seen a camel, in New Mexico Territory or anywhere else.

Lieutenant Ed Beale and his staff, consisting of some family members, friends, and a few navy associates, arrived at Indianola, Texas, in early June.

For some of the younger members of the expedition who were familiar only with the green, rolling hills of Pennsylvania, especially nineteen-year-old May Humphreys Stacey, the view of the vast Texas prairie was overwhelming. Stacey kept a "journal" during the expedition and recorded his first impressions: "A feeling of insignificance and worthlessness I felt when I gazed over the wide expanse of land."[3]

From the beginning, Ed Beale was nervous about his scheduled arrival at Fort Defiance. He had a general idea of what to expect along the trail, but his experience of expeditions before had been limited to smaller groups of men, all experts in their fields. Now he commanded a much larger group, many of whom had no wilderness trail experience.

Beale became anxious to reach Camp Verde and he pushed the men hard to "keep on the move."

Somewhere near San Antonio, as they crossed a small stream, a few wagons fell behind and Beale held Porter Heap, the young son of his cousin Gwinn Harris Heap, responsible. A heated argument between Beale and Heap lasted into the night. Heap protested about Beale's scolding, stating he had not agreed to join the expedition as a "wagon master." Driving mules was someone else's job, he claimed.

The days had been hot, with energy-sapping humidity, and Beale's quick display of temper only added to everyone's discomfort. So they waited through the night for the results of what most thought to be a family argument.

But the next morning Porter Heap resigned and Beale made a small, unsuccessful effort to convince him to remain with the team.[4]

Captain Innes Palmer, Camp Verde's commander, welcomed Beale and began at once to educate him about the care and handling of camels.

The captain warned the expedition members that camels frighten other pack animals during a first encounter. Mules might bolt and stampede, but in time, Palmer assured, they "settle down and get along just fine."

Horses and mules had had the country to themselves for two hundred years; now man had introduced a new, larger, foul-smelling beast, which appeared to be a predator. The initial panic of the animals was the main concern.

Palmer had noticed that in all cases, camels "wanted to be friends." Being herd animals, they attempted to mingle with the group, welcome or not. Once a mule or horse discovered that a camel presented no real danger, the situation returned to normal.

Captain Palmer assisted Beale in selecting twenty-five camels for the expedition, leaving behind forty-six, thirty-four adults and twelve calves.

It was suggested that they keep the camels' load light during the first few days. The animals had become "lazy" while enjoying corral life.

Then Beale met the "Arabs, Greeks, and Turks" who had been caring for the camels. They were to be the drivers (or drovers) for the experiment. Three "Middle Eastern" men refused to join the expedition, stating that the United States had broken its contract with them. They had not been paid since Major Wayne departed, six months earlier.

Beale quickly appointed three of his own men, including Peachy Gilmer Breckenridge Jr., to care for the camels. Of course, before receiving their assignment, none had even seen a camel, but with the assistance of Hi Jolly and Greek George, they would have three months of "on-the-job training" in the wilderness.[5]

On June 19, 1857, Beale's expedition rolled out of Camp Verde, making only sixteen miles the first day. They would need almost to double the pace to keep on schedule.

Captain Palmer remained at Camp Verde as commander for another year and the camels left behind soon had new assignments.

Ten years of information—charts, maps, notes, and diaries from adventurers like Jedediah Smith, James Pattie, John Frémont, Francis Aubry, Captain Sitgreaves, and Lieutenant Whipple—all that knowledge, like a gathering of spirits, would help lead the way for Beale's expedition.

The military, actually the nation, needed an all-weather route to the Pacific Ocean. And, of course, the army was waiting to learn if the camels really could outperform mules and horses. Considering the dangers, logistics, and distance to travel, Beale wasn't given much time to complete his mission.

By fall, the American army was expected to be at Utah's border. Intrusion into the territory could come anytime after that.

With all Beale's information and experience considered, nothing guaranteed success in the wilderness of the "Great American Desert." Water, he well understood, would be the major problem. Streams and springs, once recorded as plentiful, might now be dry. They might be forced to scout for new sources. Grass for the animals might now be nonexistent. June came to a close; the landscape before the expedition became barren. The area they crossed was known to be Comanche territory.

On June 29, 1857, while Beale's column was averaging more than fifteen miles each day, President Buchanan in Washington declared Utah "in rebellion against the United States Government" and ordered Colonel Alexander to march toward Utah. Colonel Johnston would follow later, with additional troops.

As Beale's expedition entered its tenth day of movement, the U.S. government officially escalated the already-tense Mormon situation, and Colonel Alexander and his troops still had not been told what they were expected to accomplish.

Beale's men were concerned each night about attacks from mountain lions (cougars or pumas), which they heard screaming and growling near the camp. And there was the constant threat of Indian attacks. Since the wagon train often stretched more than a mile, Beale worried that they were vulnerable to "hit and run" assaults, but none came.

All the Native American tribes in the West were labeled "unpredictable," friendly one moment and aggressive another. The men were cautious and concerned, not fearful. There were forty-four of them, more than half in their late teens or early twenties. And each was well armed, with Colt revolvers and percussion rifles.

On June 11, 1857, far north of Camp Verde, Dr. Charles Brewer of the United States Army was riding with a small squad of soldiers along the Platte River when he encountered a lone emigrant wagon train near Fallon's Bluff.

Since the Gold Rush of 1848 and 1849, the doctor and the men had seen many emigrants traveling along this particular route. It was an excellent trail, with an abundance of water and grass.

But this train was different from the others they had seen. It consisted of forty wagons and at least six hundred head of fine cattle, unhitched mules, and over one hundred horses, some of which were obviously excellent breeding stock.

The owners, about 120 men, women, and children, were all dressed in "elegant" clothing. The men and older boys all carried revolvers and high-quality single-shot, percussion rifles.

The doctor and his men accompanied the emigrants for a while, sharing news and information about the trail, weather, Indians, fresh springs, the things usually discussed by travelers in 1857.

The doctor recorded, "They were respectable people, well-to-do, orderly, genial, with three carriages."

The emigrants reported that they were on their way to California by way of Salt Lake City, and then planned to follow a route south to Cedar City and Santa Clara. Near Santa Clara, they would rest and depart in September, "before the first snowfall." By following the Spanish Trail though the desert, camping, and reorganizing at Las Vegas Springs, they seemed convinced that they would celebrate Christmas in California.

The emigrant leaders were a "Mr. Perkins" and "Colonel Alexander Fencher," both experienced wagon masters and Indian fighters, each of whom had traveled the route to California before. The name of their leader, the doctor reported later, depended on whom he was speaking to. Some claimed to be with Perkins and others called themselves the

"Fencher train," but everyone agreed on one fact: they were all from "Arkansas."

Some days later, Dr. Brewer and the soldiers met the train again. This time they were camped at Ash Hollow on the North Fork of the Platte.

Again the doctor "visited" with some of the emigrants and admired a carriage driven by a beautiful young woman with three equally attractive female passengers.

There was only time for smiles and a brief exchange of "pleasantries," but something other than the girls froze in the doctor's memory—a peculiar design on the carriage's side and rear panels. They displayed the picture of a "stag's head, in a bronzed coat of arms."

That image of beautiful girls in a carriage on a bright, sunny June morning with the crystal-clear Platte River flowing swiftly by was a pleasant scene, often recalled (and a topic of conversation among the soldiers for the next few miles).

Army surgeon Dr. Charles Brewer saw the carriage once again, far away from the Platte River. He remembered the coat of arms and the picture of the head of a stag on its panels. Only this time the four beautiful girls had vanished.[6]

CHAPTER 18

The Camels Head West

The camel represents the go-aheadness of the American character, which subdues even nature by its energy and perseverance.

May Humphreys Stacey, Journal, 1857

Of all the small trees in America's Southwest desert, the mesquite is the most common, known mostly today for its aromatic hardwood charcoal, which is used to flavor steaks when barbecuing.

The tree, existing in three species (velvet, honey, and screwbean), is usually found along desert washes and streams, but also in thickets below six thousand feet elevation, in the Sonoran and Mojave deserts from West Texas to southeast California.

Mesquite can grow as high as thirty feet with a trunk up to twenty-four inches in diameter and requires very little water to survive. The leaves are green, slender, and sharply pointed, usually two or three inches long. Two-inch spines or thorns give the tree some protection from animals, including bobcats and young mountain lions that may seek refuge in the branches. Cattlemen today regard the mesquite as a "range weed" and attempt to eradicate it.

The Native American Indians once relied on the mesquite to provide them with a number of essentials for survival. The tree's pods contain seeds, which were a dietary staple. From those beans, Indians (and white pioneers) made tea, sweet syrup, and a ground meal called pinole. Even the coyote, in late summer, depends on the beans as an important part of its diet.

The tree's bark has been used to make baskets, fabrics, and medicine, and the roots produce a smokeless fire. War clubs were crafted from its hard wood.

As Lieutenant Beale's column moved toward Fort Davis in western Texas, the mesquite trees received some new admirers.

Beale's men were amused to see that the camels not only enjoyed the bean pods but snapped off branches. The camels proceeded to eat everything, wood, leaves, pods, and thorns.

The first camel to notice the tree approached it with curiosity. Soon the entire herd was feasting on the same tree until almost all of the branches, attached to the rust-colored trunk, were gone.

This was the second time the camels entertained the men with their unusual diet. Throughout parts of Texas and in New Mexico Territory, homeowners often arranged fences around their front yards with a variety of cacti, especially the "beaver tail" and "prickly pear."

Such fences were perfect for protecting the yard from stray dogs, coyotes, or unwanted people. Cactus fences require little or no water to survive, but often do need years to reach a useful height.

Nothing disturbed the cactus fences until the camels passed through the villages. They found the organic barriers delicious and more than once reduced a beautiful, useful fence to a few stubs jutting from loose soil.

And the camels discovered the ugly "greasewood" plant, considered by men to be almost useless. The large bush, often three feet tall, has pale green leaves and gray branches. The seeds can be eaten, but seldom did the Native Americans become hungry enough to partake of them.

Birds often use the greasewood for shelter, but only the jackrabbit depends on it for survival. Horses will not eat greasewood and neither will mules. However, camels were attracted to the plant, quickly leveling to the ground all bushes in their immediate vicinity.

The expedition soon verified what Captain Palmer had suggested before they departed Camp Verde. Camels find plenty to eat in the desert, preferring greasewood, cacti, and mesquite over grass, unless, of course, grass is the only food available.

The expedition learned that it was unnecessary to haul great quantities of oats, corn, or other foods for camels, unlike the case with horses and mules.

For the camel, at least as a dining experience, the expedition had become a wonderful adventure.[1]

On July 4, 1857, in the East, the United States was celebrating its eighty-first birthday.

In the West, Beale's expedition rolled on slowly toward Fort Davis, where they intended to repair wagons. Suddenly the Texas winds came out of the mountains, battering them relentlessly for hours. Then the cold rain followed. At first the rain rushed in, crashing in waves from the side, almost parallel to the mushy ground. The wind calmed somewhat, and the rain began to pound straight down in sheets of pulsating spray, gluing clothing to the men's bodies and chilling everyone.

Rains soaked the expedition persistently for seven days. Horses and mules and men complained, and the camels made deep grumbling sounds from time to time, voicing displeasure.

And the camels trudged on in the mud, gaining distance on the others, their wide feet having an advantage in the soft earth. When the trail became slippery, the camels slowed their pace, lifting their long, skinny legs, step-by-step, with caution.[2]

Finally the rain stopped and the heat of the sun began to suck moisture from the earth. Humidity saturated the air, causing everyone to sweat excessively. A day later the air was dry and the July sun baked them with no mercy. At times, the sun appeared to hang in the sky like a threatening orange ball, directly overhead.

On July 16, after traveling twenty-six hours without water, the horses and mules became almost wild and difficult for the men to control. Ed Beale recorded that the camels remained perfectly docile and easy to manage.[3]

Then a spring with water in abundance was found for men and animals.

On July 13, 1857, while Beale's expedition continued to suffer from the summer's heat, there was trouble brewing in Washington.

Alfred Cumming, a fifty-five-year-old distinguished politician and businessman from Augusta, Georgia, had been selected by President James Buchanan for a difficult position. He was appointed the new governor of Utah Territory, to succeed Brigham Young, who still had the support of the majority, if not all, of the Mormons.

In 1856, Buchanan had campaigned with a promise to do something about "those twin relics of barbarism; polygamy and slavery." The president wasn't having much luck with the slavery issue, especially in Kansas, so he turned his attention on the Utah Territory, the Mormons, and polygamy.

Other than polygamy, most Mormons believed they were living under U.S. law and supported the Constitution.

With the U.S. Army marching on Utah, Buchanan's next plan was to replace Young with Cumming, even though former President Millard Fillmore had appointed Young to govern the Utah Territory.

It was at this time that the issue of "states' rights" vs. centralized national authority reared its ugly head. Naturally, bitterness and a mass of misunderstandings followed. And into this fire a peaceful, somewhat moderate Alfred Cumming and his wife, Elizabeth, would be accompanied by three hard-line federal judges (and the army) to Utah.

The entire group was to depart Fort Leavenworth, Kansas, by mid-September, but no one had informed Brigham Young that he would be replaced. By coincidence, two Mormons on mail delivery to Kansas learned of the troop movements and, by some "hard riding," reached Salt Lake City with the news on the first of August.

Young immediately set plans in motion to resist the U.S. advance.

The U.S. Army, at last, had some idea of their mission and knew it could turn out to be anything but peaceful.

Fort Davis, named for former secretary of war Jefferson Davis, was established as a key outpost in western Texas to protect travelers from Comanche and Apache attacks.

In spite of monotony, harsh discipline, tardy pay, and the constant danger of Indian attacks, Fort Davis was regarded by some "troopers" as a pleasant post. That opinion was mostly due to its location, with its impressive landscape, as well as to "off-duty" opportunities for fishing and hunting. The post was located in a box canyon with beautiful cliffs, plentiful wood, grass, and water, and blessed with a pleasant climate the entire year.

In later years, between 1866 and 1875, African American infantry and cavalry troops called "Buffalo Soldiers" by the Indians occupied the compound.[4]

On July 16, 1857, Fort Davis welcomed Edward Beale and the camels. Here, repairs were made to wagons while the animals enjoyed a short rest. "Saddle and pack" sores were doctored.

Hi Jolly made an interesting discovery while caring for the camels and reported to Beale that sores on the camels appeared to heal faster than similar ones on horses and mules. Beale noted this positive feature in his report.

On July 27, the expedition was rolling again, following the Rio Grande north toward Albuquerque, which they reached on August 1. They set up camp two miles outside the city.

By this time Ed Beale had become fond of a camel called "Seid," a male much larger than the others and with the unusual color of white. Some days Beale rode on Seid rather than his horse.

Once the camp was established, Beale journeyed fifty miles north to Santa Fe, where he negotiated a business deal with General Garland, the area's military commander. Beale traded (or "sold," as he reported) five wagons and thirty mules for a military escort to Fort Defiance 260 miles west of their camp.

While Beale was busy in Santa Fe, the men of the expedition prepared for some much-needed rest. They had traveled over 880 miles in forty-two days. But most were young and in good physical condition, and in a short time they became restless. A visit to the city seemed necessary.

Albuquerque was the largest city the men of the expedition had encountered thus far, with a population of over three thousand. (The actual count of souls was difficult due to the continual flow of emigrants passing through.)

The city had a central plaza that faced numerous shops, small hotels, and a variety of taverns. Here the U.S. government maintained a quartermaster depot and an army garrison, complete with storehouses, officer homes, and stables mostly constructed of adobe. In spite of its busy appearance, the entire metropolitan area was surprisingly clean. Yet there was no way of escaping the odors of animals and wood smoke that smothered the city like a cloud, refusing to disappear or even disperse in the constant, pleasant breeze sweeping in from the hills.

Alex Smith, the expedition's supply manager, young May Stacey, and manager of the camels Peachy Gilmer Breckenridge Jr. (who preferred to be called "P.G." but was addressed as "Breckenridge" by Beale, who gave him his important assignment) decided to visit the town. Smith wanted a haircut from a "real" barber. It cost him "four bits" (fifty cents).

Those men were followed by Hi Jolly and Greek George, but not to the barbershop. The "Turks" or "Arabs" (they were called both by expedition members) wanted to experience some of the pleasures of the city, namely the taverns.

Not all of the men went to town. Most remained at the camp and were soon treated to an unexpected adventure. Some enterprising Mexicans living nearby recognized a great business opportunity and announced that they planned to hold a "fandango" in honor of the "camel men." It would be in a lone adobe building and start at nightfall.[5]

The men were promised music, liquor, and "many beautiful girls" to dance and drink with, all at a price, of course.

The timing for such a party seemed perfect, or so they believed. Ed

Beale and his staff were at Santa Fe, the Arabs (or Turks) were some-where in the city, and the animals were grazing peacefully or sleeping.

Almost every man in camp, wearing their Colt revolvers and a Bowie knife, headed for the fandango at nightfall. Their excitement mounted at they neared the building, as music, totally unfamiliar, and female voices filled the cool evening air.

Never have liquor, beautiful girls, young men, guns, and knives been an ideal mixture. A few of the men began to realize this fact about 10 P.M. and left the fandango only to gather outside and discuss the evening's events.

No one at the fandango party had any knowledge that Ed Beale and his navy associate Lieutenant Charles E. Thorburn had returned from Santa Fe and were spending the night at the home of one of Beale's old California friends in the city. The two were exhausted and retired early.

Things would not be so peaceful two miles away at the fandango.

CHAPTER 19

On to El Morro

Whatever fortune is before us we are impatient to meet
it and be done with all suspense . . .

Lieutenant Edward F. Beale, Journal, 1857

10:15 P.M., TUESDAY, AUGUST 11, 1857

A cool evening breeze ruffled the gray tattered curtains, which hung
loosely about the windows of the old adobe building two miles south
of Albuquerque.

The fandango's band members had already soaked up a sizable
quantity of alcohol, as had most members of the camel expedition
except for the few who left the party minutes earlier.

Inside, the cigar smoke wafted in heavy clouds and the noise had
become almost unbearable. The "gringos" shouted and sang in an impossible attempt to drown out the band. None of the camel men understood the Spanish words to the songs the band members sang to the
strumming of their guitars, so they created their own lyrics, which
began to sound more like babbling.

It didn't really make any difference to the musicians. The manager
had met his promise. Indeed, he provided music, liquor, and many
beautiful girls, or at least most seemed attractive after 10 P.M.

By ten-fifteen, John Hoyne, a mountain of an Irishman, had passed his limit of alcohol. His usual carefree, jovial personality gradually faded into a crude-speaking rowdiness, and for reasons known only to him, he called a Mexican woman "some very bad names."

His friends knew it was time to remove Hoyne from the party, and fast! Hoyne, as could be expected, was having too much fun to listen to anyone. His friends became more insistent. John refused to leave.

John Hoyne, like most of the others, wore not one but two Colt Navy revolvers and a Bowie knife. Even without those weapons, he had no equal when it came to fighting.

His friends needed a plan, and one developed. They would ease him toward the door while Joe McFeeley slipped behind John and removed one of Hoyne's two revolvers from its holster. John Tribbit was selected to take the second pistol and the Bowie knife. All of this was to be accomplished quickly while others distracted Hoyne with conversation about the girls.

McFeeley, Tribbit, and Hoyne stumbled out the door. McFeeley succeeded in removing one of the pistols. Tribbit grabbed the knife but failed to snatch the second revolver.

Hoyne, in his drunken stupor, suddenly realized he had been tricked and drew that second pistol. He pointed the Colt at Joe Mc-Freeley and cocked the hammer.

"I will shoot you," the others heard Hoyne mutter. "I will, by God!"

Everyone but McFeeley dove to the ground, praying that the darkness would save them from an accurate shot.

The gun fired with a flash of flame, sparks, and a cloud of smoke. The ball passed over McFeeley's head and smashed harmlessly into the adobe wall. Inside, the mariachi band continued to play; only the music seemed louder now, while the girls whirled about the floor, faster than before.

Outside, no one could grab Hoyne fast enough to prevent his next action. He cocked the hammer of his Colt again. McFeeley dove to disarm his friend. The gun fired, the ball striking McFeeley's hand, "passing between the bones of the second and third finger."

All the men appeared to leap at the same instant, knocking Hoyne to the ground (some believed Hoyne "passed out" from the alcohol).

At 10:30 P.M., according to Stacey's journal, "Hampden Porter dressed Joe McFeeley's wound."[1]

The next morning Ed Beale learned of the fandango shooting and immediately "discharged" both John Hoyne and Joe McFeeley.

Beale, of course, was furious but showed no anger openly. No doubt he might have wanted to punish the entire group of fandango attendees, but wisdom blocked anger. He needed all those men for the dangerous adventure ahead and now he was two men (and four guns) short.

At first, no one could find the "Turks." But an eyewitness reported he had seen Hi Jolly and Greek George in a tavern near the plaza at dawn.

That report angered Ed Beale, who was in no mood for more bad news. He had studied the Quran years earlier and even spoke and understood a few Arabic words. Since his navy days, Beale had witnessed many fistfights, even a few shoot-outs involving drunken Americans, but he did not expect "drunk Muslims." Taking alcohol was supposed to be against their religion. But he found his Turks "as drunk as any Christian in the train."[2]

The same day, Beale wrote, "I was anxious, moreover, to get the men out of town as the Fandango and other pleasures had rendered them rather troublesome."[3]

But Beale's departure was delayed. He expected a delivery of packages "from home" to come through Santa Fe. When they arrived, there was considerable sentimental excitement as Beale shared cookies, cakes, and candies with his staff, many of whom also received mail with a "few treats." These would be the last treats or messages from home for many months.

Hi Jolly and Greek George did their best to appear busy brushing and washing the camels, preparing them for the movement into Albuquerque and staying out of sight of the boss until he cooled down.

In the city, the men removed items that Beale did not consider "critical" for their survival during the next eighty days. Geological specimens found in Texas were "discarded," as was the "photographic apparatus." Stacey recorded in his journal that the "apparatus" had "proved a failure" thus far and was too bulky, with its large wooden box of glass plates and jars of chemicals.

In the mid-1850s, photography was in its infancy in the United States, requiring certain skills of the photographer not only in taking pictures but understanding the complex process of developing. (George Eastman did not begin producing his first Kodak until 1888.)

Because of the expedition members' lack of understanding of the photographic process, combined with the fact that the equipment took up considerable space, history would be denied a photographic record of the first camel expedition in the United States.

Food, they believed, might become a concern, so a hundred sheep were added to the train. Farther along the trail they would purchase two hundred more.

On August 13, 1857, the train got under way, but Ed Beale and a few men waited in Albuquerque for two days expecting word from Colonel William Wing Loring, who, with a small detachment of troops, was to arrive from Santa Fe and escort the train to Fort Defiance. (Part of Beale's deal while trading wagons in Santa Fe a few days earlier.)

While waiting, Beale, at the recommendation of a number of people in the city, hired two "guides" who reportedly knew the trail Lieutenant Whipple had taken and all the springs or water holes from Fort Defiance to the Colorado River. The guides were an elderly man named Jose Manuel Savedra and his friend Lecko.

On the fourteenth, the slow-moving train came to a halt and camped at a water hole. They were in a beautiful grassy valley surrounded on three sides by tree-studded mountains, a perfect place to rest.

At 2 A.M. it began to rain "in torrents" and soon hail the size of "marbles" fell. Water rushed down from the mountains, forming a river that quickly rose several inches. The wagon master wisely moved the train to higher ground. They had just experienced and escaped their first "flash flood," so common in the West.

The next morning the skies were clear and the train rolled through a small village where the natives "all turned out to see the camelos," as they called the strange animals.

Soon they reached the town of Cubero, where Ed Beale and staff caught up with them. It was August 16 and he made a special entry in his journal: "No one can imagine the pleasant thing it was to get back to our flannel shirts, big boots, and greasy buckskins once more. It was home to us."

Colonel Loring had still not arrived and Beale directed the column to move to an area off the trail where the animals had better grass.

On August 15, Jacob Hamblin, a Mormon whose home was in southern Utah, happened to encounter a large wagon train of emigrants rolling well inside the territory's border.

Hamblin learned that the train's commander was Colonel Alexander Fencher from Arkansas. The train planned to follow the Old Spanish Trail to California, Fencher openly admitted.

Apparently, neither Fencher nor Hamblin knew anything about the United States Army's movement toward Utah.

Hamblin joined the Fencher train and on August 17 they all camped at Corn Creek, about eight miles south of Fillmore and two hundred miles south of Salt Lake City. The Arkansas emigrants had made good time since their last encounter with Dr. Brewer at the Platte River in June. Hamblin, like Dr. Brewer, noticed and would later remember the attractive girls riding in an unusual, elegant coach.[4]

Everyone in the group appeared to be in good spirits, anxious to reach California before winter.

Jacob Hamblin warned of the dangers they might encounter while crossing the "Las Vegas desert" and suggested an excellent place for Colonel Fencher to rest his train in preparation for that long journey through the desert. He recommended a large meadow with an excellent spring, sitting between wooded mountains, and offered to guide the train to Cedar City. From there, reaching the meadow he spoke of required only a day or two of travel. He knew the area well, he said, for he owned a small home at the edge of that meadow.

Thirty-nine-year-old Colonel William Wing Loring, a veteran of the Mexican War, was the kind of soldier the army needed on the frontier. The loss of one arm in that war did not slow him down. He was a handsome, dedicated horse soldier from North Carolina who wanted to fight Indians and asked only to be given a unit of dragoons to command.

The army accommodated "Old One Wing," as some of his troops secretly (but with affection) called him, and assigned him the Fort Defiance in New Mexico Territory to command.

In 1857, the trails connecting Santa Fe, the fort, and Albuquerque were used by both the army and emigrants moving west as well as Indians, both friendly and not. But beyond Fort Defiance the territory west was a vast wilderness. The trails, if they existed at all, belonged to the animals and the Indians.

On August 20, Colonel Loring and his troopers approached Cubero and learned that Beale's expedition had passed through only a few days before. The colonel dispatched a rider to inform Beale that they were not far behind and would catch up soon.

Meanwhile, while waiting for Loring, Beale's men discovered that a stream near where they camped contained a large quantity of fish. They had no nets or fishing equipment, so they opened "gunny" bags and waded into the water. In a few minutes they caught more than ninety fish, mostly trout, enough to feed the entire expedition.

During the fishing, Beale recorded in his journal, "Our camels are doing well and seem as fat as when we left. On leaving Albuquerque they were packed with an average of 700 pounds each, the largest carried nearly 1,000 pounds."

The morning of the twentieth was cool and clear, a perfect day for a ride, and a good time to show off a camel to the army. After all, Beale concluded, they were army camels and these dragoons might be riding them into combat someday in the future.

Beale mounted his big white camel, Seid, and rode fourteen miles back to Cubero at a pace of eight miles per hour. From the moment he and Beale met, Colonel Loring expressed a desire to ride a camel. Beale assured him he would have that opportunity once the expedition got under way again.

Beale bragged about his camel, reporting, "We started off together but finding his animals unequal to mine I rode on to camp alone and arrived after an absence of three hours, during which I had ridden twenty-seven miles. Seid seemed not the least tired; indeed, it was as much as I could do to hold him back on my return. The best mule or horse on our camp, in present condition could not have performed the same journey in twice the time."[5]

The camels' load-carrying capabilities were already well-known to the expedition members, but now more was understood of their strong "trotting." Everyone, including Beale and Colonel Loring, was impressed and questioned just how fast and for how long a time the camel could run.

On August 21, Beale, Charles Thorburn, and Colonel Loring vectored from the train and traveled north toward Fort Defiance. A heavy rain began and they protected themselves with something new, "India Rubber blankets."

In spite of the weather, they cooked a breakfast of "snipe, black birds, and mutton" and agreed that nothing better could "be eaten at the best hotel in New York."

Along the way, Beale recorded the location of timber and a large vein of coal, all very important if a railroad was constructed through the area.

The party, damp and cold, arrived at Fort Defiance on August 25 while the expedition continued to roll west. The train was now at an elevation of seven thousand feet above sea level and evenings found them huddled around campfires, covered with blankets, shivering from the cold.

In addition to the uncomfortable, cold nights, May Stacey recorded that he was awakened at 11 P.M. "by the mournful cry of a panther [mountain lion] quite near to the camp."

With little sleep, they pushed on the next morning, arriving at a large spring known as El Morro at the base of Inscription Rock. They camped there, then moved on to Zuni, where they would wait for the return of their leader.[6]

On August 25, 1857, as Lieutenant Beale arrived at Fort Defiance, far away in Utah Territory the Alexander Fencher wagon train neared Cedar City and was visited by Mormon apostle George A. Smith. The apostle had been traveling in southern Utah, alerting the population and instructing everyone to "stockpile" grain, food, and gunpowder.

Smith warned his people that the United States Army was approaching their border. Brigham Young, Smith said, had ordered all LDS members back from San Bernardino, Nevada, and elsewhere, wherever they might be "serving mission."

And Apostle Smith had more shocking news. Apostle Parley P. Pratt had been murdered "while on a mission in *Arkansas.*"

Smith made it clear that all the signs indicated it was time for Mormons to prepare to fight, should it become necessary to protect their religion and territory.

Apparently the Fencher emigrants were ignorant of the Pratt murder and the pending military conflict. They spoke openly with Apostle Smith, revealing facts about their journey, destination, number of travelers, weapons, food supply, and that most were from Arkansas.

With no concerns they told of plans to rest at a place "a little to the South" on or about September 8, a place known as Mountain Meadows.

Smith said he knew that valley well, then nodded slowly while smiling at the young ladies in the elegant carriage.[7]

CHAPTER 20

Crossing into the Wilderness

No one who has not commanded an expedition of this
kind, where everything ahead is dim and uncertain and
unknown, except the dangers, can imagine the anxiety
with which I set out upon this journey.

Lieutenant Edward F. Beale, Journal, 1857

Tse-hootsooi, the Navajo called it: "the Meadow Between the Rocks."
The name described the place perfectly.

An icy-cold creek flowed through the valley, supporting grassy
fields and green marshes. This had been Navajo land, a place where
they, for many generations, grazed their sheep, horses, and goats.

Then, in 1851, the U.S. Army came and constructed a sprawling
fortress, claiming they needed the land to protect white people traveling west. They renamed the place Fort Defiance, and to ensure the
safety of the army men and animals, the Navajo were prohibited from
using the land.[1]

In 1857, Fort Defiance was the last outpost on the edge of the
wilderness and sent patrols throughout the immediate area and back
east as far as Albuquerque.

When Beale, Thorburn, and Colonel Loring were about ten miles
from the fort on August 25, they were met by Captain Carlisle, a
member of the colonel's staff. The captain had a special "welcome"
treat. Beale reported, "As we stood in the warm sun of August it was
most refreshing to see the Captain's servant throw off the folds of a

blanket from a tub in the bottom of the wagon and expose several large
and glistening blocks of ice, while at the same time the Captain produced a delicate of red eye."[2]

The men, exhausted from the journey, enjoyed a few sips of whiskey "on the rocks" and then rode on to the fort, "somewhat refreshed."

Beale and Thorburn were warmly received and treated "with respect" by the soldiers while they prepared for the next phase of the
expedition—a direct penetration into the western wilderness. And, of
course, the soldiers were excited to learn news from "back east," though
the information Beale had was already three months old.

Beale for the first time revealed personal concerns in his journal.
"Today commences it," he wrote on August 27, "let us see what I shall
say in this journal, if I live to say anything on the day of my return
here."[3]

The fort's staff bid good-bye to Beale and Thorburn at 2 P.M. on
August 27, 1857. The colonel would remain, but twenty of his men
rode out to join the expedition as an escort. In another year, Colonel
Loring and most of his men would receive orders to march to Utah and
join Colonel Johnston as "reinforcements."

During the second evening after leaving the fort, Beale and Thorburn spent time examining the notes and maps made by Francis Aubrey. They concluded that most of the information was "too vague" or
difficult to understand to be of much value.

But there were the reports of Sitgreaves and Whipple, and though
these were valuable, the actual tracks left by their wagons often did not
match the recorded notes or, in places, had disappeared. Beale therefore determined that he would have to rely on the knowledge of his
two guides.

While Beale journeyed toward Zuni, the men of the expedition
enjoyed a rest at El Morro. Here was plenty of grass and water and a
large golden sandstone formation rising from the earth, decorated with
juniper and pine trees. The sandstone mountain covered an area of
almost two square miles and stood with a mesa at its top, almost two
hundred feet above the desert floor.

Travelers had cut their names in the stone for hundred of years before May Stacey and the "camel men" enjoyed the cool clear water at its base.

The first to leave messages were the ancient people, perhaps a thousand years before the Zuni ancestors, the Anasazi. Their petroglyphs told stories that, still today, are not completely understood.

But they did motivate others, including early Spanish explorers. The expedition guide translated one of the oldest: *Passed by here, the Hdelantado Don Juan de Oñate, from the discovering of the sea of the south, the 16th of April, 1605.* (The don was referring to the Gulf of California.)

Nineteen-year-old May Stacey cut his name in the stone, as did the young man in charge of the camels, Peachy Gilmer Breckenridge (only Peachy simply scratched in *P. G. Breckenridge*).

Stacey then recorded in his journal his feelings about El Morro. "It is a beautiful place, secluded and secure, fit for the echo of words of love. It is a romantic spot and one we shall all remember when years have passed and other scenes will have grown dim in the waters of memory."

From El Morro the train moved on to Zuni and camped twelve miles to the east of the village to wait for Ed Beale.

Beale arrived in Zuni on the twenty-ninth and sent an "Indian" back to the train with a letter of instruction, requesting they move forward into town as quickly as possible. On the way they noticed "enormous" fields of corn and wheat and, nearer town, large flocks of sheep and goats.

The population of Zuni at the time was about two thousand, mostly Mexicans and Indians. Beale had been busy making "bargains" for trade for corn. Successful, he got all the men busy shelling it. Though the camels had been happy eating desert plants, the horses and mules needed the corn, as well as grass, in order to complete the journey.

The expedition rolled out of Zuni on August 31, leaving many Indians very happy with hats, shirts, pants, and tobacco, which the "gringos" traded for corn and blankets.

The camels were now packed with bags of corn weighing about 750 pounds each. The weight slowed their pace only slightly; Beale wrote, "the camels got along well and came into camp only a little behind the wagons."[4]

From time to time they did find traces of Whipple's trail and located "Jacob's Well," described by Stacey as "a hole 120 feet deep surrounded by a perfectly level plain. Its circumference measured by myself with a chain is 500 yards and eighty feet."

Here some ducks were shot for dinner. Even though antelopes were grazing nearby, none were killed that day.[5]

On September 2, Stacey noted an unusual discovery. "We discovered a large piece of timber, petrified." And on September 3, Beale recorded, "The ground is strewn with pieces of petrified wood and very pretty agates."

The expedition was passing through what is now the Petrified Forest National Park, a little east of Holbrook.

The train was averaging about fourteen miles a day.

The measuring equipment used by Beale's expedition was, for the period, functional and somewhat accurate, though bulky and heavy. A special wagon they called an "ambulance" carried the instruments packed carefully for protection from the weather and the bouncing wagon.

The sextant for measuring latitude by sighting a celestial object (mostly the sun) and the horizon and the chronometer for determining longitude were both stored in felt-lined wooden boxes. The wagon also carried a surveyor's compass, which, when mounted on its tripod, could be used for a quick measurement of elevation and bearing.

The most useful or practical compass was the "prismatic." It enabled one to read the direction (or bearing) on the compass dial through a right-angle prism while simultaneously viewing the object being sighted. No doubt many of the men carried their personal flat compasses, which were usually encased in brass or wood.

Although Beale made no notes of other equipment, it is possible they carried a "wye level," used for establishing contours of the land. A barometer would tell him the difference in elevations.

But he did have an odometer, sometimes called a "via meter," which was attached to the wheel of the ambulance. This device gave a fairly accurate reading of miles traveled each day.

Of course, most of the men knew how to determine general direction from the sun's position, using the stars at night.

On September 6, they began to see signs of Indians, foot trails crossing their path and signal fires in the mountains at night. The Native Americans were constantly watching the expedition's movements, and the men knew it. They kept their weapons "at the ready" at all times.

Beale recorded a comparison of mules to camels: "The camels are so quiet and give so little trouble that sometimes we forget they are with us. Certainly there never was anything so patient and enduring and so little troublesome, as this noble animal."

He goes on with his praise: ". . . so perfectly docile and quiet that they are the admiration of the whole camp. At starting, there were many—a large majority of the men, who scouted with the idea of their going with us, even as far as Fort Davis, but, at this time there is not a man in camp who is not delighted with them."

No doubt the camels were far less trouble and much quieter than the mules, but there were some men who simply resented the animals either because of their odor or because they just could not adjust to the thought that something new and so different had entered their lives.

The next day the sighting of an abundance of wild game had everyone excited. Elk, antelope, deer, beavers, and coyotes were counted in large numbers.

Beale wrote, "What a stock country! I have never seen anything like it and I predict for this part of New Mexico a much larger population." (They were in New Mexico Territory, but what is, today, northeast Arizona near the base of the San Francisco Mountains.)

He then recorded, "Up the steep mesa we ascended . . . the camels packed their heavy loads without the least apparent difficulty and without a stop, some of them having nearly a thousand pounds."

As Beale's expedition rolled on, a forty-two-year-old dragoon officer from Vermont, Captain Steward Van Vliet, embarked on a very dangerous mission.

When Colonel Albert Sydney Johnson's army got under way in Kansas, Captain Van Vliet was ordered to ride ahead of the main body of troops with thirty men and deliver a letter to Brigham Young in Salt Lake City. The letter was from Colonel Harney and advised that the citizens and government of Utah were to accommodate and supply U.S. troops once they arrived.

Mormon travelers happened to meet the captain's unit about 150 miles from Salt Lake City and warned that they might be riding into a trap. The Mormons urged Van Vliet to return to the safety of Colonel Johnston's advancing army.

Captain Van Vliet had his orders and a letter to deliver. He thanked the travelers for the advice and, to ensure that no harm would come to his men, rode on alone into the Mormon stronghold. It was a courageous and wise decision. The Mormons would not attack a U.S. officer riding alone. They greeted him respectfully and escorted him to Brigham Young on September 8, 1857. A meeting, friendly in nature, took place over the next few days.

Colonel Harney's letter informed that U.S. troops were on the way, but the letter did not tell Young he was about to be replaced as governor (a fact Young already knew).

The captain assured Young that it was not the intention of the army to arrest him but only to establish a new government for Utah Territory.

Young and other Mormon leaders trusted Van Vliet. They had met years before during the time the Mormons were camped in Iowa, but they could not accept the possibility that the U.S. Army was coming with peaceful intent and they did not plan to permit a new governor or federal officers to enter Utah. Frustrated, Captain Van Vliet departed

Salt Lake City on September 14 and rode to join his unit, which was awaiting his return.

On September 4, the same day Captain Van Vliet rode into Salt Lake City, the Fancher Arkansas wagon train of emigrants entered the beautiful valley known as Mountain Meadows, not far from Cedar City in the southern part of the state.

The young girls in the elegant coach jumped to the soft ground, thick with grass, and ran to join their 135 companions in songs and prayers of thanksgiving.

A large spring with crystal-clear water flowed silently a hundred yards away and a few small children ran to partake of its refreshing coolness.

Captain Van Vliet, in a meeting at Salt Lake City hundreds of miles to the north, had no knowledge of the Fancher party. It would be two years before he learned of those emigrants' fate. The news, then, made him ill for several days.

On September 7, the captain's unit of thirty dragoons waiting just outside the Utah border knew nothing of the Fancher train and had never heard of Mountain Meadows. And they were not very far away.

If only a rider had reached them seeking help, if only some message arrived in time, the bugler could have sounded the charge. This time there would be no cavalry coming to the rescue.

On September 8, still no word came to U.S. dragoons. But now it was too late to stop the massacre of emigrants at Mountain Meadows.

CHAPTER 21

First Shots of the Utah War

> The scene of the massacre was horrible to look upon, women's hair in detached locks and masses hung to the sage bushes . . . Parts of little children's dresses dangled from the shrubbery . . . for at least a mile there gleamed bleached white by the weather, the skulls and other bones of those who had suffered.
>
> *Brevet Major James Henry Carleton's Report,*
>
> *May 25, 1859*

There is something about being in the wilderness that can bring out the best, but sometimes the worst, in man. Something peculiar about the isolation from civilization, producing a thrill of knowing he has a certain power, a control, influenced by nature and one's own desires without the protection or influence of society.

What can it be that hides deep in a primitive part of the brain, struggling for control, then springing out finally free, the predator in us that commands we kill our own kind?

A beautiful meadow between wooded mountains, deep inside Utah Territory, isolated from the world, hidden from California by a desert, is such a wilderness, a perfect spot to hide a horrible crime.

On that chilly morning in September 1857, the hot coffee tasted especially delightful. A light breeze brought a few snowflakes, warning the Fencher emigrant party camped at Mountain Meadows, Utah, that an early winter might be on the way. It would soon be time to leave the lovely valley and continue along the Old Spanish Trail to California.

They expected next the long stretch of desert before reaching the waters of Las Vegas Springs. But then, with another rest, they would be ready to pass through the mountains and finally reach their destination by Christmas.

Almost eight hundred head of cattle, tended by a few young men, were grazing, enjoying the thick green grass only a short distance from the wagons that morning. Women scurried about, cleaning breakfast utensils, packing family belongings, and caring for very small children. Some nursed infants, born during the long journey from Arkansas.

Two boys, in their late teen years, were discussing something of a very serious nature when one's attention fixed on a ravine at the base of a sage-covered hill one hundred yards away. He apparently saw something moving in the brush.

"Indians," he muttered. Then he screamed, "Indians!"

Suddenly the sounds of a series of rifle shots came from the hill with little clouds of white gun smoke dotting the landscape.

The two boys fell, killed in the first volley. A young girl playing nearby dropped to her knees, a rifle ball in her head.

Then the Indians leaped from the ravine, screaming as they rushed toward the wagons. But Colonel Fencher had prepared his emigrants for such an attack. Men, with rifles always within arm's reach, shouldered their weapons and fired directly into the warriors.

One Pah-Ute, the brother of a chief from the nearby Santa Clara area, fell dead, shot through the chest. Six more staggered from wounds. The charge broke apart and the warriors retreated to the safety of the ravine. Two more struck by emigrant rifle balls toppled into the crevice with fatal wounds.

The first Indian charge was a failure. Things were not going according to plan. The Mormons had assured the Indians that it would be an easy victory. The emigrants were to be slaughtered in only a few minutes. Instead, the emigrants were fighting back, firing weapons with surprising accuracy.

The Pah-Utes, armed with bows and arrows, war clubs, and only a few rifles, quickly recognized this as a battle they could not win, so they began to drive off the cattle in several directions. At least there would be some reward for their loss.

Taking advantage of the lull in the fighting, the emigrants moved into action. Wagons were pushed into a circle, their wheels linked together with iron chains. The stronger men dug firing pits almost four feet deep with dirt packed a foot or two around the sides. On this, they could rest their rifles for more accurate fire.

Twenty-eight yards away was the spring and its life-supporting water. Two emigrants rushed to defend it, but were killed by rifle shots. Indians had crept in during the predawn hours and quietly built a firing wall out of nearby stones. Now they were protected from shots fired by the emigrants and had control of the only source of water in the valley.

And so a siege began, emigrants and attackers exchanging gunfire over the next few days, and slowly the wagon train ran out of emergency water. They buried their dead inside the circle of wagons and, all being devout Christians, prayed for deliverance.

At first, they must have believed there was a chance for survival. The Indians, also suffering losses, might give up and leave the valley. But soon they began to question just who was firing all those rifles. Surely the Indians lacked such firepower. Then, as days crept by, they accepted the fact that all were doomed. There was no relief from the attack and no one to come to their rescue.

The so-called Indian attack had been orchestrated by two Mormon military leaders, Isaac C. Haight of Cedar City and John W. Lee of Harmony, Utah. They followed orders from their commander, a colonel in the militia's "Iron Mountain Brigade." Sixty men of the Nauvoo Legion were activated and authorized to participate in the attack on the wagon train.[1]

Only a month had passed since Apostle George A. Smith conducted his tour through the southern area of Utah, spreading news of the murder of Apostle Parley P. Pratt in Arkansas and the announcement that the U.S. Army was approaching Utah's border.

The people of southern Utah were fired up and preparing for war

when the wagon train rolled into their area. Each soldier of the Nauvoo Legion and the Iron Mountain Brigade believed he was acting
under orders of superiors in the LDS organization, orders, of course,
they could not question if they were to remain members of the
church.

The soldiers wanted revenge for Pratt's murder and were naturally
angry over the fact that American troops were marching on their paradise. The members of the wagon train from Arkansas were a rich,
perfect target. Blaming the killings on the Indians seemed like an
excellent and acceptable idea.

But things from the beginning did not go well for the Mormon
planners. One Pah-Ute chief refused to allow his warriors to participate in the attack, stating that the Mormons had educated his people
to believe killing and stealing were wrong.[2]

Then the first charge led by Indians fell apart as some were killed.
No one expected the emigrants to fight back with such coordinated
ferocity. The Mormons involved had disguised themselves as Indians
by wearing feathered headdresses and buckskin clothing, but now they
feared some emigrants might have noticed that not all the "Indians"
were Indians. And so as the siege continued, the real Indians were
beginning to lose their spirit for battle, relying more and more on the
Mormons to do the fighting.

The Mormon attackers agreed. There must be no emigrant survivors who could reveal the truth about the attack. They all swore an
oath. No survivors except children too young to remember.[3]

The emigrants, now short of food, water, and gunpowder, realized
that an escape to the north would lead them deeper into Mormon territory. On their east and west were mountains, and none of them knew
the trails, if they existed.

Ninety miles separated them from the Muddy River in the south,
and then another seventy-five miles of desert must be crossed to reach
the springs of Las Vegas.

On Friday, September 11, 1857, when all seemed lost for the emigrants, it appeared that their prayers for survival were answered.

A wagon appeared from over the hill and rolled down to the emigrants' perimeter. A man was standing in the wagon waving a white cloth. In minutes, a lengthy meeting was held between the Mormons in the wagon and the leaders of the wagon train.

The emigrants were convinced that the Mormons had reached an agreement with the Indians. If the emigrants left everything in their wagons, including weapons, the Indians would allow them to pass safely in Mormon wagons to Cedar City. The emigrants finally agreed.

Wounded were loaded into one wagon. Women and children led the procession out of the valley with their men following by more than a hundred yards. Mormon "guards" with rifles and pistols marched alongside for "protection."

They proceeded up a small incline where the trail passed through scrub-oak bushes and large sage. Waiting behind those bushes were Mormon militia and a few Pah-Ute Indians.

On a command shouted by one Mormon, the slaughter began. The guards turned and fired directly at the men of the train. Drivers of the wagon killed all the wounded quickly.

Some of the men and women broke and ran, screaming, trying to return to their wagons; others huddled with small children to protect them from rifle shots and arrows, but they were falling, one or two at a time.

The killers began walking among the dead and dying and, with cool precision, fired pistol shots into their heads. The women and children, considered less of a threat, were the last to die.

Then the Indians attacked the women, stripping their clothes away and killing them with clubs and knives. But some of the women and teenage girls had scattered and attempted to hide in the brush. They were found in minutes and shot in the head by the militia.

The four young girls who had crossed the country in the elegant coach ran together toward the eastern hill. Their bright-colored dresses made them easy targets.

Two girls screamed and fell, arrows protruding from their backs.

The Indians were on them, ripping at their clothes and slicing their necks with knives. In a moment the nude bodies were still.

The two other girls were almost out of the valley, but ran blindly into the arms of Bishop John D. Lee, who stood, knife and pistol in hand, next to a young Indian warrior. The older girl pleaded for protection and then mercy. Lee shot her in the head.

The young warrior suggested to Lee that the other girl be spared, remarking that she was beautiful.

Lee did not answer, but led the girl "away to a secluded spot" where she then "implored him to do anything but not take her life." Bishop Lee apparently had his own plans for the girl.

After a few minutes, Lee reappeared down at the massacre scene. The young warrior searched for the girl and found her lying near some sagebrush. "Her throat had been cut, ear to ear."[4]

The Mountain Meadows Massacre was over, some say, in less than thirty minutes. The actual number killed is still debated, but estimates range from 120 to 140 men, women, and children.

Eighteen children, from sixteen weeks to seven years old, were spared and sold by the militia to different families to be raised as Mormons.

All the bodies of the dead were stripped of clothing and searched for valuables. The bloody clothing was taken to the cellar of the Cedar City Tithing Office, where it lay in piles for three weeks until the odor became so offensive that it was sold or given away.

Most of the emigrant property was sold at auction in Cedar City; the remainder was taken to Salt Lake City and sold at auction. Some of the cattle remained with the Pah-Utes (their only reward for assisting in the massacre).

Cash taken from the train and the emigrants' pockets was carried to Brigham Young, who refused to touch it. Young had sent a letter to the Iron Mountain Brigade ordering them to let the wagon train pass through unmolested. The letter arrived the day after the massacre, too late to save the emigrants.

Within a few months, reports reached the U.S. Army in California claiming a large wagon train had been attacked by Indians and its party slaughtered. Then the Fencher party was reported to be "overdue," but believed to have entered Utah.

There were reports that the Mormons had killed emigrants and the bodies remained unburied. At first, all the stories were discounted by the army, but then claims from non-Mormon government officials living in Utah filtered into military bases in San Francisco and Los Angeles.

A year and a half after the massacre, the army decided to take action and ordered a unit of First Dragoons from Fort Tejon to investigate and bury the dead. The unit was commanded by Mexican War hero Brevet Major James Henry Carleton, assisted by Captain Reuben P. Campbell and companies of the Second Dragoons.

In May 1859, Major Carleton's report gave the country the first details of the massacre. The facts shocked the nation, and aroused old prejudices against Mormons.

". . . the remains were not buried at all until they had been dismembered by the wolves and the flesh stripped from the bones . . ."

". . . there is not a shadow of a doubt that the emigrants were butchered by the Mormons, assisted doubtless by the Indians."

". . . I observed that every skull I saw had been shot through with rifle or revolver bullets." So read part of Major Carleton's report.[5]

While Carleton investigated, Bishop John D. Lee was riding proudly about Cedar City in his new, elegant carriage, decorated with "bronzed stag's heads upon its panels."

No one had seen such a wonderful coach in Utah, no one except Dr. Charles Brewer, surgeon, United States Army. He would later testify about the true owners of the coach, the young ladies he had met along the Platte River many weeks earlier.[6]

Justice would be delayed as a result of the Utah War and the Civil War, as well as political disagreements between Washington and Salt Lake City leaders.

In 1874, nine indictments were issued by a court. Only John D. Lee was actually tried and, after two trials, convicted of murder.

On March 23, 1877, at 10:55 A.M., almost twenty years after the massacre, John D. Lee was executed by a firing squad at Mountain Meadows, claiming to the end that he and the others were "following orders" when they killed the emigrants in 1857. And he continued to deny claims that he sexually molested any of the women.

Today, a firing squad may still be used as a method of executing convicted criminals in Utah.

But the sounds of rifle fire that brought the end of John Lee also announced the end of the Utah War.[7]

On September 15, 1857, four days after the Mountain Meadows Massacre, Mormon leader (and still governor of Utah) Brigham Young officially declared "Martial Law" and activated the Nauvoo Legion with orders to stop U.S. troops should they attempt to enter Utah Territory.

On September 18, Colonel Albert S. Johnston and his reinforcements marched out of Fort Leavenworth, Kansas, and headed toward Utah. They planned to join Colonel Alexander, whose army was closing in on LDS territory.

When word of martial law reached Las Vegas Springs at the southern edge of Mormon territory, patrols of militia, often accompanied by their Pah-Ute friends, became more frequent along the Colorado River.

Meanwhile, Lieutenant Edward Beale and his camel expedition were making good progress, averaging sometimes ten to twenty miles a day.

On the morning of September 9, 1857, Beale recorded that they came upon "a plain of vast extent. The viewing of the rich green grass, the distant mountains and our moving camp wagons, sheep, horses and camels made a beautiful picture." They were near the San Francisco Mountains in eastern Arizona.

The expedition discovered, on the "cool, fresh" morning of September 10, ruins of an ancient civilization. Beale recorded it as "a curious sort of fortification or remains of homes." Many of the stone walls were three feet thick and three to four feet in height.

Whipple had recorded notes on such a place during his 1853 survey and had been especially impressed with the huge caves that were given the name Cosnurio (also spelled "Cosnino").

The caves were divided into different "apartments," which contained a large amount of pottery fragments and flint chips, indicating that many families had dwelled in them long ago.[8]

While most members of the expedition were fascinated with the archaeological ruins, Beale, Lieutenant Thorburn, and Stacey noticed that their guide, Jose Manuel Savedra, appeared to be confused about some of the landmarks and, at times, expressed uncertainty about the trail and the location of the next water hole. This, of course, had Beale very uneasy and he began to keep a close eye on the guide.

Shortly after breakfast on the tenth, an army rider approached Beale with troublesome news. One of the "military escorts" had disappeared from their camp just before breakfast and had not returned.

The closest white civilization, Fort Defiance, was behind them one hundred miles. The wagon tracks formed by the expedition would be easy to follow back to the fort, but according to reports, the soldier did not depart in that direction.

Beale was frustrated. He planned to cover at least another twelve miles that day, but now a member of the army was missing and must be found.

Did the man die of a fall or become the victim of a rattlesnake bite, bear, or mountain-lion attack? Did the Indians ambush him? No one heard a pistol shot or even a scream.

Members of the army and civilians joined together and searched a mile off their trail. Beale ordered fires to be built on surrounding hilltops, smoking fires during the day and bright ones at night. In 1857, skies were pollution-free and, of course, displayed no vapor trails from aircraft. Fires and smoke could be seen for twenty miles or more. A fellow American was missing and the camel expedition would do everything possible to find him.

CHAPTER 22

A Constant Search for Water

In the desert, water is more valuable than gold.

Arab Proverb

Some said the wilderness and the constant worry of Indian attacks finally drove him mad. If that was true, even the unspoiled beauty of trees, snowcapped mountains, and clear sky became a threat to security rather than the comfort it brought most men.

A few of the soldiers in the escort were certain he had simply deserted, perhaps disgusted with the seemingly unending march to California. But he had served five years with the army and was in his second enlistment. Nothing the expedition encountered this far should have forced a soldier of his experience to desert.

There may have been things, concerns in his mind, that he never discussed with his comrades, haunting thoughts that led him to such a reckless act, to ride off into the wild country alone.

The morning of September 10 was cool and the night had been very cold, according to Beale's journal. But the sun soon rose and the temperature became "delightful and remained so all day."

They were at the base of the San Francisco Mountains not far from modern-day Winona.

If the lost soldier managed to complete the one-hundred-mile journey back to Fort Defiance, he likely would stand trial for desertion, and as an experienced soldier, he would know that he had little chance of surviving a visit to a Native American village. He might be accepted as a friend, but that was unlikely.

May Humphreys Stacey, Hampden "Ham" Porter, and Joseph M. Bell, the youngest (all age nineteen) members of the expedition along with blacksmith "Mr. Tucker," remained at the September 10 camp, as Beale ordered, while the train rolled on. They were waiting for two "herders" who had pursued a runaway mule. The youths occupied their time during the wait counting antelope darting across the trail. Stacey shot a coyote "at forty yards" with his rifle and cut off his bushy tail "as a trophy."[1]

The herders returned, but without the mule. They'd followed his tracks to the last camp, then lost the trail. Together, the men rode west to join the train, which had moved almost fifteen miles.

The wagon tracks were easy to follow, and after traveling less than a mile, they were met by three soldiers riding toward them. The soldiers were part of a team searching for their friend. They reported that he had left the "line of march" and chased a rabbit, totally "disregarding the commands of his officer." One of the three troopers stated that he believed the man to be "crazy"; the other two thought he "deserted."[2]

Stacey's group caught up with the train, finding them camped in a "beautiful valley, surrounded by lofty pines." But the young men had missed breakfast. Hungry and frustrated, they began to rearrange their gear when they heard a loud shout and someone calling.

Absalom Reading, "Beale's black servant," was waving a wooden spoon and pointing to several iron skillets sitting on large stones next to a campfire.

Absalom was very fond of the young men, who had always considered him a friend, not a servant. That morning he expected Stacey's party to be late and saved them a nice quantity of food.

The boys called him "old Ab," but he could have been any age above thirty. None of the journals report his age, yet Ab accompanied Beale on all his cross-country expeditions as a "companion." Though

Ed Beale introduced Ab, the only African American on the expedition, as his "servant," the man was treated as an equal.[3]

Stacey recorded, "Old Ab gave us a bite which we did ample justice to and by the time we had finished the train was again ready to move."[4]

As they prepared to leave, soldiers rode into camp to report that they had found the missing man's tracks and followed them for a mile, then lost them. They had shouted and fired several shots. "The rocks, alone, answered their calls."

Ed Beale "did everything in his power" to assist the army in locating the lost soldier. He delayed the train movement another day, sent men back to their last camp to search, and through the night stayed awake to ensure that fires were kept burning on the hills until dawn. The following day, fires with heavy smoke continued to burn until dark.

Beale recorded on September 10, "I fear he will prove a total loss." Then, on September 11, "The soldier who was missing yesterday has not appeared, although bright fires were kept up all night. It seems hard to determine whether he deserted or went off in a fit of mental aberration. To track him over the rocks would be impossible and the attempt a useless waste of time."[5]

And so the expedition moved on without the "lost" man. His fate remains unknown.

That night they camped at the very base of the mountains, their sharp peaks already covered with snow, and noted the abundance of bear, deer, antelope, and partridge roaming with no fear of man.

Beale was especially interested in the "elegant squirrels with silver fur and a rich brown color down their backs."

On September 12, expedition members were up at 4 A.M. to find Ed Beale's temper boiling. He had good reason. Savedra, their guide, seemed totally lost, having no idea of where to find springs.

Now, with no knowledge of what to expect over the next twenty miles, Beale sent his trusted navy friend Lieutenant Thorburn with five men to search ahead for water.

Beale recorded, "We unfortunately have no guide, the wretch I employed at the urgent request and advice of everyone in Albuquerque and, at enormous wages, being the most ignorant and irresolute old ass extant. This obligates us to do the double duty of road making and exploring."

Thorburn and his men returned at 10 A.M. and reported "plenty of water ahead."

Along his wagon road, through what is now northern Arizona, Edward Beale named numerous landmarks after members of his party, sometimes honoring them for the discovery of a spring. Stacey's Spring, Ab's Spring (the first spring to be named for an African American in Arizona), Breckenridge Spring, Boys' Pass, Thorburn Mountain, and, of course, Beale's Spring are good examples. But thirty years later, as settlers moved into Arizona, most of Beale's names were changed.

Often, the scenery was so magnificent that Beale could not resist describing his feelings in his journal. On September 13, 1857, he wrote, "The view was so grand and extensive that we sat on our horses for a long time in silent admiration; I, on my part, only regretting that we could only go in one direction at one time."

He then went on to speak of the camels' performance: "The camels continue undisturbed by the strong character of the country and can any day go twice as far as the wagons, besides relieving us of all anxiety on their account as to food or water, for they can eat whatever they may chance to get, or do without anything and drink only when the water happens to be perfectly convenient to camp."[6]

On the morning of September 14, the men were up at four and the train rolling by five-thirty. Beale appeared in a pleasant mood . . . for a while. Then there was another disagreement with the guide, Savedra. Beale wrote, "Our guide has proven so utterly worthless that I was obligated to send him to the rear and only regret I had not done so sooner. Up to this point he has only served to annoy and mislead me."[7]

Stacey recorded on the same day that Beale began to show confidence in Lecko, the second guide, who had served with Aubrey in

1854. The expedition turned northwest, deviating slightly from Whipple's trail and following one used by Aubrey. Lecko assured them they would save time and find grass and water.

On the evening of the fifteenth, Beale sent Lecko on ahead to search for the water he believed to be close by. By noon on the sixteenth, Lecko had not returned, so Beale stopped the train and sent three men to search for him.

Late in the afternoon of the seventeenth, the search party found Lecko practically dead. He had survived forty-eight hours without food or water after becoming a victim of a simple accident. He had dismounted his mule and the animal bolted and ran off. Lecko went after him on foot, trailing the animal overnight and finally catching him the following day. They were more than thirty miles from the train when the rescue party arrived.

The next day the train was rolling again, making over twelve miles on level ground. Beale decided to continue on all night, as long as the ground remained flat. Meanwhile, he and others rode ahead, lighting fires to mark the way.

Then the next day, a new problem: Lecko admitted he was lost, having no idea where to find Aubrey's trail. He had led the train into a dead-end canyon.

The nearest water was back at their last camp, thirty-two miles away.

The expedition was now in a dangerous situation, miles from water in completely unknown country. An angry Beale recorded, "I ought to have killed [Lecko] there, but I did not."

There was no water in the area and no grass for horses, mules, and sheep. While the staff discussed their next course of action, the camels stood by, content, munching on their favorite greasewood plants.

Ed Beale came up with a plan, a desperate but necessary one. He sent two riders on camels to the east to search for water while he and several men headed west on horses.

Beale's group found no water and returned to the train, where they found the camel scouting party waiting. The men reported that after they had traveled sixteen to twenty miles east, the camels took over and led them to a stream.[8]

The camels were loaded with barrels of water and returned to the convoy. Beale wrote about "[my] camels": "Six of them are worth all of the mules."[9]

The expedition "by-passed" the dead-end canyon and continued on west. In another day the weather turned hot and the mules and horses had to be put on half water rations of four quarts daily. Beale recorded that "their distress was painful to witness . . . the camels alone seemed perfectly indifferent and chewed their cuds in cheerful contentment."

On September 24, they finally located a large spring, and the animals, almost dead, were permitted to drink and rest.

The camels had traveled more than fifty miles with no water, which amazed everyone. Stacey recorded in his journal, "The camels had not had a single drop of water since we left the last water hole. It is a remarkable thing how they stood it so well as they did, traveling under the hot sun all day and packing two hundred pounds apiece."

The camels had earned the respect of all the men. It would not be the last time they proved their value in the Southwest.

CHAPTER 23

Can Camels Swim?

We must either find water or return.

Lieutenant Edward Beale,
Journal, September 29, 1857

On September 27, 1857, the men of Ed Beale's expedition were beginning to get their first experience of a true desert as they came within a few miles east of present-day Kingman, Arizona.

The vegetation changed, as did the soil, which now had a more sandy consistency, and even though October was near, the weather was warm, sunny, and dry, very dry.

Now there were signs of Indians in the area. Tracks in the sand and remains of campfires greeted them along the way, reminding everyone that they were not alone. Beale did not appear concerned with the discoveries, at least not visibly. But the guides were uneasy and the men talked among themselves of extra precautions to be taken at night. A heightened alertness gripped everyone during the day. Weapons were checked with more regularity to ensure that they remained dust- and sand-free and that percussion caps were in good working condition.

Beale's journal indicates that he had almost no concern over the signs of Indians. He released part of his army escort to return to Albuquerque, or so he claimed: "I sent back a corporal and twelve men with four wagons and their teamsters, retaining a sergeant and six men . . . I determined to send them back from this place having no further need for them and not wishing to deprive the Quartermaster of the teams used for their transportation."[1]

May Stacey on the same date recorded, "Seven escort soldiers remain with us, determined to go to California and run all the risks. Our train is now reduced to four heavy wagons and two ambulances [carriages]. Our party numbers, all told, forty-four men."[2]

It seemed to be a critical time in their journey for the escort soldiers to return. It is not known if this action was part of an agreement between Beale and the army, or, as Stacey seems to indicate, some men wanted to return while others were willing to continue through what they all knew to be a dangerous section of the country.

Stacey was young and not privy to the plans of Ed Beale. He simply reported what he saw and felt.

It is also not known, or at least not recorded, if the man who disappeared or "wandered off" had anything to do with other soldiers leaving the train. Whatever the reason for the soldiers' departure, the lives of the other men, and the camels, were now in more danger because of the reduced protection.

Even though the nights were cold, the days continued to be extremely hot and dry. "The men frequently dried mutton by laying it in the sun and air on the bushes." The meat, according to Beale, would then "keep for a week without spoiling."

But the lack of water and the knowledge of where it next might be found remained major concerns. Beale no longer depended on his "guides" and sent teams of men out to the west, southwest, and northwest in search of enough water to keep the mules, and themselves, going.

On September 27, he dispatched Lieutenant Thorburn and ten men to search for a better trail and water. Beale and a few men searched in another direction. They all realized that if they could not find water within the next twenty to thirty miles, it would be necessary to return to the last water hole. They were trapped. The entire train, except perhaps for the camels, would perish if water was not located soon.

The search teams needed excellent navigation and tracking skills, nerves of steel, and superior physical endurance as they had to ride at least twenty miles out and then find their way back, twenty miles, to the train.

They found an abundance of deer and antelope, indicating that water must be near, but still they could not locate a spring or water hole.

The first night, Beale rode his horse ahead of his search team and stopped on a small hill overlooking the camp. The campfires were clearly visible, but no guards could be seen in the firelight. Certain the guards were neglecting their duty, had perhaps even fallen asleep, he decided to test the men, then punish the guilty later.

He drew one Colt revolver and fired it in the air as he charged directly toward the camp.

"Indians! Indians! Here they are, the damn rascals! Give them hell, boys!" he shouted, his voice adding drama to the excitement.

The guards were not asleep but wisely hiding in the shadows to avoid being easy arrow targets. They sprang into action, firing rifles in the direction of Beale's shouts. In an instant the entire camp was alert and quickly formed into firing-line ranks.

For the expedition members it was only a "false alarm," but for Beale the situation became a disaster. At the sound of the guards' rifle fire, his horse panicked and ran back over the hill and into a canyon. Beale fell from the saddle and was knocked unconscious, remaining on the ground through the night. The horse turned, his "lariat" entangled in the brush, and stood over his master, waiting for help.

Sighting the horse, a search party recovered Beale, and in a few days, he began to recover, only to have to deal with another problem. Thorburn and his team had not returned.[3]

On October 1, a team riding camels did return to camp with good news. Permitting the camels freedom to lead them through the desert, the men were taken directly to a large spring only three miles from the main trail.

A very pleased Ed Beale recorded, "My admiration for the camels increased daily with my experience with them . . . They are so perfectly docile and so admirably contented with whatever fate befalls them. No one could do justice to their merits or value in expeditions of this kind."

He ended that praise with his favorite title for the camels: "noble brutes."[4]

On October 3, Thorburn had still not returned and Beale was faced with a decision. Should he send another team out to look for those men? Thorburn had been gone six days, carrying only the water they had set out with. Few expected to find them alive.

But, on the fourth of October, just as a team was preparing to search for them, Thorburn and his men returned, all in excellent condition. They reported finding a small stream about thirty-five miles to the west, in the direction in which they were traveling.

On October 6, the train encountered some small Indian camps complete with plantings of corn and melons. Beale issued orders that no one was to do any harm to the natives or their crops, and then, with compassion, recorded in his journal, "Poor creatures! Their time will come soon enough for extermination when the merits of this road are made known and it becomes, as it most assuredly will, the thorough-fare to the Pacific."[5]

Then he made another entry about the camels: "They have been used on every reconnaissance whilst the mules were resting and having gone down the precipitous sides of rough volcano mesas, which mules would not descend until the camels were first taken down as an example. With all this work they are perfectly content to eat anything, from the desert greasewood brush to a thorny prickly pear, and, what is better, keep fat on it."[6]

Almost every day Beale made notes on soil conditions and about the availability of grass, timber, and, of course, water.

On October 10, Mr. Williams, the expedition's geologist, was out gathering specimens of gold-containing quartz when Indians crept up on him and grabbed his rifle. Williams escaped unharmed and rushed back to camp. Beale immediately sent Joe Bell, Hampden Porter, and May Stacey, armed with shotguns and revolvers, after the thieves.

Their orders were to shoot only in self-defense and then attempt only to wound, not kill.

The boys spotted two Indians who fired arrows at them, which were answered by shotgun blasts and a foot chase. Beale and Thorburn, on horses, charged in the direction of the shooting, with some of the other men following.

The group managed to capture the two Indians, a boy about fifteen and an old man. Beale believed the two captives would make better guides than the ones he had and should be able to locate water en route to the Colorado, which he now estimated to be about sixty-five miles away.

Communication between expedition members and the Indians was limited mostly to hand "sign language," a few words of Spanish, and a few in their own language, which was known by Lecko.

Beale ordered the Indians to be fed as much as they would eat and then gave them some clothing from the large stock of "trading" materials in the wagons. But Beale felt sorry for the young boy, who was extremely frightened, and released him that evening. It was a "goodwill" gesture, which paid off.

The next morning, as the train was almost ready to roll, an Indian surprised everyone by walking "boldly into camp with Mr. William's [sic] gun on his shoulder. He went up to Mr. Beale and handed the gun to him and made a long speech of which we, of course, understood nothing."[7]

The group was joined by another Indian and the party sat down for a meal of mutton while Beale handed out more interesting items: cloth, blankets, and handkerchiefs. His act of kindness in setting the boy free had helped create some new friends. The old Indian led them to a spring only a few miles away, and then another one fourteen miles farther west. Beale released the old man that evening.

Their good fortune continued on October 12, when their "former" guide, Savedra, found a spring he claimed he remembered from a journey through the area many years before. Beale was pleased and wrote, "It was the only thing old Savedra found that he set out looking for since our departure from Albuquerque." Beale named the spring after the guide. It is located a few miles southwest of present-day Kingman, Arizona.

Here, Beale reported the trail to be excellent, with "volcanic pebbles and gravel." At night they posted extra guards in case of Indian attacks, but all the men became excited when they noticed the presence of an abundance of sand on the ground. They knew they were near the river.

Then they saw a single high peak rising from the mountain range to their front. This marked the entrance to the gap through which they would have to travel. They moved on, excitement mounting with each mile, and then at last reached their goal. As Beale recorded, "The Colorado was burning in the sunlight about eighteen miles distan[t]."

Beale had been hired to conduct the camel experiment to the Colorado. Officially, his job was almost complete, but the expedition still had to cross the river and travel another two hundred miles through what is now the southern tip of Nevada and then into California, to Fort Tejon. From there, the trip to Los Angeles and the ocean would require only a day or two.

At a great distance they saw a chain of large mountains and believed it to be part of the Sierra Nevadas in California. The snow-capped mountain was, no doubt, Mount Charleston of the Spring Mountain Range, just west of modern-day Las Vegas.

As the expedition rolled down from the gap toward the river, the men began to encounter the farmland of the Mojave, full of "vegetables": beans, corn, and pumpkins.

The trail, though followed daily by the Mojave, was good for foot traffic but not for wagons. The mules had to be unhitched and the wagons lowered in places by "manpower."

Stacey described one section of the trail in his journal as "the most rocky, hilly, damnable country I have ever seen." But that night he and his friends were rewarded for their efforts. "We sat down to a good supper of pork and beans, thanks to Ab's cooking."

The next morning, October 16, 1857, all the wagons were finally lowered by "block and tackle" except for one of the ambulances, which Stacey reported to be "smashed to pieces."

On the seventeenth, excited Mojave began to surround the wagon train. One Indian, who apparently had visited Fort Yuma 250 miles to the south, approached Beale and saluted. He then shouted the only words in English he knew, "God Damn my soul eyes! How de do!" Whereupon several others chanted, "How de do! How de do!"

Soon the Mojave began to bring corn and pumpkins, which the men purchased with blankets, cloth, and trinkets. The corn was needed for the mules, and the men quickly built fires, cooked the pumpkins, and ate them that night.

Stacey described the Mojave: "They are very good-looking Indians and apparently friendly."[8]

Beale wrote, "They were a fine-looking, comfortable, and fat and merry set, naked except for a very small piece of cotton cloth around the waist and, though bare-footed, ran over the sharp rocks and pebbles as easily as if shod with iron."[9]

The Mojave were naturally thrilled to receive the woven shirts, blankets, and a variety of clothing the expedition members no longer needed in exchange for watermelons, cantaloupes, beans, and more corn.

On the eighteenth, the entire train was together at the river's edge and prepared for crossing, but then the atmosphere suddenly changed.

Some of the Indians stopped Beale at the river and with hand gestures indicated that they did not want him, or the others, to cross.

At that point the men were certain there was going to be a battle. Stacey recorded, "The camp is ready for a fight."

But the motives of the Mojave were misunderstood. They did not intend to start a fight but only desired to do more trading. In their simple minds, the wagons were still loaded with wonderful things. Why couldn't business continue? After all, such an opportunity did not come often. In fact, the last big trading had occurred when Whipple passed through a few years before. Whipple had promised that more white men would come with additional gifts for the Mojave. To the Indians, Whipple had spoken the truth.

Now the expedition faced a new and unusual problem. The Mojave wanted the trading program to continue until the wagons were empty. Beale wanted to cross the river and move on, and the men were becoming increasingly uneasy by the moment, still believing that if Beale pushed for his way (which he usually did), a fight would surely break out.

The Colorado, at that time, was four hundred yards wide and the water deep and fast flowing. They had to cross mules, horses, sheep, wagons, men . . . and *camels*.

Soldiers at Camp Verde had warned Beale that camels could not swim, but when he asked what proof they had for this claim, they confessed that they really did not know. The camels had never been tested in a deep river.

Beale had some special plans, some unusual equipment packed to assist the wagons in crossing. The animals would have to swim and so would the men, but the members of the expedition would be the first Americans to learn the answer to an interesting question: *can camels swim?*

CHAPTER 24

Beale Arrives in California

. . . to my delight, they not only swam with ease but with apparently more strength than horses or mules.

Lieutenant Edward Beale, Journal, October 20, 1857

At the Colorado River, three hundred miles north of Fort Yuma, the camels stood calmly chewing their cuds while their human friends struggled with equipment in an effort to prepare the wagons for crossing.

Then something more interesting caught one camel's attention and he moved to a grove of mesquite trees. Moments later, the other camels followed.

It was October 20, 1857, late in the season for mesquite bean pods, but some still hung from high branches. To the camels, this special treat was theirs for the taking. They first pulled the pods from the branches, then ate the branches.

A few of the animals stood on hind legs to reach the higher branches, and in minutes they had trimmed each tree down to the trunk.

The Mojave watching the dining process were shocked and angry. The bean pods were a valuable food source to the Indians, and they began to protest by shouting at expedition members, who understood nothing of the Mojave language.

Beale had selected a perfect location for the crossing. A beach, cleared of brush and trees, gently sloped to shallow water with a sandy bottom that stretched twenty-five yards out into the river. Three hundred yards away on the opposite bank, a similar beach led to a trail that ran straight into a level stretch of sage-dotted desert.

Today the spot is isolated from civilization and seldom visited, but is still known as Beale's Crossing and is located a few miles north of the southern tip of Nevada and about the same distance south of modern-day Bullhead City, Arizona.[1]

The "boys" (Stacey and his pals) were given the task of "setting up the India rubber boats" using portable bellows.

Thanks to inventor Charles Goodyear, a technique of treating cloth with "vulcanized" (sulfur mixture) India rubber had yielded some excellent "people protection" products. From 1839 through the 1850s, rubberized ground covers, ponchos, hats, and cloth, such as "Mackintosh" were impregnated with the rubber-sulfur mixtures to produce flexible water-resistant materials.

In 1848, U.S. general George Cullum of the Army Engineers introduced a rubber-coated-fabric, inflatable pontoon bridge that was put into use during the Mexican War. After that, numerous "rubber boats" were developed by both Goodyear in the United States and Thomas Hancock in England. The 1850s design of rubber boats strongly resembles that of the "life rafts" used in World War II.

The boys worked with the billows to pump up the rubber boats and pontoons for over two hours, finally producing "air bags" for the expedition to test. Some of the men doubted the strength and buoyancy of the pontoons, believing the wagons were too heavy for the new invention. But they worked perfectly. Beale recommended in his report to the secretary of war that military units continue to employ the "air bags" for river crossings.[2]

Beale, also confident with the safety of the rubber boats, had May Stacey give a few Mojave "chiefs" (tribal leaders) a ride to the opposite bank. The first voyage brought other "chiefs," all wanting a ride, resulting in Stacey having to make a second trip across the river.[3]

The Mojave were excited and impressed with the white man's accomplishments; however, they also learned something. The boat that floats on water was not indestructible. They knew that air inside cloth enabled the boat to float. Create a hole, the air will escape, and the boat will sink. This simple discovery would prove useful to the Mojave in the future.

With the wagons safely across, men began to deflate the pontoons and repack supplies. Now the time had come to swim the horses and mules. Hi Jolly was ordered to lead the camels closer to the water's edge so they could see what was expected of them.

Perhaps that wasn't a good idea. The first group of mules met disaster. Ten of the animals, unable to fight the Colorado's strong current, struggled to stay afloat but drowned and were swept downstream. The horses did only a little better. Two gave up after reaching the halfway point and let the current take them. After minutes of attempting to swim, they also were dead.

A halt to the animal crossing was called. Stacey entered in his journal: "Lost ten mules and two horses. Indians ate the drowned ones."[4]

Now the long-awaited answer to the question "can camels swim?"

It is not known if the camels could comprehend what killed their friends in the river, but they wanted no part of the procedure. Hi Jolly led the first camel to the water. The animal froze and would go no farther. For a moment Beale considered tying the camels to air bags and floating them across. But if the animals refused to cooperate, the project might end horribly.

Beale spoke with Hi Jolly, searching for a solution, but the "Arab" had never seen a camel swim. During the journey from Texas, he'd developed a close relationship with the camels and understood their moods, but he had nothing to suggest for resolving the problem at hand.

Then Beale had another idea. He told Hi Jolly to lead the largest camel in the herd to the water and try to persuade the animal to enter.

Men who had been working nearby paused a moment. All eyes

were on the big camel. Hi Jolly, dwarfed by the animal, rubbed its massive neck and appeared to be muttering words of encouragement.

Suddenly, as if accustomed to swimming rivers, the camel calmly entered the water, waded several yards from the beach, and began to swim "boldly across the rapidly flowing river." Then all the camels were eager to follow.

A relieved Ed Beale shouted with delight and patted Hi Jolly on the back. Now they had a plan to safely swim the others across. In commemoration of this event, Beale wrote a separate letter to the secretary of war: "We then tied them, each one to the saddle of another, and without the slightest difficulty, swam all to the opposite side in gangs, five to a gang. To my delight, they not only swam with ease, but with apparently more strength than horses and mules."[5]

Beale completed the historic crossing of the Colorado River on Wednesday, October 21, 1857. Then the men reorganized the train and started rolling west through what is now southern Nevada (about thirty miles south of modern-day Searchlight).

They followed what Beale called the "United States Surveyors Trail" in honor of Lieutenant Amiel Weeks Whipple, who charted it three years earlier—the same trail the Mojaves led Whipple on when they guided him to the Pacific Ocean. This route would soon carry its rightful name: the Mojave Trail.

Ed Beale recorded, "Here, my journey as far as the road is concerned, terminated." Though seldom mentioned, Beale not only completed his mission successfully, he did it on budget and on schedule, arriving at and crossing the largest river in the West about the same time as Colonel Johnston's units reached Utah Territory. Considering the distance traveled, the method of transportation, and the difficulties encountered along the way, it was an amazing accomplishment.

Beale's contracted job was complete, but his journey was not over. The expedition still had two hundred miles to travel.

They reached Fort Tejon, where Beale and his military escort parted; then he, the "Arabs," his employees, and the army camels continued a few miles to his ranch. There he turned the camels over to his partner, Sam Bishop, for a needed rest. Beale believed that the animals would be well cared for and safe from Mormon raiders. If army troops requested the camels for use in the Mormon War, he would release them. Meanwhile, he had the personnel to care for them at no expense to the government. Of course, the ranch would use them as work animals.

No reception party greeted Ed Beale upon his return to Tejon Ranch, no bands playing or flags waving or even a fireworks display. It would be months before anyone on the East Coast learned of his success. The War Department did not know if the expedition survived or if all its members had been killed by Indians.

Beale, ever the self-promoter, planned what we might call today a news conference. In 1857, Los Angeles was no longer a village but a busy, growing city of almost nine thousand people (including ranchers in the county).

The city had witnessed many unusual happenings since its days of Spanish rule: soldiers and sailors passing through, earthquakes, prospectors headed for the gold fields, and a strong U.S. Army presence at nearby forts.

But in late November 1857, Los Angeles experienced something new. Unexpectedly, Edward Beale conducted his own parade. He, Hi Jolly, and a few of the ranch hands marched into town with a herd of camels.

There may have been no bands playing, but excitement gripped the community just the same.

Lucky for Beale, newspaper writers from both Los Angeles and San Francisco were present for the event and found the "general" gracious and willing to relate "valuable" information about his experiences with the camels during that long march from Texas.

Though the writers loaded their articles with exaggerations and dramatics, the releases served a purpose. No one in California was going to forget Edward Beale.

One article read, "General Beale and about fourteen camels stalked into town last Friday week, and gave our streets quite an Oriental aspect. It looks oddly enough to see, outside of a menagerie, a herd of huge, ungainly, awkward but docile animals move about in our midst with people riding them like horses."

After the show, Beale and company returned to his ranch to rest and prepare for the return trip to Washington.

Camels in their original home territory had been accustomed to traveling mostly on sand or soft soil, but along the wagon road, they did encounter from time to time sharp stones that presented problems. The stones became lodged between their toes, slowing the animals' pace. Beale failed to mention this problem in his journal; in fact, he did just the opposite, often commenting that the camels encountered no problems on the trail.

Much has been made of this subject in previous narratives. A solution was finally found by the army. According to historian Dennis G. Casebier, author of several books on the history of the Mojave Trail, no area exists along that trail that could cause problems for camels.[6]

———————————

President Buchanan's administration misunderstood the Mormon culture, but that had nothing to do with his decision to send troops to the Utah Territory.

In October 1857, as Edward Beale and his camels crossed the Colorado River, officers under Colonel Albert Sidney Johnston still had little information as to what was expected of their men. Most marched all the way to Utah under the mistaken impression that the Mormons would not attack the United States Army. And most had no desire to fire on fellow Americans, regardless of their religious beliefs.

But the Latter-Day Saints did not fear U.S. troops and were well prepared to defend their territory and their religion from federal aggression.

Brigham Young appealed to his Native American allies to help keep Johnston's army out of Utah. "The Indians," he said, "must learn to help us or the United States will kill us both."[7]

But despite his tough talk, Young searched for a way to stop the U.S. Army without bloodshed.[8]

"Use every exertion," Young instructed his Nauvoo Legion, "to stampede their animals and set fire to their trains . . . Take no lives!"[9]

Then Brigham Young declared martial law and the legion went into action. First, they burned Fort Bridger (now in the state of Wyoming) to keep it from being useful to the U.S. Army. Fort Bridger had originally been established by mountain man Jim Bridger. He sold it to the Mormons in 1855.

When the army reached the fort in early October, they quickly rebuilt it, with plans of using its shelters for winter quarters.

Then the legion struck the large but poorly defended U.S. Army supply train that trailed the main combat units. A few shots were fired, but no one was killed. However, cattle were stampeded and most of the wagons burned.[10]

The army lacked horses and had to resort to chasing the Mormons on mules. Several small battles were fought, but again, no one was killed.

The legion had placed two thousand well-armed men in rifle pits along two narrow passages that led into the Salt Lake Valley. Inside Utah, an additional seven thousand militia completed training and were ordered to the valleys to join the legion. They prepared their defense positions and waited.

Fortunately for the U.S. Army, Captain Stewart Von Vliet, who had recently completed a meeting with Brigham Young, warned Colonel Johnston and his staff of the legion's positions.

Colonel Johnston arrived at "the front" in early November 1857 and took command of all U.S. troops. On hearing of Captain Von Vliet's report, he immediately ordered a flanking movement north along the Bear River, avoiding the legion and possible disaster.

Soon Lieutenant Colonel Philip St. George Cooke and his Second Dragoons caught up with Johnston. Washington's appointed new governor, Cumming, was with him along with a group of "administrators."

Then an early winter blizzard struck the northwest, forcing the army to halt their advance and withdraw into hastily prepared camps, including Fort Bridger.

In the south, at a much warmer Las Vegas Springs, Mormon patrols rode to the Colorado River and remained alert for a U.S. invasion through the desert. They encountered no army troops but did learn something very strange from wandering bands of Pah-Utes.

The Indians reported seeing white men riding very large animals that had humps on their backs. They were moving through the desert, west of the Colorado River.

The Mormons were shocked. Was the U.S. Army now using camels in the desert? Where did they come from?

The Indians, of course, had no idea. Fearing discovery, they did not remain in that area long enough to count the white men or their animals.

The Mormon patrol must have pondered a key question. How could they get their hands on those camels?

The Nauvoo Legion had been busy in the north. They succeeded in destroying (or stealing) most of Colonel Johnston's supplies with their "hit-and-run" attacks. They stopped his advance but not his determination to follow orders and install a new governor in Utah.

But nature stepped in, and with that blizzard the U.S.-Mormon War came to a halt, at least for a few months.

CHAPTER 25

Steamboats on the Colorado

The steam whistle of the *General Jesup* sounded the death knell of the River Race.

> *Lieutenant Edward Beale, Eastbound Journal,*
> *January 23, 1858*

People on the East Coast celebrated the New Year on January 1, 1858, but along the edge of Utah Territory, Colonel Johnston's United States Army troops shivered in the cold winter in their primitive shelters.

Blankets, clothing, and wood were rationed since the loss of their supply wagons to Mormon raiders weeks before.

In southern California, people rejoiced as heavy rain finally ended a two-year drought. But in the mountains east of Los Angeles, the rain turned to snow, which, pushed by high winds, produced drifts as deep as ten feet in some places.

California's unusual cold weather was to present a serious problem for Major George A. H. Blake and his troops, who in late December received orders to march to the Colorado River and investigate rumors that Mormons might be organizing Indian tribes to attack emigrants passing through southern Utah Territory (now Nevada) or attempting to cross the river.

Originally, the army paid little attention to rumors, fueled by newspaper articles, telling of Mormons moving large quantities of guns and ammunition to Utah, that reported that LDS squads of military men were seen roaming the desert south of Las Vegas Springs. But soon demands from the public resulted in Major Blake and his dragoons moving out to search for evidence of a Mormon-Indian movement.

Blake and his men arrived at Cajon Pass near San Bernardino on New Year's Eve 1857, and waited for additional troops led by Lieutenant John T. Mercer from Fort Tejon. They were to travel together along the Mojave wagon trail to Beale's Crossing at the Colorado, but the winter storms delayed the lieutenant until January 10.

The delay did not sit well with Major Blake, who had received orders for a second assignment. He was informed that his dragoons had been ordered to serve as an escort for Edward Beale and his "eastbound expedition" at least as far as the Colorado. But the deep snow had also delayed Beale's group, and when they did not arrive on the tenth, Major Blake ordered his dragoons forward to search the trail for signs of Mormon-Indian activity. They found none.

Meanwhile, Ed Beale, with wagons loaded with supplies in Los Angeles, mules, and ten "pack" camels led by Hi Jolly and a number of ranch hands, struggled through the snow a few days behind the army. It was slow, difficult work and the only ones who seemed to enjoy the weather were the camels, who, with their long legs, were able to step gracefully, sometimes playfully, through the deep snow.

Ed Beale was comfortable with the camels in snow for good reason. He had recently noted their performance in his journal. "In a terrible snow storm the wagon carrying provision to the camp could proceed no further. The camels were immediately sent to the rescue and brought the load through the snow to camp though six strong mules of the team were unable to extricate the wagon."[1]

Only when the camels encountered icy patches did they slow their pace and proceed cautiously, one step at a time. But as the train reached a section of trail near present-day Barstow, the ice disappeared and snow lay only in little patches in areas shaded from the sun. By that time Beale was less than a half day behind the dragoons.

By January 18, the troopers entered a much warmer area as they neared the Colorado River basin. Nights in the desert there dropped to temperatures near freezing, but during the day, the dragoons' thermometers indicated a high of fifty degrees.

Major Blake continued to order scouting squads to patrol miles out on both flanks. None reported seeing any signs of Indians or Mormons.

Then, in a few more days, they reached the Colorado and witnessed a strange sight. There at the river's edge was a steamship, floating as if it had been waiting just for them. It was former army captain George Johnson's side-wheeler, the *General Jesup*.

While the dragoons searched for Mormons along the Mojave Trail, things were changing fast along the river north of Fort Yuma. Naturally, the War Department was concerned about security on the U.S. border with Utah, and this included the Colorado River. How could U.S. forces prevent the Mormons from advancing downstream and capturing Fort Yuma? At the same time officials wondered if the river be used to transport troops and supplies from the Gulf of California to Fort Yuma and then all the way north into Utah.

To determine if this was possible, the War Department had chosen Lieutenant Joseph Christmas Ives to command the Colorado River Exploring Expedition. His assignment: to determine how far upstream the Colorado could be navigated and the feasibility of moving troops by water into Utah, should that become necessary.

Ives, an Army Engineer, was not a soldier with navy experience, and did not consider himself a riverboat captain. But having accompanied Lieutenant Whipple on his expedition that met (peacefully) with the Mojave, crossed the river, and traveled to the Pacific Ocean along the Mojave Trail, he did know what to expect in the desert through which the Colorado flowed and he was on good terms with the Indians.

Ives was a curious and brilliant officer who often formed strong opinions that he bravely offered in reports to superiors. At age twenty-nine, he also had a mind for detail and a delightful sense of humor.

The lieutenant and his team of unskilled laborers finally completed the assembly of their fifty-four-foot iron-hulled steamship, the *Ex-*

plorer, which was now ready for its maiden voyage up the Colorado on December 31, 1857.

It was a strange-looking stern-wheeler, with its giant boiler occupying one-third of its deck and the elevated cabin, which appeared much too high at the rear, just in front of its waterwheel. A cannon or "howitzer" decorated the bow.

Ives packed aboard rations and supplies, which were to support its twenty-three passengers for thirty days, including its captain, David C. Robenson, and the expedition's artist, Heinrich Möllhausen, who described the boat as a "waterborne wheelbarrow."

The river was lower than usual that January of 1858 and the underpowered *Explorer* ran aground constantly on sandbars, much to the amusement of the Indians who lined the banks, dancing and shouting each time the ship became stuck.

Captain Robenson quickly learned that the Indians knew the location of the sandbars and would be waiting at the spot of the next one in order to witness another grounding. Soon the captain was able to apply steam at just the right moment and steer the ship away from trouble.

The *Explorer* had 150 miles to travel before reaching Fort Yuma, and it captain and crew did not know that George Johnson and the *General Jesup* were waiting there, preparing to leave.

At 108 feet, the *General Jesup* was twice the length of the *Explorer,* and with its two side wheels, it had ample power for the Colorado, at least for the distance it needed to go: slightly beyond Beale's Crossing. Farther upstream, dangerous "rapids" were reported to exist.

Depending on the season and how much snow had melted in the north, the current of the river could become very swift, often in excess of five miles per hour.

Unlike large rivers in the East, the Colorado was sprinkled with sandbars and boulders hidden beneath the surface.

In 1856, Captain Johnson had convinced the California legislature to support an expedition up the Colorado and offered his *General Jesup* to be contracted by the army to deliver troops and supplies from the Gulf of California to Fort Yuma. The former secretary of war Jefferson Davis received the funding for Johnson's program, but with the change of administration, the new secretary, John B. Floyd, had a different idea. Floyd believed the army should not rely on civilian contractors but have its own ship. The army ship project then was assigned to Lieutenant Joseph Christmas Ives.

To prove his capabilities, Captain Johnson and his *General Jesup* hauled over thirty-seven tons of supplies to Fort Yuma from the mouth of the Colorado.

Strictly by chance the *General Jesup* departed Fort Yuma on December 31, 1857, the same day Ives and the *Explorer* steamed upriver from the gulf. The *Jesup* had a 150-mile, several-day head start in reaching the Utah border.

The *General Jesup* took on twenty-seven days of rations and an interesting assortment of passengers, all anxious to see if they could reach Utah. These included U.S. Army lieutenant James L. White, who was commanding fourteen soldiers from Fort Yuma, mountain man Paulino Weaver and a few of his pals, and a Yuma Indian chief called Pasqual.

The *General Jesup*, moving around sandbars with some difficulty, steamed up past the first Mojave villages, its passengers marveling at the desert scenery. Cottonwood, mesquite, and willow trees, their dark branches without leaves, lined the banks, and beyond, some several hundred yards, arrow weed, sage, and creosote offered the only green to the winter's landscape. Far off on the eastern horizon, treeless mountains, dotted with yucca, separated the river valley from what appeared to be an endless desert.

George Johnson had navigated the Colorado as early as 1854, but only as far as Fort Yuma. The waters from the fort to Mormon territory held unknown dangers.

On January 21, 1858, the *Jesup* reached the first rapids and Johnson made the decision to turn around and wait while he, Lieutenant White, and a few men paddled a small boat farther upstream. They made it to a point now known as Cottonwood Valley, from where they could see up the canyon about forty miles, and were convinced that the ship could, with proper handling, reach the first Mormon settlements upstream.

But the *Jesup* needed firewood, and food rations were running low. Dry wood was scarce along the banks, and Johnson knew that the Mojave had food and were always interested in trading for whatever the white men were willing to sacrifice.

Captain Johnson had proven that steamships could reach Mormon territory, and he had beaten the army's *Explorer* (though he really didn't know at the time that he was in a race).

The *Jesup* arrived at the Mojave villages in the early morning hours, at a clearing along the beach, discovering later that they had "docked" at Beale's Crossing. At dawn, they planned to begin trading with the Mojave for food, especially corn and beans, while two groups set out to gather firewood.

It was cold that January morning. The sun seemed to slowly struggle over the eastern mountains. Suddenly it was free, a large orange ball sending its warmth into the Colorado's valley. And its first light revealed a strange sight, unlike any witnessed before in America.

It is impossible to describe the shock that was surely felt by the assortment of humans brought together by fate that morning. The Mojave who had gathered at the clearing, at first, were speechless. They had never seen such a large boat floating in their river. Black and gray smoke streamed from a pipe, and wheels on each side of the boat slowly turned, gently splashing the water.

It wasn't the fact that the boat carried white men that frightened the Mojave; it was the realization that their nation could be invaded by water as well as by land.

Then the soldiers gathering wood were in for a shock themselves. There, standing on a ridge some twenty feet above the beach, was an unbelievable sight. Camels!

Standing next to the animals were two "Arabs," or what the soldiers, who had never seen Arabs or camels before, assumed to be
Arabs. With them was Frederick E. Kerlin, Beale's trusted "clerk," and
he too was in shock. He did not expect to see a steamship in the Colorado. Beale had sent Kerlin, Hi Jolly, and Greek George ahead with
the camels because the train, with wagons being pulled by mules, had
been delayed by a rainstorm.

Soon Beale arrived, and he was thrilled when he saw the *General
Jesup*. He felt proud and envious when he learned that the ship was the
creation and property of a civilian, not the army.

"I confess," Beale recorded, "I felt jealous of [Johnson's] achieve-
ment and it is to be hoped the government will substantially reward
the enterprising spirit which prompted a citizen, at his own risk and a
great hazard, to undertake so perilous and uncertain an expedition."

Beale and the others were unaware at the time that Lieutenant Ives
and the *Explorer* were approaching from the south.

Major Blake had already made arrangements with Captain Johnson for the *General Jesup* to carry Beale, Fred Kerlin, and wagons across
the Colorado. The mules swam, this time without mishap.

Major Blake and the dragoons prepared to escort the "Arabs" and
camels back to the Bishop-Beale ranch. None of them would see Ed
Beale for another year.

After assisting Beale with the crossing, Captain Johnson turned
the *General Jesup* downstream and started his 150-mile journey to Fort
Yuma.

Later, thinking back on the scene at the crossing, Beale recorded
in his journal: "I had brought the camels with me and as they stood on
the bank, surrounded by hundreds of wild, unclad savages, and mixed
with these, the dragoons of my escort and the steamer slowly revolving her wheels preparatory to start, it was a curious and interesting
picture.

"Here," Beale continued in an unusually emotional tone, "in a wild,
almost unknown country, inhabited only by savages, the great river of

the west, hitherto declared unnavigable and, for the first time borne upon its bosom that emblem of civilization, a steamer . . .

"But alas! For the poor Indians living on its banks and rich meadowland. The rapid current which washes its shores will hardly pass more rapidly away. The steam whistle of the *General Jesup* sounded the death knell of the river Race."[2]

Ed Beale had accurately predicted the fate of the Mojave.

Sergeant Armstrong and the small escort of soldiers who accompanied Beale on his westbound expedition had remained at Fort Tejon for a few months and now joined him in the return east. They would travel with Beale until they reached Zuni. There they split up and the soldiers moved on to their post, Fort Defiance.

About a week after the Beale's Crossing encounter, the *General Jesup* had another interesting meeting as it steamed slowly toward Fort Yuma. On January 30, the crew met the *Explorer* heading north.

The men on both ships were excited and in good spirits. They exchanged stories, gifts, and tobacco, then the ships parted to complete their assignments.

Lieutenant Ives and the *Explorer* finally arrived at the Mojave villages on February 10, 1858.

Ives's report would include detailed, picturesque descriptions of the Mojave and interesting comments: "[The Mojave] regard the steam boat with a ludicrous mixture of amusement, admiration, and distrust. The stern wheel particularly exacts remarks. It is painted red, their favorite color, and why it should turn around without anyone touching it is evidently the theme of constant wonder and speculation."[3]

Ives had an advantage over the previous visitors to the Mojave camps, having spent considerable time there in 1854 with Lieutenant Whipple's expedition. During that visit, he developed a friendship with a few of the chiefs, who remembered him with trust and fondness.

Ives often found humor in encounters with individual Mojave. One of the chiefs returned from a trip to Fort Yuma where he "picked up by ear about thirty English words without having any idea of their meaning. These, he rung the charges upon with great volubility, producing an incoherent jumble of nonsense which made him pass, with his admiring friends, for an accomplished linguist. Our friend with his jabbering proved a great nuisance."[4]

When it was time to leave the villages and continue his mission upstream, Lieutenant Ives distributed gifts and persuaded subchief Greteba and a sixteen-year-old warrior, N'ah-van-roo-par, to join the expedition as guides.

The crew waved good-bye to the villagers, including the English jabbering chief, who shouted his limited vocabulary over and over as a salute while the *Explorer* pulled away.

Ives recalled in Chapter 4 of his report an observation about the Mojave: "In most respects they think of us as their inferiors. I had a large crowd about me one day and exhibited several things that I supposed would interest them, among others, a mariner's compass. They soon learned its use and thought we must be very stupid to be obligated to have recourse to artificial aid in order to find our way."

The *Explorer* reached Cottonwood Valley. The nights were cool but the days "very warm" as they continued on to Black Mountain Canyon. Then they were hit by heavy, cold winds.

They finally reached a Mojave village on "Cottonwood Island." At this point the guides became "uneasy" and began to give "constant warnings" that "bad Pah-Utes" were "prowling about with White men with them." These Indians and Mormons had recently visited a few Mojave villages, warning that they "intended to destroy our party as soon as it should enter their territory."[5]

The lieutenant was, of course, concerned that his men could be easily liquidated as they "sat in a small boat in the center of a narrow river," but they continued on through "Black Canyon," where walls reached one thousand feet in height in places.

Finally Ives decided that they had gone far enough. He had the *Explorer* anchored and, along with two other men, rowed a small boat a mile or two farther. Ives was now convinced that the army could, indeed, invade Mormon territory by the Colorado. He and the *Ex-*

plorer had traveled farther upstream than anyone before them, including the crew of the *General Jesup*.

The *Explorer* turned and started for Fort Yuma, but Lieutenant Ives's adventures were not yet over. At Beale's Crossing he loaded up a mule pack train, and he, with a few of his party, crossed the desert east to the Grand Canyon. He would return to Fort Yuma on foot after completing a mapping expedition around the canyon.

The *Explorer*'s service in the U.S. Army was over. She had accomplished her assigned mission, and the War Department ordered her sold at auction at Fort Yuma. The little steel steamship brought only one thousand dollars. The buyer: Captain George A. Johnson, owner of the *General Jesup*.

While Lieutenant Ives was fighting the rapids, weather, sandbars, and rocks in the Colorado River, Edward Beale made good progress along "his" wagon trail as he traveled east, recording important information on snow depths, timber, grass, and water availability in February.

For the most part, Beale's eastbound expedition would be uneventful. His objective for taking a winter journey, "to test the practicability of the road surveyed last summer for winter transit."[6]

On February 21, a few miles west of Albuquerque, Edward Beale proudly entered the following in his journal: "A year in the wilderness has ended! During this time I have conducted my party from the Gulf of Mexico to the shores of the Pacific Ocean and back again to the Eastern terminus of the road, through a country, for the great part entirely unknown and inhabited by hostile Indians, without the loss of a man. I have tested the value of camels making a new road to the Pacific and traveled 4,000 miles without an accident."[7]

In two more months, newspapers on the East Coast would report Ed Beale's exact words and some mothers would name their newborns "Beale."

At Albuquerque, Ed Beale, Frederick Kerlin, Beale's "Negro Servant" Absalom Reading, and the other members of the expedition rested for a few days. During this time, word of the new wagon road spread throughout the area.

Before they even left for Washington with the official "journals" and reports, people were talking about how wonderful the new road would be to travel. Stories said that Beale would return with more camels, though exactly when no one, including Beale himself, seemed to know. Nor did anyone know if Beale would truly have more camels to travel his new road.

CHAPTER 26

Leaving Peaceful Iowa

Scattered emigrant parties with their families would offer too strong a temptation for the Indians to withstand.

Lieutenant Edward Beale,

Report to the Secretary of War, 1858

With his winter's journey east complete, Edward Beale met with Secretary of War John Floyd in the spring of 1858 and delivered the wagon trail "journal," which included the official report on the use of camels during the expedition along the thirty-fifth parallel. Accompanying the journal were a number of letters concerning related subjects, including one stating, "I regard the establishment of a military post on the Colorado River as an indispensable necessity for the emigrants over this road. Scattered emigrant parties with their families would offer too strong a temptation for the Indians to withstand."[1]

Floyd agreed with Beale's recommendation. It was a logical idea from a former military officer who had extensive experience with the Native Americans and had traveled the trail twice.

The location of a military post at Beale's Crossing along the Colorado, in the middle of the Mojave nation, could serve to maintain peace in the area but would also move the army closer to Utah Territory and the Mormons. Of course, erecting the fort was one problem; supplying it presented a much more complicated one.

At the time of the Beale-Floyd meeting, the result of the steam-boat "race" up the Colorado was still not known, though the War Department held to the dream that their plan to ship supplies and men up the river from the Gulf of California would eventually become a reality.

Congress had not reached a decision on a route for a railroad, but while debates on the subject continued, as far as the War Department was concerned, Beale's wagon road would be completed and ready for wagon traffic within a year.

Beale's report on the camels convinced Floyd that the animals should be used by the army as often as was practical. Interestingly, he even began to work on a proposal to ask Congress for funds to purchase more camels.

While the secretary of war weighed his concerns about the pending war with the Mormons, the battles in Kansas over slavery, problems with Indian attacks, and supplying western forts, the wagon road still had top priority. Ed Beale was ordered to prepare for a new expedition, not from Fort Defiance this time but from Fort Smith, Arkansas. He would have only a few months to organize a construction crew.

No one doubted Beale's suggestion about the necessity of an army post along the Colorado. Floyd surely shared his concerns about the Mojave people.

None in the government had actually seen a member of the Mojave nation, but still fresh in their minds were the newspaper accounts of the Oatman family massacre and the enslavement of their two young daughters.

It had been a few years earlier and the Mojave had nothing to do with the massacre, but a book published in 1857 by Pastor Royal B. Stratton, detailing the lives of Olive and Mary Ann Oatman in Indian captivity, became a bestseller. The newspapers, as could be expected, picked up the story and soon, it seemed, everyone was reading how whites were being slaughtered in New Mexico Territory and "young, beautiful, white women" were assaulted, murdered, or taken as slaves by Indians.

"Indians" meant *all* Indians in the West. But, in reality, the Mojave might well have been the "good Indians" in this story.

In 1851, the emigrant family of Royce and Mary Oatman with seven children ranging in age from one year to sixteen were attacked by a group of Apache Indians (some say they were Yavapais) about sixty miles east of Fort Yuma in present-day Arizona. All were clubbed and hacked to death except for a fifteen-year-old boy, Lorenzo, who was left for dead, and his two sisters, Mary Ann, age seven, and thirteen-year-old Olive. After a year, the two girls were traded to the Mojave, who treated them more like family than slaves. The girls were given shelter and a plot of land on which to raise their own crops, more or less equal to everyone in the nation.

But the Mojave suffered from a drought, which smothered the area for over a year. Many died of starvation, including Mary Ann Oatman, then in her tenth year.

When Olive was sixteen, a Yuma messenger arrived at the Mojave village with a request from the Fort Yuma commander, who had learned that a white girl was being held captive. Blankets and horses were offered by the U.S. Army as a trade for Olive.

At first the Mojave suspected a trick and held back, but after a few days of tribal debate, they agreed to the transaction and escorted Olive to Fort Yuma, where she was soon reunited with her brother Lorenzo. He had never given up his search for his sisters. For months afterward, front-page news stories presented all western Indians as murderers and rapists.

The Bloody Kansas years had led many to consider relocating west to California. There was still talk of gold being found there in 1858, but that and the battles over slavery in Kansas were not the only motivating factors. Some believed the country to be spiraling toward a Civil War. Many citizens had friends or relatives already living in California who reported a "peaceful" life near the warm ocean.[2]

With the results of the U.S.–Mormon conflict still unknown in early spring 1858, the emigrants preparing to leave the Midwest were warned about the wisdom of traveling through Utah Territory. Except for the presence of Indians, the southern route through Fort Yuma seemed acceptable, but there had been rumors of a new road along the thirty-fifth parallel. The first part of the journey west would take them through Albuquerque. There, influenced by the "locals," emigrants made their decisions and chose a trail to follow to California.

At age twenty-two, Leonard John Rose, a Jewish emigrant from Bavaria, left a prosperous business in Illinois and relocated to Keosauqua, Iowa. There he started a mercantile business, which quickly became a success. He then married Amanda, the daughter of a community founder, Ezra Jones.

Through business dealings, Rose met and became friends with Alpha Brown, a poor but well-respected man in the area. Brown had joined the "great gold rush" of 1849 and, despondent over the passing of his wife, traveled to California to seek his fortune. In two years, he was back in Keosauqua with no gold but "rich in experience."

Brown worked hard at a number of jobs, gained back some of his financial losses, and married the widow Mary Fox, who had four daughters, including twelve-year-old, vivacious Sarah, whom everyone called "Sally." Alpha and Mary, in a year, had their own child, a son.

In the winter of 1856 and 1857, Rose and Alpha Brown formed a partnership with the common desire to relocate to California. According to the arrangement, Rose would provide the funds necessary to outfit an emigrant train, and Brown, because of his experience crossing the country, would manage the expedition.[3]

They first purchased 150 head of cattle and hired seventeen adventurous young men to drive the wagon teams and serve as herders. The employees were willing to work for free just to join the train and reach "the land of gold." Among them were nineteen-year-old Billy Stidger, twenty-year-old Will Harper, Ed Akey, age twenty-six, and Lee Griffin, about the same age as Akey.

The young men may have dreamed of finding gold, but Rose was a creative businessman and planned to start a ranch to raise champion horses. Brown and family simply wanted to farm in a warmer climate.[4]

In the middle of April 1858, the train started rolling toward Kansas. It consisted of four heavy prairie schooner wagons, each drawn by six oxen, and a large buggy that Mr. Rose called an "ambulance" (the young men called it the "avalanche," mocking Rose's strong German accent).

Fourteen trotting mares; a stallion named Black Monell; Picayune, a special breeding mare; "Old Bob," a driving horse; six mules and 140 oxen and the cattle completed the list of animals in the train.[5]

The first destination of their journey, 850 miles away, was Albuquerque, but before that, they had to cross the Missouri River and avoid the fighting in Kansas.

After that, the wagon road out of New Mexico Territory seemed perfect for their trip west and an easy way to avoid problems with the Mormons in the north.

CHAPTER 27

Peace in Utah Territory?

... offering the inhabitants of Utah, who shall submit to
the laws, a free pardon for sedition and treasons ...

President James Buchanan,

April 6, 1858

In late May 1858, the Rose-Brown caravan from Keosauqua reached
Kansas City and was joined by a "Dutch" family named Bentner who
was also going to California.

The Bentners, husband and wife and three children, loaded everything they owned into a small wagon pulled by two mules. Their
twelve-year-old son and fifteen- and eighteen-year-old daughters were
taking turns riding in the wagon, but they knew they would have to
walk most of the way to the "golden state."[1]

Before the families reached Albuquerque, they were joined by another train, commanded by John Daily with his family, including his
daughter Adeline. Within a few miles they encountered four other
families—those of Gilliam Bailey, Right Bailey, Joel Hedgespeth,
and Thomas Hedgespeth—and after a short distance were joined by
Isaac T. Holland and sixty-three-year-old John Udell, who recorded
the trip in his journal. An older man with Udell, introduced only as
the "Missouri Preacher," was reported to be the "best shot" with a rifle
in Missouri.[2]

This giant train consisted of twenty wagons, forty men, fifty to sixty women and children, several milk cows, twelve mules, five hundred head of cattle, and the horses belonging to Mr. Rose.

At Albuquerque, time was spent gathering supplies, repairing wagons, and visiting with excited locals who told of the new trail created by Lieutenant Edward Beale. They claimed it to be the "best" trail, though only one man had actually traveled it. That man was Jose Manuel Savedra, the guide who'd been punished by Beale for incompetence.

The local military commander warned the emigrants that Beale's trail might not be complete in some places and he issued some very strong orders. First, the train would not be permitted to proceed without a guide. That meant Savedra had a new job, since no one in the city but him had traveled the total distance of the trail.

Next, he instructed all the families to keep their wagons close together. No one should venture far from the train. He explained that Indians were less likely to attack large groups. The emigrants ignored this rule, with disastrous consequences.

The families were falsely assured by some of the citizens that the Mojave were peaceful and that they could expect to encounter no hostile Indians from the Colorado valley into California.

As a young man, John Udell had crossed the northern wilderness and almost perished when Indians stole his horses and supplies. He was not in agreement with the idea of taking Beale's trail and recorded concerns in his journal on June 25, 1858: [3] "Through the influence of the citizens of this place our company had, all except myself, agreed to take Mr. Beale's newly explored route and undertake to travel 900 miles through an altogether savage, mountainous country, all the way without any road except the trail of a few explorers, which could not be found much of the way by a stranger. I opposed the move at that time, but to no avail."[4]

Udell complained again, this time over the amount Rose suggested should be paid to the guide. Rose had not included Udell in the negotiations regarding just how much each family must pay. Udell resented the decisions. On June 25, he entered the following in his journal:

"Such an insulting expression from a German aristocrat caused the blood in a free-born American to rankle in my bosom."

Hard feelings between Udell and Rose continued as a number of disagreements developed during their journey. These were usually the result of Udell's objecting to ideas presented by Rose. The resentment Udell felt for Rose apparently had nothing to do with the fact that Rose was a Jew; rather, it was because Rose, a younger man, was foreign-born, aggressive, and very successful in business.

Ever the skeptic, Udell doubted the story told by the "citizens" that Ed Beale would arrive soon with more camels. Beale had assured the people of Albuquerque that he would return, but when, no one knew.

Beale was still busy with business and personal affairs in Washington and the camels used on the first expedition were at the Beale-Bishop ranch near Fort Tejon, California. There, they hauled supplies between Los Angeles, the ranch, and the little village of Tejon (not the army post, Fort Tejon).

Ironically, the primary cause of concern about traveling the northern route through the Utah Territory, the pending "Mormon War," was about to be eliminated. It would be late in 1858 before people in New Mexico Territory learned that the Mormon conflict had ended peacefully, thanks mostly to negotiations between Brigham Young and an attorney friend of the Mormons, Thomas L. Kane.

While Colonel Albert S. Johnston and his troops waited for the winter snow to melt, negotiations were under way between the U.S. government and Brigham Young.

This effort to avoid bloodshed was a blessing in many ways for the U.S. Army. Even though Colonel Johnston received reinforcements through the winter, he still lacked adequate supplies. The army also had very little knowledge of the terrain in which they might need to fight.

Some months earlier, Brigham Young had written his old friend Thomas Kane in Pennsylvania requesting that Kane use his political influence in Washington to help settle the conflict peacefully.

Kane succeeded in convincing President Buchanan that negotiations could be successful. The president told Kane to assure Brigham Young that a full pardon would be issued for all Latter-Day Saints if they submitted to American government authority and did not block the installation of the new governor.

Traveling from Washington, across Panama, then by sea to Los Angeles, and guided by Mormons through the desert on the old Spanish Trail, Thomas Kane arrived in Salt Lake City in February 1858. After a series of meetings with Mormon leaders, Brigham Young stated that he would honor and accept President Buchanan's appointment of Cumming as territorial governor.

In March 1858, Kane traveled to Colonel Johnston's camp and persuaded Cumming to go with him, without a military escort, and meet with Young.

By mid-April, as the Rose emigrant party planned to leave Iowa for California, Cumming was installed as the governor of Utah and Thomas Kane departed the territory for Washington to report on the success of his mission.

In June, a "peace commission" sent by President Buchanan presented the promised "pardon," which read in part: "Now, therefore, I, James Buchanan, President of the United States of America, have thought proper to issue this, my Proclamation . . . offering the inhabitants of Utah, who shall submit to the laws, a free pardon for sedition and treasons heretofore by them committed, warning those who shall persist, after notice of this proclamation, in the present rebellion against the United States, that they must expect no further leniency."[5]

The United States agreed that it would not interfere with the Mormons' religion and Brigham Young could remain the LDS "religious" leader.

At the end of June, as the Rose party departed Albuquerque, the army under Colonel Johnston entered Salt Lake City unhindered.

In Utah Territory and surrounding areas, a fragile peace began, but in the East, the "Mormon War" had become a political disaster for the president. The press labeled the entire event "Buchanan's Blunder," mostly blaming the president for the expense of committing the army, without adequate supplies and without completely investigating the reports of Mormon disloyalty to the United States. At the same time the same editors and papers continued to condemn the Mormons for their religious beliefs.

A full "shooting" war was averted, but damage had already been done by Mormon scouts in parts of Utah and along its borders. Scattered Native American Indian tribes were convinced by those "scouts" that other white men were coming to take their land. It was not that most of the Indians sided with the Mormons. To the contrary, the Indians had no concern for the whites' religion or politics. But they did worry about losing their land and knew they might need to resort to fighting to save their homes. Those who were the most fearful were, perhaps, the Mojave. They had their river and farms but nowhere else to go. They didn't trust the Mormons, but they believed the story that echoed through the villages: more whites were coming.

As the summer of 1858 brought an end to most of the tension in Utah Territory, the Rose emigrant train became the first to test Beale's new wagon trail. They started rolling toward the Colorado River, not fully understanding what might be waiting.

CHAPTER 28

The Rose Train Heads for Disaster

Because of the torrid heat which prevails in the Colorado
River country there is a legend that a soldier from Fort
Yuma who died there and had gone to Hell, sent back for
his overcoat.

Leonard John Rose,

Journal, 1858

On July 4, 1858, with spirits still high, the Rose wagon train followed
Beale's trail past Laguna, New Mexico Territory. John Udell entered
in his journal, "plenty of water and grass, wood scarce. Travel today 14
miles. 908 miles from the Missouri River."

The wagons used by most members of the train were reinforced
farm equipment made of oak and maple wood, about ten to fifteen feet
long, with an arched waterproof canvas cover that could be closed by
drawstrings at each end, making them somewhat watertight.

The bottom and sideboards were usually caulked with tar to protect
valuables when crossing streams. Some wagons would float, but most
would not, due to their weight.

Each had containers or compartments along the sides for tools and
spare wheel parts. Even though barrels were attached for drinking
water, the emigrants soon learned there was never enough for themselves during summer months and finding water for the animals was
to become a serious concern.

The wagons broke down frequently and were uncomfortable to
ride in, but they were an efficient means of hauling goods at the time.

Women and children usually rode inside the wagons but often walked alongside for exercise. Once an emigrant family reached its destination, the wagon became a temporary home until more suitable housing could be erected.

With the exception of the Bentner family, who employed mules to pull their small wagon, the wagons in the Rose party were pulled by powerful oxen. These animals, bulls castrated early in life, were slower than mules, averaging two or three miles an hour, but had superior stamina, were gentle, and survived off of prairie grass. Oxen were normally yoked in pairs, three pair per wagon. At three miles per hour, the "teamster" could easily walk alongside the animals and guide them with a staff.

On July 16, 1858, the Rose train passed an area that is present-day Winslow, Arizona. They had traveled 1,091 miles since crossing the Missouri River.

By July 27, they arrived at the base of Arizona's San Francisco Mountains. Here, at an altitude of eight thousand feet, the days were mild and the evenings cool. They rested for a few days, enjoying the pleasant weather and crisp, clean air, speaking very little of the scorching desert that awaited them.

They relaxed under massive pine trees, breathing the sweet fragrance, and listened to the wind as it moved through the green needles of the higher branches, where blackbirds fluttered about and called as if they were discussing the creatures on the ground below. Hawks circled in a blue sky decorated with white puffs of clouds, which had broken away from the taller mountain peaks. Wild game roamed seemingly unconcerned with the visitors; antelope, deer, bobcats, rabbit, and fox were in such quantity it was difficult to count them.

Wrapped in feelings of peace, the emigrants discussed the urge to stay forever at this wooded paradise, but destiny called and they were determined to travel on. Many weeks of walking and riding and another nine hundred miles had to be endured before they reached their destination.

But other emigrants would soon follow, and some surrendered to nature's beauty and remained to carve out a town in this wilderness. From the abundance of tall, straight pine trees, they selected a very special one from which to fly the American flag. And they named that little village Flagstaff.

In early August, the Rose wagon train encountered their first of many dangerous situations. Springs marked on their map had often dried up in the summer's sun.

But on August 13, a sudden hard shower lasted over an hour, with rain filling water holes and barrels. The emigrants' spirits were once again lifted and they gathered together to pray, and "hymn singing by excellent female voices [lasted] until late at night."[1]

Within a few days, they noticed the first Indians following the train, but at a safe distance. The men were instructed to keep their weapons within easy reach and to exercise "greater vigilance."

Two days later, when the herders began to round up the stock for another movement, they realized that some of the oxen and six cattle were missing. After a brief search, they found the remains of the butchered animals but wisely elected not to pursue the thieves. Water was still in short supply, they did not know the territory, and no one wanted to take a chance on encountering a large group of Indians.

The train needed water within a day, perhaps two at the most, or the animals would begin to perish. The leaders decided to break the rules and go against the warnings issued at Albuquerque. They divided up, sending several wagons with a few animals ahead to search for water. If successful, they planned to send a messenger back with orders for others to follow.

Rose moved on to a section of trail just west of present-day Kingman and located a large spring. He sent eighteen-year-old Ed Jones to tell the Brown party to come forward. Jones, described as "absolutely fearless but a headstrong youth," decided to rest in the shade of a mesquite tree after delivering the message. He was suddenly greeted by a flight of arrows from a group of Indians waiting in ambush.

Jones, "in one bound," vaulted into the saddle of his "running mare," Picayune, who quickly outdistanced the Indians and carried her wounded rider to camp.

Jones fell unconscious to the ground, bleeding from several arrow wounds in his back.

No one had medical equipment to remove all the arrow points, but they were able to stop the blood flow. Ed Jones lingered near death with a high temperature for four days but, perhaps with the advantage of youth, eventually began to recover.[2]

The entire train rested at the spring, fearful of the possibility of attack by Indians and concerned about the availability of water between their current location and the Colorado River.

They were now only seventy miles from the river, having traveled 1,450 miles from the Missouri. Rolling on slowly, they finally reached the mountains eighteen miles from the Colorado, but both men and animals had become so weak from lack of water and the desert heat that their leaders doubted they could push much farther. Wind and sun had caused lips to crack, burned eyes, made heads throb with pain, and throats and tongues had become so swollen it was difficult to speak. Mothers dampened cloths with precious drops of water and bathed the faces of their young. Oxen and mules could no longer pull the wagons. Men were unable to pull the loads and morale sank to the lowest since the wagon train had left the Missouri.

In desperation, a decision was made once again to break the rules and divide the group. The Rose and Brown families proceeded on to the river with six wagons, the "ambulance," and most of the oxen and cattle. Bentner joined them with his two mules, leaving his wife and children in their wagon with the Udell and Hedgespeth families.

Bentner planned to water and rest his mules for a day or two, return to his family, and then move them to the river.

The leaders expected that all the animals would be physically fit to pull the wagons within two days.

The older men remained behind at the camp to guard the women and children. Here at least they had water from a spring. Those moving ahead (Rose, Brown, and Bentner) would have to reach the river without water.[3]

On August 27, 1858, the advance group crossed the crest of the mountains, leaving the eastern side of the river, and paused to marvel at the sight below. Less than eight miles away, the waters of the Colorado River snaked their way through a valley lined with grass and thick patches of willow and cottonwood trees.

Some of the group fell to their knees, praying aloud, expressing thanks to their God for the deliverance. The river not only meant water, it also marked a threshold. Beyond the river, they had been told, Beale's trail was smooth, there were no more Indians, and only two hundred miles remained between them and the settlements of white people.

They still had a few miles of rocky desert to travel in scorching heat. Along the way they discussed how they might construct a raft large enough to carry a wagon across three or four hundred yards of fast-moving water. They could see a good supply of trees, the perfect size for the project.

Suddenly they were greeted by the Mojave, who seemed to appear from behind every boulder. They were smiling and laughing. The emigrants relaxed. Perhaps the Mojave were friendly, maybe even helpful.

Twenty-five warriors accompanied the emigrants to the river and then inquired through Savedra if they planned to remain in the valley long.

Their guide assured them that the emigrants only wanted to cross, then proceed west. But Savedra expressed the opinion that the Mojave did not believe his answer. Nonetheless, the warriors indicated that they had no objection to the emigrants crossing.

Meanwhile, the young men broke from the group, rushed to the river's edge, and, joined by the cattle, began to enjoy the cool, muddy water. The men drank too fast and were "racked with violent nausea" for hours. Others drank, then collapsed from exhaustion in the shade and fell asleep, with no concern that they were surrounded by curious Indians.

ABOVE LEFT: Major George H. Crossman (taken 1865) was one of the first to suggest the use of camels in the U.S. Army. He served in the Quarter Master Corps, where he befriended Major Henry Wayne. Together they attempted to convince the War Department to purchase and test camels. *National Archives*

ABOVE RIGHT: Gwynn Harris Heap, author, artist, explorer, diplomat was sent to the Near East by the War Department in 1855–1857 to assist in purchasing camels. *National Archives*

ABOVE: Major Henry Constantine Wayne (right) was dispatched to the Middle East to purchase camels for the Army. He resigned his commission in 1860 and joined the Confederate Army (left) as a general. *National Archives*

LEFT: The grave marker for Old Douglas, a decorated member of the 43rd Mississippi Infantry Regiment, C.S.A., who was killed during the battle of Vicksburg, 1863. *Wayne McMaster, Civil War Historian*

ABOVE LEFT: Lieutenant David Porter devised ingenious systems to protect the camels on board the USS *Supply*. This sketch by Gwinn H. Heap shows a camel firmly secured during an ocean storm. *National Archives*

ABOVE RIGHT: David Dixon Porter as an admiral in 1865. In 1855 Lieutenant Porter commanded the USS *Supply* on two trips to the Middle East to assist in purchasing and transporting camels to the Army in Texas. *Library of Congress*

Lieutenant Amiel Weeks Whipple, U.S. Army Corps of Engineering led a scientific expedition along the 35th Parallel in 1853, crossed the Colorado River with the help of the Mojave Indians, and continued on to the ocean. As a brigadier general in the Civil War, he was wounded at the Battle of Chancellorsville, taken to Washington, and promoted to major general. He died a few hours later on May 7, 1863. *National Archives*

Francis Xavier Aubry (or Aubrey) was known in the early 1850s as "the most daring man on the prairies," and set endurance records for the Santa Fe Trail. Later, he drove sheep into California crossing the Colorado River in the South but returning on a northern route, which would become a key passage during the Camel Experiment. Aubry was stabbed with a bowie knife in a barroom fight and died in 1854 at age twenty-nine. *National Archives*

ABOVE: Mojave Native American Indians from a drawing believed to be by Heinrich Balduin Moll-hausen, a member of the Whipple Expedition in 1852. In early reports the Mojave were said to be "friendly, healthy, the men well over six feet tall." *National Archives*

LEFT: Olive Oatman. Surviving an 1851 massacre in Arizona, Olive was traded to the Mojave, who marked her with ritual tattoos, but otherwise treated her well. The Mojave released her at Fort Yuma in 1855 and, at age sixteen, she was returned to relatives. Oatman, Arizona, was named in her memory. *Arizona Historical Society*

RIGHT: Weapons of the 1850s. (Top): Colt percussion revolver, Model Navy 1851, .36 cal.; (middle): Colt percussion revolver, Model Pocket, .31 cal.; (bottom): bowie knife. This one was designed by custom knife maker Dan Harrison. *Author's photos*

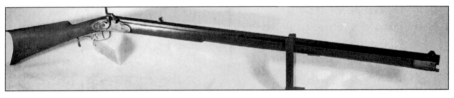

ABOVE: Percussion rifles carried by frontiersmen in the 1850s. (Top): Long Rifle or Kentucky Rifle. (Bottom): Sharps rifle, .52 cal., with "falling block" breach loading action. Designed by Christian Sharps in 1848, it was very accurate up to about five hundred yards, giving us the modern term *sharpshooter.*" *Author's photos*

Lieutenant Edward F. Beale, U.S. Navy, in his "Mexican" disguise used as he crossed Mexico with samples of gold and word that it had been discovered in California. Drawing, circa 1848–1849. *U.S. Naval Historical Center*

Edward F. Beale (1822–1893). Perhaps the most published photo taken, circa 1861. Beale was a navy lieutenant, hero of the Mexican War, first to bring proof of the gold discovery in California to the government, California superintendent of Indian Affairs, general of the California Militia, supervisor of road construction from New Mexica to California, first to test camels for the Army, rancher, surveyor general of California, Minister to Austria-Hungary, and, the title he most enjoyed, American explorer.
Santa Clara Valley Historical Society, Laws Railroad and Bishop Museum, Bishop, California

ABOVE LEFT: Edward F. Beale, circa 1871 when he served as Minister to Austria-Hungary.
U.S. Naval Historical Center

ABOVE RIGHT: Mary Beale (circa 1876 at age fifty-five), wife of Edward Beale. In later years the Beales were leaders in Washington society using their Decatur House as a center for entertainment. A year after Edward's death, Mary was stricken with blindness. She died in 1902.
Kern County Museum, Bakersfield, California

1857—The Camel Express. Painting by Carl Rakeman. Artist impression of the camel experiment, along Beale's wagon road.   *The Federal Highway Administration, U.S. Dept. of Transportation*

Hadji Ali. Better known as Hi Jolly. Born Filippou Tedora to a Greek mother and Syrian father, Hi Jolly converted to Islam at an early age and joined the American camel buying expedition as a camel driver. He was with Lieutenant Edward Beale during the 1857 Road Building project and Army testing experiment. This photo was taken by a "Mr. Rose of Phoenix" in 1896. An aging Hi Jolly was prospecting for gold and searching for stray camels not far from Tucson.
Courtesy of Arizona Historical Society/ Tucson AHS #19193

"Greek George the camel driver." Born George Caralambo in Greece, he grew up in Turkey, and came to the U.S. with the camels and worked on Beale's Wagon Road in 1857. Caralambo became a U.S. citizen in 1867, changing his name to George Allen. He died in 1913, and is buried in Whittier, California.

California Historical Society, Dohney Memorial Library, Pierce Collection

ABOVE LEFT: Colonel May Humphreys Stacey in 1872. In 1857, at age nineteen, Stacey accompanied Ed Beale on the first camel expedition and wrote his own journal describing his experiences. During the Civil War he was commissioned as a lieutenant in the Union Army. He would later be wounded, but continued to fight in several more battles, and eventually promoted to colonel. He was called the "little colonel" by his men (he stood five-foot-five). After the war, he was assigned numerous frontier posts. *Arizona Historical Society, Tucson, Arizona*

ABOVE RIGHT: Mary "May" Banks Stacey, at age twenty-seven, in 1872. An expert shot with her own revolver, which she carried for protection, she accompanied her husband, Colonel Stacey, to frontier outposts. The petite (five foot tall) Mrs. Stacey actually had blond hair. The studio elected to change the color to dark red in this picture.

Arizona Historical Society, Tucson, Arizona

Beale's Wagon Road along the 35th Parallel, still visible in places. (Top): Northern Arizona; (bottom): Mojave Road (Beale's Trail) heads west from the Colorado River through Southern Nevada. *Author's photos*

TOP: *Search for Water.* Painting by Ernest Etienne de Francheville Narjot, oil on canvas, 1867; at Decatur House, Washington, D.C. A scene, believed to be in Northern Arizona, described to the artist by Ed Beale. Camels in the background. Beale dressed in buckskins (center).
The National Center for White House History at Decatur House, a National Trust Site, #9268

BOTTOM: *Horses eagerly quenching their thirst, camels disdaining.* Painting by Ernest Etienne de Francheville Narjot, oil on canvas, 1867; at Decatur House, Washington, D.C. A scene described to the artist by Ed Beale. Camels in the background.
The National Center for White House History at Decatur House, a National Trust Site, #9267

RIGHT: Lone Camel. Somewhere in the South-west, circa 1861. Photographer and exact location unknown. *Dave Alexander, LegendsOfAmerica.com*

TOP: *Edward F. Beale and the Camel Experiment.* Oil painting by Bill Ahrendt. "I had brought the camels with me and as they stood on the bank, mixed with the dragoons of my escort and the steamer . . . it was a curious and interesting picture." Lieutenant Edward F. Beale, journal entry, 1858 *Painting by William Ahrendt*

BOTTOM: The steam ship *Explorer* on the Colorado River as sketched by Heinrich Balduin Mollhausen in 1858 during the expedition led by Lieutenant Joseph Christmas Ives. *National Archives*

Beaver Lake today is dry. Once almost a mile in length formed by backwater from the Colorado River. Here, in the southern tip of Nevada in 1859, Samuel Bishop, with his army of twenty men mounted on camels, battled the Mojave. *Author's photos*

ABOVE LEFT: Samuel Addison Bishop (1825–1893). Prospector, rancher, business partner of Edward Beale, sergeant in the California Militia, justice of the peace, designed the street car system for San Jose. Perhaps best remembered for leading twenty young men in a charge through attacking Mojave Indians in 1859. Bishop California is named for this pioneer.
Laws Railroad and Bishop Museum, Bishop, California

ABOVE RIGHT: Francis Ella Young (1840–1923). The Los Angeles beauty married Sam Bishop in 1856 and raised three children at Tejon Ranch. Later, the family moved to what is now Bishop, California. Sam named their new ranch "San Francis" in her honor.
Laws Railroad and Bishop Museum, Bishop, California

Three U.S. Army officers who resigned their commissions to fight for the Confederacy. (Left): Lewis Addison Armstead. As a captain, he was the first commander at Fort Mojave in 1859. As a C.S.A. general, he was killed at Gettysburg in 1863, leading his unit in Pickett's Charge. (Center): Richard Brooke Garnett, as a captain, commanded a company at Fort Mojave in 1859, As a C.S.A. general, he was killed at Gettysburg in 1863 leading his unit in Pickett's Charge. (Right): Colonel Albert Sidney Johnston led the expedition to put down the Mormon "rebellion." As a general in the C.S.A., he was killed in action at the battle of Shiloh in 1862.
National Archives

ABOVE: A rare watercolor recently discovered in the archives at the Decatur House, Washington, D.C., titled *Uncle Sam's Camel Corps Wintering at Fort Tejon, California*. Artist and date unknown. This was, no doubt, painted between November 1858 and March 1859, the only time the Army camels were actually based at the fort.
The National Center for White House History at Decatur House, a National Trust Site, #9266

RIGHT: Camel in the Southwest appears to be standing in a dry lake bed, believed to be a member of the Owens Survey Expedition, 1861. Photographer unknown.
Dave Alexander, LegendsOfAmerica.com

Camels in Texas. Oil painting by Tom Lovell. A very accurate scene from Lieutenant William Echols's July 1860 expedition into the Big Bend section of Texas. A camel had slipped and fell on the smooth stone trail. It was not hurt but the kegs carrying valuable water were smashed.
Courtesy of Abell-Hanger Foundation and the Permian Basin Petroleum Museum, Library and Hall of Fame of Midland, Texas

ABOVE LEFT: William H. Echols (1834–1909). As a lieutenant in the Engineering Corps he led the camel expedition into the Big Bend, Texas, area. He resigned his commission in 1861, becoming a major in the Confederate Army. Photo taken after the Civil War when he was the director of the Huntsville National Bank. *Huntsville, Alabama Madison County Public Library*

ABOVE RIGHT: Edward L. Hartz as a captain. He lost contact with his friend Lieutenant William H. Echols at the beginning of the Civil War and died at age thirty-six in 1868 at an outpost in Dakota Territory. *National Archives, Brady Collection*

The "Nut Tree," Vacaville, Caliornia, circa 1937. Sally Fox, survivor of the 1858 Mojave attack at the Colorado River picked up four nuts in New Mexico while recovering from her arrow wound. Later, she carried the nuts to her uncle's farm near Vacaville and planted them in 1859. The landmark black walnut died in 1952 but the area is still remembered as the Nut Tree Family Park and Plaza and visited by thousands of tourists each year.
California Historical Society and the National Archives

Camel Train in Nevada, also titled *Mr. J.J. Couch, Mr. Francis Murphy and camel train. Harper's Weekly*, June 30, 1877. Wood block engraving of camels transporting supplies to mines in Nevada. *California Historical Society (Fine Arts), National Archives*

ABOVE: Confederate General Sterling Price had a "pet" camel between 1861 and mid 1863. *National Archives*

LEFT: Hi Jolly with new bride, Gertrude Serra. Wedding portrait dated April 21, 1880. Records show Hi Jolly used the name "Philip Tedro." *Courtesy of Arizona Historical Society/ Tucson AHS #19482*

The tomb of Hi Jolly and his monument at Quartzsite, Arizona. Buried with Hi Jolly, who died in 1902, are the ashes of "Old Topsy," the last Army camel to die in captivity, in 1934. *Courtesy of Arizona Historical Society/ Tucson AHS #58288*

ABOVE: They are still with us! Wild camels in Texas. Photo taken in 2003 by railroad historian Bullet Bob Smith. *Robert "BulletBob" Smith*

RIGHT: Author Forrest Bryant Johnson (five-foot-eight) meets much taller "Mojave" the camel. *Photo by Dale Koprek. Camels from Rancher Maggie Rapp, of All's Welcome Camels in Colorado*

In an hour, the situation changed drastically. Some of the warriors separated a number of cattle from the herd, slaughtered them, and began to cook the meat. They had apparently planned this barbecue. Numerous fires had been blazing along the banks when the emigrants arrived.

Mr. Bailey, his horse watered and rested, mounted and started back to the Udell camp to report that the Mojave were not friendly and, in fact, were stealing cattle. At the camp the leaders discussed a course of action. If they mounted all the men and rushed to the river to help Rose, the women and children would be unprotected. The decision was to wait for further word from Rose.

At the river Rose and Brown decided against any retaliation against the Mojave. No one knew the exact number of warriors they might have to face in a battle.

After breakfast the next morning, Bentner seemed convinced that his mules were ready for the trip back through the mountains to Udell's campsite. He assured Rose that he planned to retrieve his wagon and family and rejoin them at the river the next morning.

On August 29, one of many Mojave chiefs entered Rose's camp with twenty-five warriors and inquired of the emigrants' intentions. He was assured that they planned to cross the river. Rose then gave the chief, as gifts, "blankets, butcher's knives, shirts, tobacco, bells, and beads."[4]

Permission to cross the river was granted.

An hour later, another chief, accompanied by about twenty warriors, appeared and asked the same question. Again, gifts were given and permission to cross granted.

With growing apprehension, the Rose group knew they had to construct a raft as quickly as possible.

On this day, there was nothing unusual about the behavior of the Mojave, or at least nothing occurred to cause additional alarm.

But there was concern among the Mojave leaders. They had been warned more than once by the Mormons from Las Vegas Springs that white people were coming to the river. They listened to the words of the Utes who accompanied the Mormons. Though they did not trust either the Mormons or the Utes, their predictions had come true. These new white people were not soldiers like the ones who came with Beale or Whipple, for they traveled with women and children, which indicated, to the Mojave, that they might decide to erect homes nearby.

The chiefs could not agree on a course of action. Some had promised the soldiers at Fort Yuma that they would never fight the white men again. Not all the chiefs made such a commitment, and their code dictated that if one chief and his clan decided to fight, they must all join together.

The tactics used in combat successfully in the past, they felt confident, would work again. They were simple and effective: attack and force the enemy into the river, where they usually fled to escape hand-to-hand combat; then, from both shores, shower the enemy with arrows. Those who survived would be clubbed to death as they crawled back upon the shore.

CHAPTER 29

The Indians Attack

The Indians are coming! They will kill us all!

Twelve-year-old Sally Fox,

August 30, 1858,

(L. J. Rose journal)

For two days the Mojave had stolen and slaughtered the emigrants' cattle and oxen. The warriors were now convinced that the white men were cowards since no one tried to resist them or to retaliate for the losses. The Mojave did not believe they were committing a crime. Rather, it was payment for the emigrants' intrusion into their territory. The emigrants violated the land by cutting trees and crossing cultivated fields with their wagons. The crops and trees were Mojave property, important to their survival.

Drifting in and out of the emigrants' camp gave the Mojave the opportunity to study the exact numbers of their enemy and their routine. They also learned that the wagons were loaded with wonderful treasures: clothing, blankets, knives, cooking pots of metal, and other things just waiting to be taken.

But most important in the minds of the Mojave was what the Mormon scouts had reported a few months earlier. More white people were coming to take their land and women and enslave them forever. Their survival, they believed, depended on preventing foreign intrusion, then and in the future.[1]

The Mojave were capable of committing more than one thousand men to battle. Since the emigrants numbered fewer than forty, such a large force of warriors would not be necessary for victory. Thus far, the emigrants had been passive, but the Mojave could not be certain just how the white men would fight once under attack. For this, the chiefs knew they needed a good battle plan. By midmorning, they had such a plan, but then the situation changed.

The emigrants were relieved but puzzled the morning of the thirtieth. For the first time the Mojave did not appear at the camp during breakfast.[2]

Mr. Rose decided to move the wagons one mile downstream, where there was an abundance of grass and cottonwood trees—perfect for building a raft they needed to ferry the large wagons across the Colorado. Here (actually Beale's Crossing) the river was only three hundred yards in width and shallow, suitable for men on horseback and the remaining livestock to cross.

Everything was moved to this second camp, part of which was a hundred-foot clearing along the riverbank. The camp stretched several hundred feet toward the eastern mountains. Into this clearing they rolled the wagons in two parallel rows, perpendicular to the river. No attack was expected from the water. The opposite end, facing the long, flat clearing, remained open so men and horses could swiftly move in or out of the camp.

Rose's covered buggy was pushed into the camp's center and the women began to prepare lunch. Children were ordered to remain inside the perimeter of wagons.

The story of what occurred on the thirtieth of August, 1858, was recorded in the diary of L. J. Rose's teenage son, who witnessed the events. Although a few details have surfaced recently, the younger Rose's account is considered the most complete.[3]

About 10 A.M., two Mojaves strolled near the camp, studying the wagon arrangement. They said nothing and were gone in a few minutes. A lone Mojave appeared at 11 A.M. He did not speak as he walked casually around the outside perimeter of the wagons. Then he too disappeared.

The emigrants were somewhat distracted by the visits. However, one of their men called attention to a large group of Mojaves crossing the river from the "California" (now Nevada) side. They counted 250 armed warriors.

Everyone's suspicions were now aroused, especially those of Savedra, who seldom had much to say. The old man spoke loudly for all to hear: "I don't like the way them Injuns is acting. We're going to have trouble with them, I bet, before night!"[4]

Was it Lieutenant Beale who'd led them to believe there were no Indians in California? After some discussion, they all agreed that the false information was based on gossip they'd heard in Albuquerque.

They now faced the reality of the situation. If escape from the Mojave was possible and if the other wagons could safely be brought to the river, they still had to cross three hundred yards of fast-moving water and endure at least two hundred miles of California desert before reaching any civilization. Now they knew that desert might be inhabited with more Indians.

As lunch was served, the emigrants discussed a more immediate, disturbing fact. The German, Mr. Bentner, and his family were expected that morning and were overdue. Bentner had departed the first camp more than twenty-four hours earlier, after feeding, watering, and resting his mules. He was supposed to retrieve his wagon and family, waiting eighteen miles east. Rose and Brown discussed the possibility that Bentner had reached the first camp and was waiting there.

After lunch, nineteen-year-old Billy Stidger and "a man named Young" mounted horses and rode toward the first camp to find the German party and guide them to the new camp.[5]

"Old Man" Alpha Brown, twenty-six-year-old Ed Akey, and his thirty-year-old friend Lee Griffin returned to the trees to continue work on the raft. Brown was mounted on his horse, Akey and Griffin walked close by.

Four other men left camp to tend to the remaining cattle, which were grazing about two hundred yards away.

The time had come for the Mojaves to activate their plan. The emigrant camp was now reduced by nine defenders.

The group of 250 warriors divided, one-half circling between the cattlemen and the camp, the other positioning themselves near the raft side. Thus far undetected, they had isolated the working emigrants from the camp and were ready to launch the attack.

Then about twenty warriors began a stealthy advance upon the camp, moving silently from tree to tree and through the brush.

The emigrants, though nervous for almost two days, oddly had posted no sentinels. It would be a matter of pure luck if someone sounded an alarm in time to prepare for a defense. The women went about camp life as usual, cleaning after lunch and gathering supplies for supper. Some children napped, while others played with one another. For a while everything seemed peaceful that hot August afternoon at Beale's Crossing.

Sally Fox, the twelve-year-old stepdaughter of Alpha Brown, was playing alone by one of the wagons. Using its spokes as a ladder, she reached the top of a large wheel and then froze. She saw warriors darting from bush to bush less than thirty yards away. At first she thought they were playing a game, but they had never approached the camp in such a way before, and now they carried weapons. Then she realized the camp was about to be attacked. Fear ripped through her as she leaped to the ground shrieking, "The Indians are coming! They are going to kill us all!"

Her warning was quickly followed by Mojave screaming and yelling and dozens of arrows raining into the camp. Pandemonium seized the area as emigrants raced about locating weapons and safety from the falling arrows.

The Mojave had lost the valuable element of surprise. Their plan for a fast victory with war clubs was gone. Now they would have to destroy the intruders from a distance with arrows or risk the unknown by charging in.

When the shafts struck inside the camp, boxes, blankets, and bedding were hastily stacked next to the wagon wheels to serve as a barricade to protect the women and children. Sally Fox, who was hovering together with her four little sisters and brother next to one barricade, ironically became the first casualty. An arrow impaled her abdomen from side to side. Though the wound was serious, the arrow miraculously missed vital organs. Sally would survive to endure another ordeal.[6]

Twelve screaming warriors raced into the clearing headed for the camp's entrance. But the emigrants had organized a "firing line" and greeted the attackers with a barrage of revolver fire. As the gun smoke drifted away, the bodies of seven warriors lay scattered on the sandy soil. The others retreated.

At the same moment the battle began, Stidger and Young reached the site of their first camp. No need to search further. The German family had arrived sometime earlier. Their wagon stood empty. The mules, Mr. Bentner, and his wife were gone.

Then the men's eyes became locked on a horrible scene before them. The Bentners' three children, a twelve-year-old son and the two daughters, ages fifteen and eighteen, lay on their backs near the wagon. They had been stripped of all their clothing. Their heads were smashed, apparently by war clubs, and the older girl's face was "frightfully mutilated."

Stidger reported later that there was no time to search for the senior Bentners. Proof of their deaths came later. The sounds of gunfire back at the camp snatched their attention. Quickly, they turned their horses, drew pistols, and galloped toward the camp to aid in the defense.[7]

The four cattle herders, also alerted by gunshots, raced their horses around the attacking Mojaves and charged through the clearing, entering the camp without injury. Stidger and Young arrived only moments behind them. The six men took positions along the firing line at the camp's entrance.

While reloading his pistol, Young began to report what they had discovered at the Bentner wagon. Stidger, seriously traumatized, would not speak of the murders for several hours.

A few minutes earlier, when the first report of gunshots reached the men working on the raft, Lee Griffin puzzled, "What's that mean?"

"Great God! It's the Indians!" Alpha Brown exclaimed as he flung himself on his horse. "To the camp!" he shouted.

He broke through a group of Mojaves at a full gallop. But Brown had no chance of surviving the gauntlet. As he sped on, a shower of arrows from both sides zipped past. A few hit their mark and one pierced his back, traveling through his body, close to the heart.

He entered the camp bleeding from the wounds. Mrs. Brown and several boys rushed to his aid.

"Where's my gun, Mother?" Alpha Brown spoke almost in a whisper, and he added, "Boys, I'm done for. Help me down!" Then he toppled from his horse, dead.[8]

Meanwhile, back at the construction site, Lee Griffin and Ed Akey, who were not mounted, began a zigzag run for camp, revolvers in hand. They lost sight of each other momentarily in the thick brush.

Suddenly Akey stopped. A Mojave, "not more than 20 feet away," stood with bowstring drawn, the arrow pointed at him. Akey raised his Colt and fired. The enemy fell backward, the arrow whizzing harmlessly by. Akey started to run again, but in a few paces found himself face-to-face with another warrior. Akey fired his pistol a second time. The warrior fell to his knees, then rolled over on his side, still clutching his bow.

Startled by a noise, Akey spun, cocking the pistol hammer. There in a small clearing stood Lee Griffin. He appeared to be dazed.

"Why in the world are you standing here?" Akey shouted.

Griffin did not reply but turned slightly, revealing two wounds. An arrow protruded from his right arm. Another shaft had passed through his right breast and out his armpit. Blood already covered that side of his body.

Akey gave Griffin a shove and yelled, "Run! Run for your life!"

The two youths rushed through the clearing in front of the camp and broke past the firing line.

Akey turned to shoot point-blank into the pursuing warriors who had reached within fifteen feet of the men who were aiming Colt revolvers directly at them. An arrow struck Akey's shoulder, hit his collarbone, and bounced out, causing no serious wound.

The charging warriors made a fatal mistake. At such close range, pistol fire killed most of them. At this point the Mojave gradually retreated to a safer distance, aiming their arrows in a high arc in the hope that some would strike a target inside the camp.

"Grandmother" Jones cradled the year-old sister of L. J. Rose Jr. One arrow fell directly down from its zenith and pierced her wrist, missing the infant's head by inches.

Soon the Mojave had moved back out of pistol range, but they were not safe from rifle fire. As the emigrants studied the retreat, a warrior appeared near the riverbank waving a long pole while chanting loudly in a shrill voice to gain attention. He waved the pole several times. The gruesome fate of the Bentner family was then confirmed. Five blond scalps hung from the pole.

The emigrants realized that their situation was desperate, but they fought on, coolly firing rifles only at sure targets in the distance. After ninety minutes of battle, their ammunition was running low.

Black Morrell, the Rose family stallion, became the next victim. Not far from the camp, Rose had fastened the horse by a long chain with a lock to a mesquite tree so the animal could enjoy some shade in the torrid heat. Black Morrell was intended to be the important stallion for a breeding farm in California, but the warriors had other plans. Unable to loosen the chain, they cut the animal's throat and left him hanging by the halter.

Then, suddenly, all the warriors withdrew from the battle area. The emigrants guessed they were regrouping for another attack.

The men at the camp's firing line were all worried by the same thought: if the Mojave organized into a single force and rushed the camp, stopping them would be impossible. True, a number of warriors would die in the charge, but the emigrants' defenses were not enough. Were the Mojave ready to pay the price for total victory?

During the brief lull in the fighting, the emigrants reloaded weapons and discussed their plans for survival. There was clearly no other option but to continue fighting.

Some thought that perhaps their friends who remained with the Udell party, waiting eighteen miles to the east, might arrive and their numbers (about forty) would frighten the Mojave away. A foolish idea. The group was composed mostly of old men, women, and children. They would all be slaughtered in minutes.

A few others suggested that Lieutenant Beale might be on the way with his camels. This was his trail and his river crossing. Perhaps he had followed their wagons and would be coming through the mountains from Albuquerque in time to rescue them. Another hopeless dream. Ed Beale was in Washington, planning a journey along his trail. It would be a year before he reached the Colorado.

Hope had forsaken the emigrants when an incident occurred that turned the tide of battle in their favor. A tall Mojave "in gaudy war paint and an array of furs and feathers stood in a clearing on a small hill about 200 yards from the camp." He obviously wanted to attract everyone's attention.

He waved his war club and shouted with defiant gestures while patting himself on his chest. To the emigrants, the huge Mojave looked like some sort of leader, maybe a chief.

Perhaps he was simply taunting the emigrants while proving to his men that pistol fire could not harm him at that distance, or he was attempting to encourage his warriors to make a massive charge.

As the emigrants watched the show, one young man, his face smeared with blood from an arrow wound on his forehead, turned to the older man next to him, the "Missouri Preacher."[9]

"You have the reputation of being a crack shot, Preacher," the wounded man said. "Why don't you shoot that fellow?"

"My gun won't carry that far with accuracy!"

"Here, take mine! I cannot see to sight with blood in my eyes. But this rifle will hold up true that distance."[10]

The preacher accepted the rifle and took aim, but from fatigue or excitement could not keep the long, heavy barrel steady. He lowered it, confessing, "I cannot hold it for the shot."

"Try again," the wounded man persisted. "If I could only clear my eyes, I know I can hit him. Try again, Preacher!"

Once more the Preacher raised the rifle, this time placing the barrel upon the top of the wagon wheel. No weaving. He took careful aim, held his breath, and slowly squeezed the trigger. The rifle fired with a loud "crack."

Almost two seconds passed; then the ball smashed into the warrior's chest. The club fell from his hand and the chief pitched forward to the ground, dead.[11]

Four warriors leaped from concealment, picked up their fallen leader, and carried him out of sight. More warriors appeared to retrieve wounded and dead and quickly disappeared over the hill. They then returned for the unguarded livestock, estimated to be about 408, and drove them south toward their main village. Minutes after the chief fell, the Mojave had completely vanished.

Apparently, all this activity indicated a cessation of hostilities, at least for the immediate future. Then an eerie silence fell over the valley, broken only by the occasional sound of women and children sobbing.

The battle had lasted a little over two hours. At least seventeen dead warriors were counted in sight of the camp. Emigrants estimated an equal number were killed or severely wounded by rifle fire at a distance of one to two hundred yards.[12]

Casualties among the emigrants: five members of the Bentner family and Alpha Brown killed, a total of six dead. Three—Lee Griffin, Sally Fox, and "Grandmother" Jones—were seriously wounded. Eight men suffered superficial wounds, including the man who loaned his rifle to the Missouri preacher.

As the smoke and smell of burned gunpowder began to clear away, the emigrants met to decide their next course of action. Escaping the area, of course, was paramount and no one knew how long the lull might continue.

A few mules and six head of oxen survived, along with Alpha Brown's horse and another named Old Bob, a favorite bobtailed riding horse, along with ten workhorses.

The oxen were enough to pull one wagon and essential supplies. All possessions had to be left behind in the other wagons.

Crossing the river without a raft was impossible and the construction of one required at least three days, during which time an attack from the Mojave could certainly be expected. Even if they managed to cross unscathed, there was still a thirty-day walk to the first white settlement in California.

Almost three hundred miles to the south stood Fort Yuma, but to get to the protection of the army required that they walk the entire distance through Mojave territory along the Colorado.

To stay and fight invited certain disaster. A check of ammunition revealed enough gunpowder and ball for perhaps one more battle. After that, the fighting would be hand to hand—a fight they knew they would quickly lose.

The emigrants decided they had only one hope for survival and escape. They would have to retrace their steps and return to Albuquerque, five hundred miles to the east.

In eighteen to twenty miles, they would meet the John Udell train, which they assumed to be waiting for the return of oxen and cattle. Those emigrants were unaware of the disaster that had befallen the Bentner family and the rest. Without oxen and mules, Udell and his party would also have to abandon their wagons. If fortunate, they might encounter another westbound train before all supplies were exhausted. Then new plans could be considered.

At 4 P.M., they wrapped Alpha Brown in a blanket and wound log chains around it. They "buried" him in the Colorado, praying the Mojave would not find and mutilate the body.

A little before 5 P.M., "Grandmother" Jones and all small children including Sally Fox gathered with a few personal possessions and climbed aboard one wagon.

Mrs. Brown mounted her dead husband's horse and for a moment tried to scratch some of his dried blood from the saddle. Mrs. Rose rode Old Bob and, with a few of the others, led the group toward the eastern mountains.

The somewhat senile "Grandfather" Jones was given the task of driving the mules hitched to Rose's large buggy, the so-called ambulance, which was, for now, earning its title. Lee Griffin, with serious arrow wounds, rested inside on an improvised stretcher.[13]

Twenty-five men, including Mr. Rose, walked or limped from their wounds. Their flight from the river valley started shortly after 5 P.M., and no one looked back at the deserted camp, where five large wagons, loaded with all their worldly possessions, sat unattended, waiting for new owners.

They halted after traveling only four miles into the mountain pass. Darkness had enveloped the desert, making it impossible to see the trail. They would have to wait until after midnight. Then the moon would be high enough and provide light to continue.

Those who once held the unrealistic hope that Lieutenant Beale was rushing to their rescue must have finally given up the dream.

Were the Mojave already in pursuit? The survivors huddled together in the darkness, fearful of revealing their location by building a fire or lighting a lantern. Ears strained in the deathlike stillness of the desert in the effort to hear of approaching danger.

CHAPTER 30

Escape!

Death seemed to stare us in the face. We had nothing to
expect but immediate death from the hands of merciless
savages, or a more lingering death from starvation.

John Udell, Journal,

September 1858

If they spoke at all, it was in whispers. The emigrants waited patiently,
like animals, for the moon to provide enough light to start the escape
through the mountain pass. Some shivered from fear, stress, and exhaustion, not because of the dry mountain air. Summer might have
ended in their native Iowa, but September nights in the desert are usually blessed with warm breezes.

The night had remained oddly quiet; not a howl from a coyote or a
cougar, none of the bobcat screams to which they had become accustomed during the long journey to the Colorado River.

Suddenly the stillness was shattered by the sounds of human shouts
and yells in the distance. This was instantly followed by the loud bang-
ing of metal. Sometimes the noise had the deep tone of iron pots or
kettles being beaten; at other times it was the higher pitch of glass
shattering.

The Mojave had finally stormed the emigrants' river camp and,
discovering it vacant, began to enjoy the loot from the abandoned
wagons.

Then, while the night's breeze carried the sounds of the Mojave's celebration, the moon reached its zenith, providing the light the emigrants needed to begin the slow, tedious grind through the gap.

Why didn't the Mojave pursue the fleeing emigrants? The tracks were easy to follow and the whites could easily have been overtaken.

It is possible that the Indians were satisfied with the treasures left behind by the emigrants. In a way, despite their loss of at least twenty warriors, they had won a victory. The whites had been driven from the River People's home, and the River People were enjoying that victory. It would require hours to divide the treasure from the wagons and the four hundred head of cattle. That meat, once dried in the September sun, could feed the entire village for months.

The emigrants had left their food and equipment and were moving east from the mountains into the desert. In the Indians' mind, there was no need for revenge. Why lose more warriors? The desert would finish the emigrants in a few days.

The morning sun soon brought smothering heat. The emigrants rationed their small supply of water and shared it with their animals.

Grandfather Jones, in the rear, driving the mule-team ambulance, fell back from the party. At dusk, his mules stopped and refused to continue. Jones set the animals free and then began to limp along the trail, trying to catch up with the others. Fortunately, the party reached the Udell camp. At first there was celebration. The Udell wagons had food and water. But then Udell learned the hard facts of the Mojave attack, and as he listened to the horrible report from Rose, Grandfather Jones shuffled in. It was dark and Jones confessed that he had left Lee Griffin lying in the ambulance more than a mile away.

In spite of his own wounds, Ed Akey, without eating supper, started back on foot in the darkness to retrieve his pal. He had saved Griffin at the river during the battle. He wasn't going to leave him in the desert to die. Akey found the ambulance and gave Griffin a drink of water. Then the two hobbled toward camp, Griffin "half carried" by Akey.[1]

The next morning the full reality of their situation brought everyone to shocking awareness. The Bentner family had been murdered at the Colorado; one of their leaders, Alpha Brown, was dead, killed in the battle; and practically all the cattle and oxen were in the possession of the Mojave.

Mr. Rose had his team of oxen to move one wagon, but there were no animals to pull the other ten wagons. They, like the five at the river, would have to be left behind with all the emigrants' possessions.

The temperature hit the hundred-degree mark as the emigrants began their five-hundred-mile walk to Albuquerque. Within a few days, most of their shoes and boots had fallen apart due to the rough trail of lava rock and hunks of quartz. The water supply was scarce and continued to be rationed, making it especially difficult for the wounded and sick.

Some hobbled on blistered, bloody feet, exchanging prayers with one another. Then, as they began to count the hours to life's end, those prayers were answered.

They encountered another train heading to California. Coincidentally, it was from Iowa, and was commanded by a Mr. Hamilton, a friend of Rose.

The Hamilton party had lost a number of their animals during Indian attacks along the way and some had died from lack of water, but, at once, they began to distribute food, clothing, and medical supplies to Rose's group.

Upon learning of the Rose disaster at the Colorado, Hamilton announced that he too was turning back. The women and children of the Rose party could take turns riding in his wagons.

At dawn on September 11, three men guarding Hamilton's remaining cattle were attacked by an unknown number of Indians who were driven off by Colt revolver fire. The guards returned to camp with one Indian scalp and bows and arrows as "trophies of their success."[2]

Before their journey, the guards had not been gunfighters or even hardened frontiersmen, but simply farmers. They had suffered enough Indian harassment, and this time they fought back.

While resting on the night of September 12, about sixty miles east of present-day Kingman, Arizona, the group encountered another train heading for California. E. O. Smith and his brother T. O. Smith of Decatur, Illinois, commanded this one. There were no women or children with this train, but the Smiths did have a number of horses and five hundred cattle.

With true American spirit, or what the emigrants called "pioneer kindness," the Smiths began to butcher some of their cattle to feed the starving Hamiltons and the Rose group. That night, Mrs. Brown's horse died of exhaustion. He had survived the Mojave arrows that killed Alpha Brown, but one hundred miles with so little water was more than the animal could endure. Mrs. Brown now joined the others who had been on foot since leaving the Colorado.

On September 26, about twenty miles west of present-day Flagstaff, her son, the youngest of her children and her only child by Alpha, became ill. Like his mother, the three-year-old had walked until his swollen bloody feet could no longer support his tiny body. For days, he had stumbled every few paces. Mrs. Brown had no strength to lift the child, so his twelve-year-old sister, Sally, still suffering from her arrow wound, attempted to tote him piggyback. But soon they both fell. The compassionate Smith brothers made a bed for the boy in the back of a wagon, but there was nothing anyone could do to restore his health.

The emigrants recorded that it was an unknown "illness" that finally caused the child's death. Some claimed dehydration and the heat, the horrible merciless heat of the desert, which draws energy and smothers the breath while the sun seems to smile at it all.

Mrs. Brown was not yet thirty-five. She had already lost two husbands, all of her belongings, and her horse, and now her son was gone.

The wagons paused only long enough to dig a small grave a few yards from the edge of Beale's trail. The earth was soft and dry, and the dust from each full shovel appeared to float a moment in the hot air, as if waiting for a breeze to carry it away.

Sally Fox insisted she be allowed to help dig her little brother's grave, but the adults refused, pointing to her arrow wound and explaining that it was not yet healed. She stood by, sobbing, holding her bloodstained apron to her face.

Mary Brown joined in the prayers led by the Missouri preacher. They all sang a hymn; then the wagons, with dry, squeaking wheels, began to roll.

Mrs. Brown, Sally, and her sisters were the last to leave the grave, but in minutes they followed, limping and shuffling, tears streaming down unwashed faces, until caring hands lifted them into a wagon.[3]

The train rolled on slowly, leaving behind in the unsettled dust a lonely cross made from mesquite branches. There was no place for a name or date or age on the cross. Future travelers remember it as an "unknown emigrant" grave. In a year, all traces of it disappeared.

On October 2, they reached the base of the San Francisco Mountains and winter welcomed them with pelting, cold rain, sweeping down from the peaks with chilling winds. The snow came, a few flurries at first, than so heavy it began to form drifts.

They pushed on and were near Zuni when thirty of the strongest men volunteered to walk ahead the 240 miles to Albuquerque. There, the plan was to seek help from the army.

The Smith brothers slaughtered more cattle and prepared a sizable amount of jerky for the men to survive on until they reached their destination.

The men made the journey to Zuni ahead of the train and told the curious population of the Colorado massacre and the poor condition of the emigrants who were following them. Then they continued toward Albuquerque.

When the emigrant train arrived at Zuni, the citizens, mostly Christian Indians and Mexicans, provided them food, blankets, and a place to rest out of the cold. On November 1, 1858, sixty-one days after the massacre, the United States Army came to the rescue at Zuni with wagons loaded with food, shoes, and clothing. The advance party of thirty men had made it through to Albuquerque, and the army, fearful at hearing such news from the Colorado, responded immediately.

By the middle of November, what was left of the emigrant train arrived in Albuquerque. Again, citizens provided food, clothing, and shelter.

The Rose, Brown, and Udell parties had lost everything except the one wagon belonging to Rose and his horses, Old Bob and Picayune. The Hamiltons and Smiths had sacrificed practically all their cattle during the retreat; everyone had beef to eat. They now had clothing, shoes, blankets, and a few other items to see them through the winter, thanks to the good people of New Mexico Territory and the U.S. Army.

Mary Brown lost her husband and her youngest child. She and the travelers were destroyed financially and emotionally. Dreams of farming or retiring in the land of gold and sunshine seemed shattered forever. But the spirit of the pioneers, wounded as they were, had not died. A month later, as a cold, sad Christmas came and went, there was talk of new ideas, of new possibilities to reach California.

The Hamilton and Smith parties said they might take the southern route through Yuma, and then they said they might wait and follow Ed Beale if he ever returned to New Mexico.

L. J. Rose worked in Albuquerque a short time as a waiter, then moved his family to Santa Fe, the business center for New Mexico at the time. With funds borrowed from a brother-in-law in the East, he purchased a hotel and bar named La Fonda, a local drinking establishment with a poor reputation. But, as a good businessman, Rose turned the place into a true moneymaker and sold it for a large profit. In 1861, the Rose family, with Old Bob and Picayune, resumed their journey to California. They made it safely this time.[4]

By January 1859, rumors once again flooded through New Mexico Territory. Lieutenant Beale was coming with "many men" to improve his wagon road, punish the Mojave, and cross the Colorado. This time the rumors were not false. Their hero would soon be there to help.

Beale was indeed on his way with a large party of men and had entered New Mexico, paid a visit to his old friend Kit Carson, and then waited out the winter, planning his spring expedition.

As a Mason, Alpha Brown had made friends with lodge members in Albuquerque during their stop as they prepared for the westbound trip. Now Mary Brown was greeted warmly by the Masons, who cared for her and her children over the winter. The Smith brothers, who had given so freely of their cattle and supplies, invited Mrs. Brown to join them in the spring for another attempt to reach California. Sally Fox-Brown was so excited with the news that she gathered some odd-looking nuts along the banks of a stream and vowed to plant them at her new home someday.

Now they needed to wait for Edward Beale, who would lead them all safely across the Colorado. But Beale commanded a construction crew, not an Army, and he had no idea of what waited for him in Albuquerque.

CHAPTER 31

The Army Investigates

Wipe out the Mojaves!

Citizens' War Cry, California, 1858

Rumors of Edward Beale's journey flashed through New Mexico Territory during the winter of 1858, moving ahead of his expedition like today's news bulletins.

As is often the case, most information on heroes of the frontier was either untrue or highly exaggerated. People learned that the wagon road construction crew had entered New Mexico and camped for the winter, but some stories told of a huge army and a camel corps under Beale's command, coming to punish the Mojave.

Beale had not yet learned of the emigrant massacre at the Colorado, so he had no plans to punish anyone. There was no camel corps, no troops, and there were no camels with the expedition this time.[1]

Beale did have a sizable workforce of over fifty well-armed men, prepared and eager to take on any trouble along the route. These men were civilians, not members of the military.

The expedition departed Fort Smith, Arkansas, on October 28, 1858, with orders from the War Department to improve the wagon road from Arkansas through what is now Oklahoma, New Mexico, and Arizona to the Colorado River. There, at Beale's Crossing, the trail used by the Mojave continued past present-day Barstow, California, ending in the Los Angeles area.

They made good progress with the construction until they entered New Mexico Territory in mid-December and winter set in with snow and ice, making it impossible to continue. Three days after Christmas, they camped at a ranch leased by the army from rancher Alexander Hatch. This army post, commonly called Hatch's Ranch by the military, was a convenient supply stop between a larger post, Fort Union, and Santa Fe, and was situated about twenty-five miles northeast of present-day Las Vegas, New Mexico (not Nevada).

Hatch's Ranch was protected from Comanche attacks by a ten-foot-high adobe wall. Inside the compound were several adobe buildings, including one large 115-by-288-foot structure.[2]

Beale's team, consisting of an interesting list of characters, would share living quarters for the next two months at Hatch's Ranch. Hampden Porter, Joe Bell, and the small but energetic May Humphreys Stacey, who accompanied Beale on the first expedition, were not with him this time. Stacey planned to become an officer in the army and dreamed of returning west someday. (Years later, his dreams came true.)

Greek George and Hi Jolly remained in California at the ranch with Sam Bishop and the original camels, but Peachy Gilmer Breckenridge, now an experienced "trail hand," joined Beale on this journey, as did the "black servant," Absalom Reading.[3]

Some new men on this expedition were Beale's brother George, Dr. William Floyd, Dick Brown, called "the Delaware" by Beale, and Little Ax, "the Shawnee." (Dr. Floyd believed Little Ax to be a Creek.)

Beale stated that he hired the two Native Americans as "hunters" to provide fresh meat for the managing members of the party, but they, along with "half-breed" Jesse Chisholm, also served as guides.

"The Delaware's" real name was Black Beaver, and he was born near present-day Belleville, Illinois. As a young adult, he emigrated to the Canadian River area of Oklahoma and became chief of about five hundred Delaware. He served with the U.S. Army during the Mexican War, leading mounted volunteers composed of Delaware and Shawnee, then became a guide after the war.

Jesse (also spelled Jessie) Chisholm, half white and half Cherokee, married the white daughter of James Edwards, a local trading-post owner, and lived with the Creek people.

Little Ax was Shawnee and friends with both Chisholm and Black Beaver. All were recommended as excellent guides and hunters, and were hired by Beale in Oklahoma in October 1858.[4]

Though Beale would not be testing camels on this journey, he did bring along his five greyhound dogs: Nero, Fannie, Prince, Buck, and Ramus.[5]

There were sheep for food, supplemented by wild game killed by the "hunters," more than one hundred horses and mules, and a construction work crew, identified by Beale as "fifty willing hands." Beale also had about twenty men who were friends or employees.

Fourteen wagons hauled the necessary tools, equipment, and food supplies.

Beale knew that fourteen wagons might not be able to carry everything his crew needed to complete the expedition and he suspected that he might run seriously low on food by the time they reached the Colorado. Expecting to arrive at the river by late April, he devised a plan to have supplies waiting for him.

Concerned with the unpredictability of the Mojave, he decided to send a messenger to Los Angeles by the southern route through Fort Yuma, thus hopefully avoiding snow and the Indian villages along the Colorado.

The man he selected for this dangerous mission was his friend and "clerk," Frederick E. Kerlin. Trusted by Beale for years, Kerlin proved to be no ordinary "clerk." In physical appearance, perhaps, he fit the stereotype of an accountant rather than a rugged outdoorsman, yet Kerlin possessed not only loyalty to Beale but stamina and extraordinary courage.

His success was critical to the road crew's survival. This, he understood.

Beale's plan, though simple in concept, proved complex in execution.

Kerlin's orders were to purchase supplies in Los Angeles and have them delivered to Beale's Crossing along the Colorado by Samuel A. Bishop, Beale's Tejon Ranch partner. Bishop might need to wait at the river and prepare to cross and proceed east if Beale sent a request to do so. This phase of the program could be very unsafe, depending on the mood of the Mojave.

With that concern, Kerlin was also to request an army escort for Bishop from the California military commander, General Newman S. Clark, to ensure a safe arrival (and crossing) at the river.

Kerlin's journey would take him over 1,200 miles of rugged wilderness. First, he had to travel alone south to El Paso, Texas, and there board a stagecoach belonging to the (less-than-two-year-old) Butterfield Overland Mail Company. These coaches, pulled by eight mules, completed almost 70 miles a day on the "snow-free" trail from El Paso to Tucson, then to Yuma, and the last 280 miles to Los Angeles. In good weather, with no breakdowns or Indian attacks, that final section to Los Angeles was often completed in a remarkable seventy-two hours.

The coaches were driven by tough frontiersmen, who faced hardships in all weather while attempting to travel a required sixty miles before being relieved by other drivers waiting at one of the many Butterfield stations (assuming they had not been killed by Indians). The southern trail they traveled was guarded, partially, by patrols of dragoons from Fort Yuma.

It would be four months before Ed Beale learned if Frederick Kerlin survived and completed his mission.

While the Butterfield company was having some success delivering the mail along the southern Fort Yuma route, the Post Office Department continued to experiment with other ways to deliver mail from the eastern states to California. This would include Beale's new but uncompleted wagon road from Fort Tejon to Santa Fe and then along the Santa Fe Trail into Kansas.

The mail service on this route started in October 1858 and quickly became a disaster, partially because of Indian attacks and the Mojave's refusal to permit mail carriers to cross the river. However, the first westbound mail did arrive in Stockton, California, in late November 1858, bearing news of the August emigrant massacre at the Colorado. As the story spread, the number of white people murdered by the Mojave quickly climbed, and within a month, no one knew the actual figure. It made little difference. Emigrants had been killed, and the mail, so important to human existence, could not get through because of the Indians.

From town to town, citizens demanded that the army take action with the cry, "Wipe out the Mojave!"

General Newman S. Clark issued orders for the Sixth Infantry to send four companies under the command of Major William Hoffman to the Colorado and establish a post in Mojave territory along the river.

Hoffman, a highly decorated officer during the Mexican War, had been promoted twice for "gallant conduct." With twenty-nine years of service and a superior combat record, he should have been most capable for the assignment. Certainly, no one could question his bravery or his devotion to the United States Army. However, his tactical decisions during the next two or three months might leave historians to wonder about his ability to analyze a situation and proceed in a logical fashion.

Major Hoffman's "reconnaissance" of the Colorado River seemed in order before a post could be established. That decision, at least, seemed logical. At the end of December 1858, he departed with one company from the Sixth Infantry and an escort of fifty dragoons from Fort Tejon.

Hoffman's men were armed with the latest weapons available for the army. The California Ordnance Department received the 1853 breech-loading rifles and carbines and the 1851 Colt Navy revolvers in the summer. Soldiers had four months' practice with the weapons and were anxious to test them in combat.

The major wanted to employ a few army camels on his journey to the Colorado, but his request was rejected. According to Secretary of

War Floyd, the camels and the wagon road would remain in civilian control, a fact that irritated Hoffman.

Floyd had become so convinced of the potential of camels that in December, he recommended to Congress that the army purchase a thousand more. Preoccupied with other expensive projects, Congress ignored the request.

In a later report, Hoffman was less than complimentary about the quality of Beale's road from Fort Tejon to the Colorado. He claimed it was difficult to follow, though the Mojave people, Lieutenant Whipple, and even Ed Beale's expedition had successfully followed it. Hoffman falsely reported that it might be too sandy and soft to support loaded wagons, a claim that would be disproved in months to come as various wagon trains, military and civilian, rolled along the trail.

At midmorning, on January 7, 1859, Major Hoffman's unit, chilled from days of travel in the cold, dry desert air, arrived at the Colorado basin. From a twenty-foot ridge above the "bottom land," they could clearly see the trail lead up to the water's edge. They descended into the flatland.

A large body of water, perhaps a mile long, known as "beaver lake" separated them from the river. The lake, created by backwater of the river, appeared dark and green. The entire area on all sides was a tangle of arrow weed, sagebrush, vines, and mesquite trees. And there, waiting in the clearing between the underbrush and the river, stood more than two hundred Mojave warriors armed with wooden clubs and bows and arrows. The Indians, aware of Hoffman's movements, were ready for combat.

Many of the warriors had visited Fort Yuma, hundreds of miles to the south. There they observed soldiers marching and target practicing, so the sight of dragoons did not intimidate them at all. To the contrary, the Mojave were full of confidence since their victory over the emigrant party just a few months before.

Major Hoffman ordered the first rank of dragoons to prepare to charge into the warriors.

But before the charge began, the Mojave executed a tactic of their own. Warriors suddenly appeared on each side of the trail, ready to attack the dragoons' flanks. Hoffman's men found themselves in a trap as arrows rained down from the front and sides.

The major quickly ordered a retreat and his men withdrew two hundred yards, safely out of the range of arrows. Two squads dismounted to fight a delaying action while the remainder of the troops scampered up the hill and waited. Covering the retreat, the squads on foot cocked their Sharps carbines and prepared to fire.

A group of warriors charged toward the waiting soldiers, who took careful aim as they had been trained to do, and fired. They quickly reloaded and fired a second barrage, then turned and raced up the hill to join the waiting units.

As the gun smoke drifted from the clearing, soldiers could see four dead warriors and several more, apparently wounded, crawling for the protection of mesquite trees.[6]

The Mojave paused in their attack and appeared to be regrouping for another charge. But now the army had the advantage of elevation, occupying the high ridge.

A quick check of the soldiers revealed a few with very minor arrow wounds. Major Hoffman had remained perfectly calm during the engagement, barking orders as expected of an experienced combat officer. Then he gave the final order: "RETREAT!"

And withdraw they did, first back to a temporary camp at Cajon Pass, then all the way to the safety of Los Angeles.

In his after-action report, Major Hoffman could not blame the Mojave completely for his mission's failure. If he did, some would question how "savages" armed with clubs and bows and arrows sent the United States Army, armed with revolvers and carbines, into a full retreat.

The major had issued the correct order. He was completely outnumbered, almost surrounded, and withdrew from the field of battle without losing a man, while inflicting enemy casualties.

So Major Hoffman elected to direct attention to the condition of Beale's road. At least part of his failure, he concluded, was due to the difficulties his troops had managing the trail.

And this, somehow, began to fit into a ridiculous plan he'd concocted for total victory over the Mojave nation. He presented these ideas to his superiors. This plan, of course, could not include a full movement along Beale's road. Such a suggestion might contradict his "complaints" regarding the trail's condition.

Meanwhile, at the Colorado River, the Mojave celebrated their first victory over the United States Army. The river remained in their possession, as it had for hundreds of years. But some tribal leaders warned that many soldiers might return and bring more death. These chiefs suggested they go to Fort Yuma and seek peace with the soldiers.[7]

But the news of the Mojave attack on Major Hoffman's men spread fear and inflamed the people of California. Emigrants were murdered and mail carriers driven off. Now a unit of "American Dragoons" had been attacked and forced to retreat. There could be no peace with the Mojave.

Citizens, encouraged by newspapers, continued to cry, "Wipe out the Mojave!"[8]

CHAPTER 32

Heading for a Showdown at the Colorado

I believe the world might be picked and not find a better
set of men than I have with me.

Samuel A. Bishop, March 13, 1859

In March 1859, at Jamul Ranch near San Diego, U.S. Army captain
Henry S. Burton packed for a new assignment. The orders, which he
studied in detail, posed a number of questions in the mind of this
Mexican War veteran.

The California Department of the Army was mobilizing a number
of units for something they called "the Colorado Expedition." Captain
Burton and a company of his Third Artillery were to report to Major
William Hoffman aboard the ocean steamship USS *Uncle Sam*, which
would be arriving in a day or two at San Diego. The ship was to carry
his men and other troops already aboard to the Colorado River. Captain Burton had enjoyed a social life on his sprawling ranch with his
beautiful wife, Maria Ruiz. They had married shortly after the war, in
1849, and purchased the Jamul property in 1853.

Maria, the daughter of a wealthy landowner in Baja, had taken
advantage of emigration agreements in the Guadeloupe-Hidalgo
Treaty and moved to California with her mother. Both became U.S.
citizens.

Captain and Mrs. Burton were involved in the "social circles" in

San Diego and developed friendships with a number of landowners, both "Anglos" and "Latinos." The couple complemented each other in this endeavor. Burton, a New Englander and American army officer, had the necessary manners and reputation of a true gentleman. Maria charmed everyone with her grace, beauty, and "air of aristocracy." She quickly mastered English, and as she did so, the captain became fluent in the Spanish language, an accomplishment that was about to prove very beneficial to the U.S. Army.

The *Uncle Sam* usually carried passengers up and down the West Coast, often all the way to Central and South America, and was capable of speeds up to nineteen miles per hour. From first class to steerage section she could carry nine hundred passengers. In early March 1859, she had on board almost five hundred U.S. Army troops, who boarded in San Francisco with Major Hoffman. Then she received Captain Burton and the company of his Third Artillery Unit at San Diego.

They traveled around the Baja peninsula to the mouth of the Colorado River. From there, the army would march upstream to Fort Yuma. Now Captain Burton and other officers learned just what the Colorado expedition was all about.

Major Hoffman, with orders from his California command headquarters, had organized a huge army consisting of seven companies plus the one from the Third Artillery. In addition, some two hundred civilian workers joined the expedition. Hoffman's mission: move against the Mojave nation, force a peace agreement, or, if necessary, destroy them.

Major Hoffman's army lacked the necessary field intelligence for the mission and did not even know how many warriors the Mojave could muster. The Mojave nation consisted of many villages scattered for miles along the Colorado, each controlled by a "chief" and various "subchiefs."

Some estimates of warrior strength were three thousand. In reality, there was half that number.

Hoffman had never traveled the Colorado basin. Now he planned to march his army up the river from Fort Yuma and confront the Mojave from the south, capturing village after village, if necessary, until he reached the thirty-fifth parallel and Beale's Crossing, a distance of about three hundred miles.

He also ordered another company of soldiers to march from San Francisco, join a unit based near Cajon Pass, and together move, not to the thirty-fifth parallel and attack from the west, as might be expected, but travel at an angle through the California desert to Fort Yuma and link with the entire force.

The men released from the USS *Uncle Sam* at the mouth of the Colorado had a 150-mile march from there to Fort Yuma. That was simple when compared to what lay ahead.

This preposterous plan seemed necessary only in the mind of Hoffman and became a heavy burden, financially, for the government when the investment of troops, animals, wagons, and supplies was considered. A more logical option existed: assemble the troops at Fort Tejon and march east along Beale's wagon trail, striking the Mojave at their center (Beale's Crossing). But Hoffman already held negative opinions about that trail from his "reconnaissance" a few weeks earlier and was careful not to contradict his own reports. It is very possible, also, that his dislike of anything related to Edward Beale played a part in his decisions. The Beale wagon trail, the Beale Crossing, and most of all "Beale's" camels on Beale's Ranch. In his mind, they were not Beale's camels. Those animals were U.S. Army property, and Major Hoffman had been denied their use, not just once, but twice. Evidence of the resentment Hoffman felt for Beale would bloom again before the Colorado expedition came to a finish.

But Major Hoffman was a good old soldier and went about putting his plan, no matter how strange, into effect, and with efficiency.

Soon after the first troops arrived at Fort Yuma, Hoffman ordered Captain Henry S. Burton and his Third Artillery unit north about forty-five miles to establish a supply post on the west (California) side of the Colorado. They called it Camp Gaston in honor of First Lieutenant William Gaston, killed by Spokane Indians less than a year before.

Tons of supplies began to arrive at Camp Gaston (near present-day Palo Verde, California) by pack mules and mule-drawn wagons.

During Camp Gaston's creation, Hoffman made arrangements with Captain Johnson and employed the latter's two paddle-wheel steamboats: the successful, 103-foot-long *General Jesup* and a smaller boat. These were to haul troops up the river while those less fortunate rode mules or walked.

The steamships, fighting the Colorado's three-mile-an-hour current and with a maximum speed of six miles an hour, did not move much faster than marching troops. But now the Colorado expedition had a psychological advantage over the Mojave, being able to advance both by land and water.

The expedition was not entirely blind to the conditions expected along the Colorado trail. During the failed reconnaissance in December, Hoffman employed the famous mountain man and explorer Joseph Rutherford Walker, described by his peers and various army officers as "reliable, cool, firm, and dignified." Walker had served under Andrew Jackson during the Indian Wars of 1812 before coming to the western frontier. Unlike Hoffman, Walker knew the difficulties facing the army as they marched out of Fort Yuma.

There was no road for the wagons along the Colorado, only trails used by Indians. Surely, based on his excellent reputation, Walker must have discussed the problems the expedition was likely to encounter, but we can only assume that his ideas were ignored. There could be no changing of plans for Hoffman. His massive army of six hundred soldiers plus two hundred armed civilian employees (called "workers") moved out of Fort Yuma on March 26, 1859, and headed north to face the Mojave, three hundred difficult miles away.

Meanwhile, back in Los Angeles, Beale's clerk, Frederick E. Kerlin, had completed his thousand-mile journey and arrived safe but exhausted on February 2, 1859. Ignoring the need for rest, he began work on the assignment Beale had given him. Part of his mission was the purchasing of provisions and sending messages. The first one he sent was to Sam Bishop at Tejon Ranch. Bishop was to organize a team of men and prepare to move with the supplies to the Colorado, there to either wait for Beale or deliver a quantity east.

The next message went to army headquarters in San Francisco. It requested a military escort for Bishop. The wagon road was, after all, a pet project of the secretary of war and the protection of the work crew and management staff (Ed Beale and associates) should be a military priority. This, however, would not be the case.

Kerlin had no knowledge of the Mojave's attack and murder of emigrants at Beale's Crossing that past September, nor of the army's plans to attack the River People. All this he learned shortly after his arrival in Los Angeles. By then, Major Hoffman and his men were already on the way to Fort Yuma.

On February 21, Kerlin sent a letter to the military commander, General Clark, officially requesting an escort. Major William W. Mackall, the adjutant, answered on February 25: "It is not practical to send you a sufficient escort . . . General Clarke regrets his inability to secure your march to the River but the demands on the troops at Tejon forbids [sic] it."

Major Mackall also sent a letter to Ed Beale on the same date, which stated, in part: "Brigadier General Clarke directs me to notify you that the Mojave Indians have become hostile and that he has sent a force to bring them into submission; this force will not probably reach the thirty-fifth parallel on the Colorado before the 15th or 20th of April and if your party is not strong and well-armed you will be endangered should you reach the crossing before the troops."

Mackall went on to assure Beale that he could find the troops south of the thirty-fifth and they had orders to "offer assistance," but there were no soldiers available for Kerlin at the time.

While at Fort Yuma, Major Hoffman received a letter, also dated the twenty-fifth, from Major Mackall instructing the Colorado expedition to give Ed Beale any assistance he needed.[1]

Fred E. Kerlin was a man of honor and Sam Bishop possessed the same qualities. Beale needed food supplies in a few weeks and the army would not furnish an escort. The Mojave had become "hostile." That was nothing new to the people of southern California.

Samuel Bishop had to make a serious decision. Should he wait for Beale to get closer to the Colorado, or should he take action, move the supply train east, and risk a confrontation with the Mojave?

Bishop understood the thinking and culture of the Native Americans in southern California, having lived and worked with them, first in the San Joaquin River area and later at the Tejon (San Sebastian) Reservation. From the beginning, he had proven himself brave, considerate, and resourceful.

He began, at once, to organize a team of forty men whom he personally selected. But while he was involved with that process, something very personal was on his mind. His wife, Ella, delivered their first child, a daughter, on February 10. They named her Jennie Josephine.

In two weeks, Sam Bishop would leave his family with servants and embark on a dangerous journey.

Bishop's team left the Los Angeles area on March 1, 1859. It consisted of forty men, six wagons pulled by six mules each, a few pack and riding mules, and twenty camels from his ranch.[2]

A controversy exists over how many camels went on this adventure. Partly this is the result of a letter written on March 24 by W. W. Hudson, sent to the Los Angeles *Southern Vineyard* (printed in its May 3, 1859, edition). Hudson accompanied Bishop's party until about April 1, when he returned to California. In his letter he reported, incorrectly, that Bishop had ten camels.

Bishop did take ten *pack* camels (which could be ridden by men if their packs were removed), but he took ten *riding* camels as well.[3]

His men were well armed. Some carried shotguns, but most preferred percussion, single-shot rifles. Each wore a Bowie-type knife and at least one Colt Navy .36-caliber percussion revolver. Bishop and a few others carried two revolvers.

They would cover more than 330 miles of rugged desert, averaging about twenty miles a day on the Mojave Trail.

Crossing over the Cajon Pass summit, they followed the Mojave River bed toward Soda Lake and Marl Springs. On the evening of March 12, the party camped along the Mojave River and was joined by a small group of men from the "Overland Central Route Mail Party," which included Charles H. Graves, John Eckhart (spelled Eckart in some reports), William Pool, and a Mr. Hoag. Pool carried a new breech-loading Sharps rifle, which received admiring attention from Bishop's men.

At this time they were "45 miles from the Salt Lake Road" (Old Spanish Trail).[4]

The mail company had been unsuccessful in crossing the Colorado or even getting close to the river. Naturally, they were excited to join Bishop's party.

The combined group made good progress, and paused at Merl Springs and Rock Springs to dig out the area, improving the springs for future travelers.

A confrontation was about to occur at Beale's Crossing as three determined groups moved toward the Mojave.

From the east, somewhere in what is now Arizona, Edward Beale and his crew of sixty to seventy men worked their way west along the wagon road. Estimated arrival time at the Colorado: the second week of April.

From the south, Major Hoffman and his massive army moved slowly north, following the Colorado. Estimated time of arrival: the second week of April.

And from the west, Sam Bishop and his forty armed men (plus four from the mail company) were ahead of schedule. Estimated time of arrival: the end of March.

None of these three groups knew the exact location of the others. Beale was not aware of Major Hoffman's march; nor did he know if

Fred Kerlin had made it safely to Los Angeles. He assumed the re-sourceful Kerlin not only reached the city but was on the way east with Sam Bishop, supplies, and a military escort.

But Beale was realistic. Suppose Kerlin did not reach Los Angeles. Perhaps he had been killed somewhere in New Mexico Territory or the California desert. Maybe his body lay along one of those trails and no supplies were waiting anywhere.

Ed Beale knew how to plan in difficult situations and he needed a good one if he was to cross the Colorado River without losing men to the Mojave.

There was one group, though, that did know where the others were: the Native Americans along the river. They observed the move-ments of the white men and calculated correctly that Bishop's smaller group from the west would arrive at the river before the others.

The Mojave were confident in their ability to defeat, even annihi-late, Bishop, but they needed reinforcements to ensure a victory over Major Hoffman.

For many generations the Mojave maintained a relationship with neighboring Pah-Utes and Yumas. Sometimes those relations were amical and beneficial (at least from a commercial point of view), but often they were bitter. It all depended on various factors and the pe-riod in history. But with so many whites approaching, some tribes of Yuma and Pah-Ute agreed to fight alongside their sometime friends the Mojave.

The actual number of warriors waiting for Sam Bishop at the Col-orado in late March 1859 is not known, but the best estimate is 1,500.[5]

Sam Bishop, with a force of forty-four civilians, prepared to chal-lenge the Mojave nation. His little army was a true representation of Americans. A few were first-generation European emigrants, but most were second-generation German, English, Dutch, Scottish, and Irish plus one Native American (Georgine, a member of the Chowchilla tribe of California), a Greek (Greek George), and one Syrian "Arab" (Hi Jolly).

On March 13, 1859, Sam Bishop wrote a letter to the Los Angeles *Southern Vineyard* in which he said of his group, "I believe the world might be picked and not find a better set of men than I have with me."[6]

In a few days, Bishop's survival would depend on the fighting ability of those men and something never attempted before in American history.

CHAPTER 33

The Battle Begins

Samuel A. Bishop was perfectly fearless in the time of danger.

Lewis Spitzer, Wounded at Beaver Lake, March 20, 1859

There was no wind that day. The gray smoke from the Indians' signal fires nearby drifted upward, straight into the clear morning sky, as if pulled by some invisible magnet.

Sam Bishop studied the smoke with understandable concern. The signals were coming from small hills dangerously close to their trail, and now his men were whispering to one another, discussing their belief that it must be some kind of omen.

Bishop turned in his saddle to look at Hi Jolly, who was riding a mule close to the line of twenty camels, all loaded as pack animals. The animals were moving along peacefully and in silence, as usual. The little Arab smiled back at Bishop as if they shared a secret, something the others knew nothing about.

Before departing Tejon Ranch, Bishop ordered Hi Jolly to select the camels for this journey very carefully. He wanted him to pay special attention to the ones he believed to be the "fastest" and in the best physical condition. And the orders were to pack them with a lighter-than-usual load.

Hi Jolly must have assumed Bishop had a long trip planned before they met Ed Beale. But then, why the emphasis on speed? He'd never indicated that speed was important before.

Everyone, including Hi Jolly, knew Sam Bishop meticulously planned things this way. He was a man who tried to think of different contingencies for every situation. He had learned that process years earlier from Major Savage and the system of thought paid off many times.

Bishop did not expect trouble from the Mojave at such a distance from the Colorado River. He estimated they were still three days from those river valley villages. But the vast desert the team crossed was also visited by several other tribes, some friendly, some not. But they all communicated in some way, including smoke, announcing the arrival of intruders. This time the Indians had something special to broadcast: forty-five white men with wagons were traveling toward the river on the Mojave Trail.

The nomad tribes were too few in number to pose any danger, but their messages would be received by the Mojave days ahead of Bishop's arrival at the Colorado. The direction, exact number of men on the team, animals, wagons; the Mojave had all the information they needed to prepare their defenses or be ready for some serious trading.

But this time trading was not on the Mojave's agenda.

Bishop's team suddenly came to a halt. The Mojave had dug a wide line in the dirt across the road. No one dared cross it without Bishop's permission. They knew the line was clearly a message of warning. They were to proceed no farther.

Sam Bishop sent a letter to the *Los Angeles Southern Vineyard* describing for their readers the situation: "The Indians, he said, were 'warning us not to cross the line on the peril of our lives. On the East of this line they drew in the sand figures representing themselves, and on the West were drawn only a few figures of Americans to represent us, as they have an idea that they far outnumber us. In the breast of each figure representing Americans they stuck an arrow, about one foot of the end of which was colored with blood . . . The twelve arrows sticking in the breasts of the Americans was to show us the fate that awaited us if we cross the line.'"[1]

Bishop went on to remark that when he wrote the letter, his group was "forty miles east of the line and still advancing. They were now close to an oasis known as Pah-Ute Creek, about twenty one miles west of the Colorado" (today, the spelling is often "Piute").

For centuries, the spring had given her waters to travelers before Spanish explorers. The Pah-Ute and other Indians made this oasis a temporary home, but before those people, a prehistoric race pecked messages on the side of large stones, blackened by volcanic activity.

Pah-Ute Creek flows from a spring hidden beneath black and reddish-brown boulders, and appears from a distance like a mirage. It seems its vegetation, willow trees, barrel cactus, cholla, yucca, and creosote bushes, simply should not be there in the barren desert. But eventually the water disappears, swallowed by the desert floor.[2]

At Pah-Ute Creek there was ample water and grass for the Bishop team, so they camped overnight before proceeding to the Colorado. In the morning they began the next twenty-one-mile journey, to Beaver Lake, which sat two miles west of the river.

The lake was over a mile long and in places a few hundred yards wide, filled with sometimes clear, but often greenish water from the Colorado, which continually overflowed its banks in the area. Here, Bishop had been told, was grass for the animals and an abundance of desert willow, mesquite, and a few cottonwood trees, an excellent place to camp and make preparations to cross the river . . . providing the Indians did not have other plans.[3]

On the way to Beaver Lake the party traveled on a well-packed trail descending through a treeless desert. On each flank, stretching for several miles, were sage, desert grass, and yucca, but no large boulders, not even a small hill. As they neared the lake, the trail became heavy with gravel and then began to blend into sandy, clay-like soil.

Samuel Bishop were now almost thirty-four years old, truly an "old man" in the eyes of the young men riding with him. But a life of hard work, especially the previous ten years, had produced a muscular man, small in stature but always big in determination, highly motivated, and like his friend and partner Edward Beale, constantly moving with seemingly endless energy.

Bishop's narrow-slit eyes, accented by dark, bushy brows, added to the impression that he was an older man, preoccupied with deep thoughts. He was creative but not particularly brilliant. His lack of formal education often haunted him, especially when it came to writing. But then again, he was equal to most of his fellows in southern California, who were also self-educated frontiersmen.

His friends and coworkers knew Bishop to be businesslike, calculating with a busy mind, but someone who found it easy to smile and give personal attention to others' needs.

And now Samuel Bishop was leading a strange army of men (with an assortment of weapons but no uniforms) into history and adding a new word to his personal description—fearless.

At 2 P.M. on March 19, 1859, the Bishop party rolled to a halt about five hundred yards west of Beaver Lake.

The lake area appeared at first as it had been described: with many trees, the types one expects in or near a river basin; only the land was much more sandy than reported and the vegetation very dense. Arrow weed, sage, vines, and small cactus were tangled between the trees, making it impossible for Bishop's wagons to pass through to the river except on a few wide trails, which, like fingers, fed into the flat, treeless river bottom for another mile to the river's edge.

Bishop and his men had ignored the warning of the Mojave they had encountered forty-five miles back along the trail. They rolled on into Mojave territory, confident they could overcome any obstacles or problems upon reaching the Colorado. They did not expect what now waited for them two hundred yards away.

A combined force of Mojave, Pah-Ute, and Yuma Indians in an estimated number of over seven hundred blocked their way to Beaver Lake.

From that moment, and over the next few days, the events were recorded and sent to California newspapers by Charles H. Graves of the Central Mail Route party; W. W. Hudson, adventurer and independent news reporter; and Sam Bishop.

The warriors along the flanks moved slowly, quietly toward Bishop's column until one-third of his men were surrounded on both sides. The warriors to the front, believed to be mostly Mojave by their red-and-black-striped body paint, remained three hundred to four hundred feet from the column, out of pistol-shot range and at the very extreme distance for most percussion rifles.

Bishop's men cocked their weapons, preparing for a warrior charge. Tension and breathing was heavy for the next three minutes. Then fifteen warriors stepped from their ranks and walked toward the column.

Bishop had been riding near the rear and now moved forward slowly, attempting not to attract the attention of the warriors until he was in a desired position.

At the front, two men, John Eckhart and Mr. Hoag, rode forward to meet the fifteen Mojave. It is not recorded what was said during the brief meeting. Neither Eckhart nor Hoag spoke Mojave or Pah-Ute, and it is doubtful if the Indians understood more than a few words of English. But by hand gestures, waving, and pointing, one thing was understood: the column must not proceed farther.

By this time Sam Bishop arrived at the front of the column and paused long enough to study the situation. Then he waved his arm and shouted, "Forward!"

The column began to move closer to Beaver Lake and the waiting line of Mojave.

Before the men reached the row of warriors, they came to new lines drawn across the road. Placed on each side was a four-foot-long war club and a shorter one made from the wood of a mesquite tree. To Bishop's men, it resembled a "potato masher." Apparently, this represented a final warning.[4]

Bishop halted the column when he reached the line and, using dramatic movements to capture the Indians' attention, handed his rifle and two revolvers to the men riding next to him.

Then he turned, stood up in his saddle, and shouted, "Boys! I will do everything which is right! We will not submit to anything that is wrong. I did not come here to fight Indians but to meet, as you know, Lieutenant Beale with supplies. You see that water?" He pointed to the lake. "Our mules want water. To that water we shall go, in peace if we can . . . if not, we will fight for it!"⁵

Accompanied by four unarmed men, Bishop rode toward the warriors, indicating in "sign language" that the chief, identified by a costume of feathers, animal skins, and the design of his black-and-red-lined body paint, should set aside his weapons and come close enough to talk.

A few suspenseful moments passed.

Each member of the team understood the odds they were facing. They were outnumbered more than ten to one. If the Indians charged them, perhaps the team might kill two hundred with rifles and revolvers, but there would be no time to reload. Those team members not killed in the initial fight would be taken prisoner. The Mojave's reputation for treating prisoners with no mercy was well known. Each prisoner would be scalped while still alive, then tortured as he roasted to death on a stake.

The chief complied and laid down his clubs. Again using sign language and speaking slowly the few words of California Indian language he knew, Bishop explained that they wanted to camp, then pass peacefully through the Mojave ranks, and cross the river the next morning.

The chief hesitated at first, then, nodding, appeared to give permission, but indicated he wanted some tobacco in return for the favor.

Bishop had purchased a good supply of gifts for the Indians, including tobacco. He handed a few packages to the chief, who, seemingly satisfied, signaled, and the warriors' ranks parted.

The column moved on to the lake's edge, where they set up camp for the night. A heavy guard was established around the perimeter, but few members of Bishop's party slept well.

Bishop recorded his concerns. "Being acquainted with the treachery of Indians I was not fully satisfied that all was right." His suspicions would soon be confirmed.[6]

Early on the morning of March 20, the mules were hitched to the wagons, then four Indians suddenly appeared. They were thought to be more "curious" than spies, and offered to lead the party through the barren flatland to Beale's Crossing.

Bishop realized that this was a trick but decided to go along with the offer and see what the Mojave planned.

They reached the river without incident and the men went to work pumping up an India rubber boat and preparing the inflatable rafts to float the wagons (the same equipment Beale had used a year earlier during his westbound expedition).

Four men rowed the rubber boat across, towing a rope, which they tied to a cottonwood tree on the east bank.

By 10 A.M. the wagons were secured on the rubber floats and ready for the crossing. Then the situation changed.

A few Indians emerged from a grove of trees at the bank and approached Bishop. They demanded some shirts in exchange for permission to cross. Bishop gathered a few of his own shirts and distributed them to the warriors.

The leader of the group, apparently a chief or subchief, indicated by pointing to the east bank and moving his arm in a circle that each warrior must be given a similar gift.

On the opposite bank, four hundred warriors armed with bows and arrows and the usual war clubs waited for a reply. Another group of warriors, estimated to be about two hundred in number, was swimming toward Bishop's men from the east bank.

As expected, the Mojave had no intention of permitting Bishop to enter the river and were only "toying" with the whites.

Bishop indicated that their demands could not be met. He recorded later that they were "not right and unfair."

The negotiating warriors left and joined others still waiting in the grove of trees.

Dividing his men to cross the river would be disastrous and exactly what the Mojave wanted. Bishop decided to retrieve the rope and try something else. John Eckhart and William Pool volunteered to row the rubber raft over and untie the rope.

As they entered the water, the Mojave tried a new tactic. Three young women emerged from the tree grove, walked directly up to Bishop, and began to tug on his arm playfully.

W. W. Horton described the girls as being "very young and very good looking."

The girls giggled and continued to pull Bishop's arm, trying to coax him into following them to the trees and visit with their own chief. But regardless of their true intentions, Bishop was in no mood to be tempted by beautiful girls into anything. He indicated to the girls that he would visit their chief *after* his men crossed the river.

While that conversation continued, Eckhart and Pool reached the east bank, untied the rope, and began paddling as fast as they could. When they were about twenty yards from the bank, arrows rained down, one passing between Eckhart's arm and body. Midway in the river they were safely out of arrow range, but a few had already punctured the rubber boat, which began to deflate and take on water; nevertheless, they reached the west bank unharmed and found the team ready to move out of the area.

Now the warriors on their flanks released arrows that, at first, fell harmlessly. Then one pierced the blanket on the back of a mule, wounding the animal slightly, but none of the camels were hit.

Eighteen-year-old Lewis Amiss Spitzer, like the others, had volunteered to join the expedition, but Bishop initially objected because of his age. The determined young man offered to work for no pay and Bishop finally gave in, remembering his own youthful quest for adventure.

Spitzer became the first human casualty. He was struck in the leg by a Mojave arrow. Though painful, the wound was not serious, and when his friends pulled the arrow shaft from his leg, the hardwood point came with it.[7]

On seeing Spitzer wounded and having survived his own near-death experience on the rubber boat, William Pool decided to take action. He retrieved his new Sharps rifle, took aim on a warrior standing on the bank across the river, and fired. A second or two passed. The warrior, who had been waving his war club, let it drop, and fell backward, dead.

Pool had proven the deadly accuracy of the Sharps rifle. The warrior was almost four hundred yards away when the rifle ball struck and killed him.

Bishop now led the column almost six hundred yards north to another location along the river. Here, he calculated, they had a slight advantage over the Indians and a better chance to cross.

The river was only two hundred yards wide at this point and about three feet deep, but the current, disrupted by two large sandbars, moved at an estimated four miles per hour.

Between the new location and Beale's Crossing was nothing but flat, river-bottom land. To attack, the warriors would have to cross that open country and become easy targets for rifles.

The position of the two sandbars gave Bishop an idea. It might be possible to pull the wagons across rather than try to float them. But first it would have to be determined if the sand was packed firm enough to support the weight of the wagons without them sinking.

This time Bishop himself decided to conduct the investigation. If the plan failed, the team would be trapped in the river, just where the Mojave wanted to catch them. If this happened, the responsibility would have to be his alone.

Another rubber raft was quickly inflated, and Bishop, joined by John Eckhart, rowed toward the opposite bank.

The Mojave, now aware of Bishop's new plan, raced up the east bank and were waiting. Their number had swollen to about 1,500 warriors.

The rubber boat became stuck on the east sandbar.

The Indians recognized a perfect opportunity to attack and rushed toward Bishop and Eckhart, who were frantically trying to free the boat.

Finally, in desperation, Eckhart leaped out and onto the sandbar and began to push the boat, first left, then right, as Bishop paddled backward.

Suddenly the boat broke loose just as arrows began to fall.

The pair made it to the west shore safely. Neither had been wounded, and though a few arrows struck the boat, none punctured its rubber skin. Bishop handed one of his men several arrows, souvenirs of those that fell around them.

The river crossing, at that point, was abandoned, but the area did have an abundance of grass, so Bishop decided to camp there for the night while he thought of another plan. He knew the Indians would not attack that night. If they tried, they would lose too many warriors while crossing open territory. And besides, they had a funeral to attend.

The warrior, killed by Mr. Pool's Sharps rifle, by tradition had to be cremated before dawn. Fires could be seen on the opposite bank, both north and south of the camp.

Early the next morning, March 21, the expedition prepared to withdraw from the river and return to Beaver Lake.

Bishop issued a new statement to his men: "We have done all we can do to convince them that we do not want to fight. And now . . . Boys, prepare to fire your guns! Do not fire unless you think you can kill an Indian! Then, scalp them if you think you can do so!"[8]

And so they started the two-mile dash to the lake followed closely by the Mojave.

By noon, the men were in the process of "corralling the wagons" and placing them in a semicircle while others hastily dug a ditch, tossing the dirt out and forward to form a firing pit or breastworks.

They moved the animals inside the perimeter so they were safe from the Indians and had easy access to the lake water. The firing pit was about ten yards from the lake and averaged four feet in depth. It was almost completed when arrows from different directions began to fall into the camp. One man staggered in shock, an arrow protruding from his chest. He reached up to grab the shaft as his friends stared, unable to speak. The wounded man jerked the arrow out. Lucky for him, a "plug of tobacco" had stopped it from penetrating and saved his life.

Volleys of rifle fire began to take a toll on the Mojave. As the gray-white smoke drifted off, Bishop counted six dead warriors only a few feet from the pit. More dead were scattered in between bushes several yards away.

But the attacks did not stop. The Mojave regrouped and charged again and again, losing more warriors. Often they reached the row of wagons only to be driven off by revolver fire. Bishop reported later that it seemed as if his men were "killing two warriors for every three shots fired." It was not enough. Still the warriors charged and still more died. Gun smoke, after two hours, hung over the camp like a white cloud, affecting visibility in some places.

Then, into the third hour, all became quiet. By late afternoon, the Indians began to carry their dead and wounded from the field and to set fire to bushes and grass behind them as the procession of death returned to their villages.

Bows and arrows had proven no match for the frontiersmen's rifles and revolvers. Even with superior numbers, the Mojave did not come close enough for hand-to-hand combat.

None of Bishop's men was killed and no one except Spitzer was wounded.

Silence fell over Beaver Lake as the sun slowly disappeared. The cold evening wind caused everyone to shiver and wrap themselves with blankets. They waited, weapons reloaded, eyes and ears straining for sounds of the enemy. But no Indians came toward the lake. Bishop's men had won the first battle against an overwhelming force. Yet they knew there were more enemies out there, perhaps at the river.

At dawn, Bishop and a few men rode to the river once more. On the east bank, at least 1,800 warriors were waiting, anxious for revenge.

Discouraged, Bishop returned to the lake. Now that the Indians had burned much of the grass around the lake, Bishop needed a new plan. The camels were content munching on mesquite branches and nearby cactus. They had remained calm during the retreat from the river and through the afternoon battle. But the mules, during the same time, were on the verge of panic. Their eyes were wide with fear and their ears lay back against their heads. The mules would need grass, and soon.

With the air still strangely quiet, the breeze diminished and night came upon them suddenly. Many collapsed into deep sleep only to be awakened for guard duty on the perimeter. Sam Bishop did not sleep well that night. He knew his men would have to withdraw and he wasn't certain of his next course of action.

A warm sun smiled down on Bishop's column the next morning as they retreated west through the desert, up the gradual incline, twenty miles to Pah-Ute Creek.

The men had fought bravely and won a battle, but their mission was not yet accomplished.

By the time they reached Pah-Ute Creek and began to set up camp, Bishop had formulated another plan. He would send messengers to find Major Hoffman and the American army, which he assumed to be somewhere south along the Colorado River, with a request for a detachment, perhaps a small unit, of soldiers to come to their rescue. He did not expect the soldiers to engage the Mojave in combat but simply to protect his men while they crossed the river. Then they could return to Hoffman's main force.

But this idea only brought more worries. Suppose the messenger was killed before reaching the army, or became lost and died in the desert from lack of water. The solution: send *two* messengers. But even if they were successful, would Major Hoffman send troops to help civilians?

Bishop realized that Hoffman held a grudge against Ed Beale over the fact that army camels had remained in possession of civilians, and Hoffman knew that he, Bishop, was a friend of Beale. But surely, an officer in the army would not let personal feelings block a request for rescue . . .

CHAPTER 34

The Charge

It takes much to bring down a charging camel!

Lieutenant Colonel T. E. Lawrence (of Arabia)

Sam Bishop's little army arrived at Pah-Ute Creek as daylight dissolved into a glowing red-and-orange sunset. Both men and mules were exhausted. They had continued from Beaver Lake, almost twenty-two miles, without a pause.

The camels appeared as calm as always, showing no indication of strain from the march, even though they carried packs of at least 250 pounds.

With the help of the remaining minutes of daylight, the men established a primitive camp and a perimeter of defense with guards posted every few yards.

The men rested, then attended to duties, checking for necessary repairs on the wagons, cleaning weapons, and reloading those that were empty.

They felt safe at Pah-Ute Creek, with its unending supply of sweet-tasting water. The Mojave were unlikely to travel so far in any group large enough to attack the camp. Nonetheless, Bishop got the men busy with two projects.

First, a suitable place was selected for a lengthy stay. A small mesa about fifty feet above the creek offered an excellent view of the desert and clear firing in all directions should they need to defend the position. Though the mesa was above the creek, an easy path led down to the water. The men were ordered to ensure that their canteens and water barrels were always full.

By midday on March 23, the next project began: the erecting of a chest-high stone wall, about forty by one hundred feet, to enclose the camp area. One side of the rectangular structure ran along the cliff, which dropped off to the creek below.[1]

While the men were busy with the wall, Bishop did some serious thinking about their mission and the immediate situation. He knew Major Hoffman's army would be facing difficulties moving wagons and troops along the Colorado, but he did not know their exact location or when they might arrive at Beale's Crossing.

Yet Bishop remained convinced that he could get across the river if he had help protecting his men while they crossed. So he began to write a lengthy letter to the army requesting assistance.

He finished the letter early in the morning of March 24 and asked for volunteers to deliver it. From the seven who came forward, he chose two who already had proven to be resourceful, brave, and full of energy: John Eckhart and Isaac (Ike) Renfroe, both twenty years old.

Of course they knew the mission was extremely dangerous. They would have to travel one hundred miles or more in some of the most rugged, rocky areas of the Mojave Desert, through Indian territory, and find the American army. Bishop could only give them an idea of where that army might be.

Eckhart and Renfroe selected good riding mules, filled extra canteens, placed fresh percussion caps on the chambers of their Colt revolvers, packed food rations of dried beef, and within an hour were ready to depart. They could not build a fire along the way: the enemy might see the smoke. So they tied extra blankets behind the saddles, as the nights in the desert in March are still very cold. These two skilled frontiersmen not only understood the risks; they also fully appreciated the importance of their mission. They had no maps, not even a drawing of the part of the desert they were to traverse, and the only information given them was that they should find Hoffman on the east side of the river, moving north, perhaps one hundred miles from Yuma.

The boys shook hands with their friends, Bishop being the last. He handed Eckhart his letter to Major Hoffman and, with a slight smile, wished them "God Speed!"

The boys rode out of camp, heading southwest at 10 A.M., on March 24, 1859. In thirty minutes, they appeared as tiny dots far out in the desert.

Bishop's letter to the army was addressed "To Colonel Hoffman or Captain Burton, or, the Commanding Officer present." It began with details about his group's first meeting with the Mojave at Beaver Lake when he requested permission to cross the Colorado, the Indian demands, and the gifts he gave in compliance to them.

It covered his efforts to cross the river and the Indian attacks and stated that while he believed he had defeated them on the west, the Indians still had a sizable force waiting on the east side. The last paragraph of the letter outlines his request:

I have forty men and as I believe we have whipped them on this side of the river, I think I could do the same on the other, were it possible to cross the river with all my men. But, as I should be under the necessity of dividing my company, as well as having the river, which is one fourth of a mile in width, to obstruct my movements, I think it would be dangerous to attempt without assistance. I am satisfied that 50 men would be ample, knowing as I do, that I could whip them had I not the river to cross. If, therefore, you can with propriety, and in accordance with your duty, or without transcending your official power, you will send to me a detachment of men. Hoping to hear from you soon, I am, Respectfully, your obedient servant.

(Signed) Samuel A. Bishop

After these words, Bishop added in a final line: "WROTE IN A HURRY"[2]

Bishop's men would not be idle during the messengers' absence. He put them to work improving the wagon road in the area, especially an "impassable" incline known as Pah-Ute Hill. This was his second project.

The construction program accomplished two things. First, while doing physical labor, the men were less likely to worry about Renfroe and Eckhart or the results of their mission. Second, the road in the area needed improving anyway.[3]

On March 26, Eckhart and Renfroe managed to survive their journey through the desert and located the American army. It had covered only sixty miles since leaving Fort Yuma.

The army fed the boys and ordered them to rest. But sometime during their short stay, Renfroe's pistol fired an "accidental discharge," the ball striking him in his leg. The wound was serious and prevented him from returning to Bishop's camp.[4]

Renfroe had to remain with the army while his wound healed. Now Eckhart was forced to return alone with Hoffman's answer.

Shortly before departing, Eckhart witnessed a meeting between a few Mojave "chiefs," whom he recognized from his first encounter with the tribe at Beaver Lake, and some army staff officers. It appeared to Eckhart that the chiefs were offering to "make peace" with the army, but it was difficult to know with any certainty because the negotiations were carried on in Spanish, with Captain Henry Burton speaking for the army.

Eckhart's assumption was no doubt correct. The Mojave chiefs present at the army camp had learned a lesson while trying to protect their river. Bows and arrows could not equal the white man's firearms. In hand-to-hand combat, the huge Mojave, being more than a foot taller than the average white man of the time, had an advantage, but the Indians never got close enough to use their war clubs.

The chiefs spoke only for their own villages. Convincing the other chiefs to settle for peace was not going to be easy, and at Beale's Crossing, warriors were still gathering, waiting for the next fight.

Unfortunately, John Eckhart made no maps, nor did he keep a

journal containing any information regarding the route he traveled back to Pah-Ute Creek. Nothing is known of his experiences along the way. The army offered no escort for him and he did not plead for one. But with Hoffman's letter hidden somewhere in his belongings, Eckhart set out alone, arriving at the Pah-Ute camp on April 5. He had traveled more than 150 miles since leaving the army camp.

Eckhart was never promised a bonus, an increase in pay, or any special privilege if he completed his mission. His reward after handing Hoffman's letter to Bishop was a chance to rest and visit with his friends to tell them of his adventures and of Renfroe's accident.

The moment Sam Bishop saw Eckhart approaching the camp alone, with no escort of soldiers, he knew Hoffman's reply was negative.

The army's reply read:

April 2, 1859

Colonel Hoffman directs me to acknowledge your letter of the 25th Ultimo and to say that he expects to be in the Mojave Country in ten or fifteen days. As you represent your party is in no danger he does not think it advisable to detach any portion of his command in advance of him.

(Signed) Lt. Joseph L. Corley,
Adjutant, Colorado Expedition,
Fort Gaston, California

(Hoffman believed they were marching in California, but he was actually on the Arizona side of the river, in New Mexico Territory.)

Bishop doubted that the army would make it to Beale's Crossing by April 17, considering their slow progress thus far. He knew his next course of action if Hoffman's answer came as a negative.

The American army had refused to send fifty troops out of a force of over one thousand. Bishop was, of course, angry, even though the refusal did not come as a total surprise.

From Hoffman's point of view, it would be too risky to divide his force and lose the element of surprise. Fifty soldiers might have difficulty defending themselves once they assisted Bishop at the river. Major Hoffman may have also been suffering from a case of paranoia, since the Mojave drove his units into retreat three months earlier. Now he wanted complete conquest.

Furthermore, the army had recently warned Bishop of the dangers he faced if he entered the Colorado River territory. Regardless of Hoffman's reasoning, whether it was based on military strategy and/or a personal grudge, the citizens of the Southwest became outraged when they learned of the army's refusal to assist civilians, including Bishop.

Charles H. Graves of the Central Mail Route party reported the rejection of Hoffman to the Los Angeles *Southern Vineyard* on April 12, 1859, in a sarcastic tone. The article read in part, "When our express, which has been sent to Col. Hoffman came back without any satisfactory news from him, he having only seven Companies of soldiers and 200 civilian workers . . . it appearing he did not deem it safe to divide his command. Mr. Bishop took 20 men from his grand force of 43 men and went forth like a true American to clear the road for what is called the American Army!"[5]

Of Sam Bishop, Graves concluded, "Mr. Bishop is a bold, daring, and a prudent man, never asking any man to go where he would not go himself."

Dr. William Floyd, on Ed Beale's westbound road-building expedition, learned later of Major Hoffman's refusal to help Bishop and recorded an emotional opinion in his journal on April 18, 1859: "There is disappointment, I think, on the part of the officers of the Army. One of the things, bleeding Uncle Sam[,] they are now doing, and most lavish. Congress had better disband the Army, dismiss all Indian Agents, and let keeping the Indians quiet by contractors. The life of no citizen is protected by the Army and the death of none has been avenged by it."

At their camp on Pah-Ute Creek, Sam Bishop calculated that

Hoffman's army might not arrive for another twenty to twenty-five days. He could not wait that long. Each day gave the Mojave more time to reorganize and recruit warriors from other tribes.

Bishop set his new plan, one he had contemplated for some time, into action.

He ordered all the supplies unloaded and informed the men that the wagons were to be sent back empty to Tejon Ranch.

Most of the food would be buried inside the walls of the camp except for a small amount, which was to be repacked and loaded onto several mules.

Bishop then announced that he needed twenty-three volunteers who were willing to risk their lives for another dangerous mission. Three men would stay at the camp as "guards," but twenty must ride with him, on camels, and attempt once more to cross the river. Those remaining were to return with empty wagons and extra mules to the ranch.

Practically every member of the party volunteered to ride with Bishop. From those, he chose twenty-three.

He appointed his wagon master, Robert Wilson, as commander of the convoy returning to the ranch and Mr. Chambers, his "clerk," as second in command, to take charge should Wilson become unable to perform his duties.

Riding with the wagon convoy back to "civilization" were W. W. Hudson, bearing his historic reports for the *Southern Vineyard* that he titled "Mr. Bishop's Journey to the Colorado," and Charles H. Graves of the Central Mail Route Company, with his narrative of their "adventure."

These men knew Bishop planned to "clear the road," break through the Mojave lines, and cross the Colorado at a place called Aubry's Crossing. That crossing was apparently known to Bishop, but he wasn't certain of its exact location. And just how Bishop planned to accomplish all this with only twenty men remained his secret.

All the men assisted in the digging of trenches inside the stone walls and buried the bulk of supplies, leaving that which Bishop's mules would carry and the rations required by the three guards for a few weeks' survival.

About 1,700 pounds of bacon, 2,700 pounds of flour, 600 pounds of beans, 200 pounds of coffee, along with tobacco, dried beef, rice, pepper, mustard, ginger, sugar, and soap were covered by a few feet of desert soil. These supplies would sustain Ed Beale's expedition until they reached either the ranch or Fort Tejon.[6]

The guards were to stand watch over the cache until either Bishop returned or Beale's work crew arrived. For protection, the guards were given extra rifles and ammunition.

Shortly after 1 A.M. on April 7, 1859, they shook hands and bade one another "good luck." Then the wagon convoy headed west into the darkness.

A few minutes later, Bishop's twenty men mounted camels and, leading the pack mules, started east for Beaver Lake. At this point none had any idea of what Bishop planned.

After traveling about ten miles, Bishop called a halt to give men and animals a rest. He was uncertain of what awaited them at the lake or between their current location and the river. This seemed a perfect time to reveal his plan and give anyone with a "change of heart" the opportunity to ride west and join the wagon convoy back to civilization.

He promised that those deciding to return would receive full pay and never be criticized for their decision.

He told them his plan in cold, hard detail and all twenty men elected to remain.

Perhaps devotion to Sam Bishop, combined with youthful desire for adventure, were the deciding factors. But some felt strongly that they had an obligation to Edward Beale and his road-building crew. And then they also believed it to be basically wrong for the Mojave to have denied them the right to cross the river when they requested nothing more.

Bishop reported that a light, balmy breeze carried the sweet aroma of sage and creosote during that hour in the darkness as his men listened to his plan. Success, he told them, depended on "shock." The Mojave had seen camels before, but they knew them only as slow-moving pack animals used by the white men. What the Indians did not know was how fast a camel could run with only the weight of a rider on his back. This was the basis of the surprise and, hopefully, the shock he counted on for success.

He reminded the men that they were outnumbered at least "fifty to one" and emphasized it would be impossible to reload rifles or pistols while riding a running camel.

Hi Jolly and Greek George were standing together talking softly with a Chowchilla Indian who had also volunteered to remain with Bishop. The conversation was a garbled mixture of English, Spanish, Greek, and a few words in Gabriel's language. No one but the three of them understood any of it, but they assured Bishop that the camels were in excellent condition. Unlike mules, which are unpredictable and often difficult to control if excited, they knew the camels would remain together and perform exactly as Bishop directed.

Then they all mounted and rode on without speaking, arriving at the western edge of Beaver Lake about 6:30 A.M.

They were given another rest, but during that time it was necessary to conduct a final check of weapons and saddles.

As dawn brought a dim glow of light to the river valley, the group got their first glimpse of what lay ahead. An estimated five hundred warriors, expecting Bishop's arrival, had crossed the river from the east side before daylight and were now moving directly toward the lake. They had already traveled a mile in the darkness over the barren, sandy floodplain.

At Beaver Lake, hidden among mesquite, willow trees, and long-stemmed arrow weed, Samuel A. Bishop, California rancher, and his men waited.

Bishop's narrow eyes squinted in the dim light as he studied the advancing warriors. He seemed calm, confident, as he watched the enemy lines moving closer in a tight formation, four hundred yards wide, blocking the trail to the river.

He moved his little army to the edge of the underbrush so the camels would have a clear field in which to run, without having to dodge the trees. Then he ordered the men to dismount and gather near him for final instructions.

Bishop faced his men. In reality, most were not yet men but "beardless boys," tough sons of pioneers who journeyed to southern California to search for gold or work the land as farmers. None wore a uniform because no one belonged to the military. None even had prior military training. They were all civilians, but they were experts with their weapons. Survival in the wilderness demanded that proficiency.

The camels were resting in their kneeling position, waiting for a command, content after enjoying a snack of fresh, young mesquite leaves.

Hi Jolly moved around one camel, whispering something in Arabic in his ear while gently stroking the long, massive neck. Then he moved to the next camel and then the next, until he had spoken to each one.

Sam Bishop's eyes searched the youthful faces of his little army. They reflected no fear in the early morning light, only excitement and admiration for their leader. Surely they must have wondered how twenty boys and an old rancher could defeat hundreds of Mojave warriors. Would they be successful? Would any of them survive?

"Boys," Bishop began, "I have told you the Army refused my request for help. Not even a detachment of dragoons can they spare. As Americans we understand that the government cannot always come to the rescue. As citizens we understand we must sometimes fight alone for our survival. Your fathers knew that and you shall know it too."

Bishop paused, waiting for a comment on his words. Silence. Everyone's eyes were fixed on him.

"A few days ago," he continued, "I said we did not come here to fight Indians. But, they deny us the right to cross the river! They sent arrows in reply to our gifts! By treachery, they tried to wipe us out!"[7]

Bishop turned and nodded to Hi Jolly. The little Arab returned the nod. The camels were ready.

"Mount!" Bishop shouted as he climbed into the saddle of Seid, Ed Beale's favorite white camel.

Hi Jolly mounted the camel next to Bishop, then, when everyone was in their saddles, he barked a sharp command. The camels rose to a stand, grumbling and growling as they often did before a movement.

Hi Jolly spoke again and the camels moved into four rows, five in each row, side by side, six feet apart.

Then the camels became quiet, holding their heads high, awaiting another order.

Bishop turned to his men. "You see that river?" The soft-spoken man's voice became a shout as he drew a revolver and pointed it toward the Colorado. "To that water we shall go. As before, we will fight for the right to cross! Prepare yourselves! We will charge directly through their lines!"

Then he faced the advancing warriors. They were five hundred yards away. He glanced over his shoulder and yelled his last order: "Make every shot count, boys! To the river! NOW!"

Seid sprang forward. The front row of camels quickly followed. They broke free of the tree line and entered the flatland.

Then, two seconds later, the next line chased after the first, and then the next, until all four lines were in the open, followed by the mules.

The camel charge had begun.

If the riders felt any fear, it must have instantly disappeared, replaced with the thrill of speed. They had never traveled so fast before.

The Mojave at first would have seen what appeared to be a wave of dust rushing toward them.

The camels were now at top speed, over forty miles an hour, and holding their pace steady, rapidly closing on the enemy.

Three hundred yards!

The boys' shouts were muffled by the pounding of hoofbeats on the soft, dry earth.

Two hundred yards . . . one hundred yards.

The camels' long strides made them appear as if they were floating gracefully above the ground.

Fifty yards.

Now the Mojave clearly saw men riding large animals charging at them. Some warriors, clutching their weapons, began to run like startled rabbits, darting in different directions.

Then the cracking sounds of pistol shots cut through the yells.

Suddenly the camels smashed into the Mojave's formation. Warriors leaped aside to avoid being trampled.

In moments, except for the yells, screams, and dust, it was over. The camels had easily sliced through the Mojave's lines. Bishop shot a glance over each shoulder. All the camels had a rider. None of the men had fallen.

Two hundred yards from the river, Bishop turned Seid to the left. The others followed. Then they began to race parallel to the river, heading north, leaving the Mojave far behind.

CHAPTER 35

The End of the Mojave

I have the honor to inform you that I have, at their ear-
nest solicitation, made peace this day with the Mojaves.
They wanted a good whipping, which they got.

Captain Lewis A. Armistead, Fort Mojave, August 31, 1859

Ed Beale arrived in Albuquerque during the first week of March 1859 and became deeply disturbed as he learned of the details of the Mojave attack on the Rose wagon train seven months earlier. The possibility of such a massacre had worried him for over a year after he first encountered the Mojave and recommended to the secretary of war that the army establish an outpost at his "crossing" on the Colorado.

Of course, Beale could not be blamed for the civilians' decision to take chances in the wilderness and test his road. Nonetheless, he felt he bore some responsibility for the disaster. He also puzzled over another thought: what changed a happy race of people in the river valley into murderers? At the time Beale had no knowledge of the Mormon visits to the Mojave villages and the trouble they may have created.

During the winter of 1858–1859, the Rose family moved to Santa Fe and opened a business, but the families of John Udell and the Hedgespeths remained in Albuquerque (a place Udell called "unpleasant, half-civilized, half-savage"), surviving with the help and generosity of local citizens and a variety of small "paying" jobs furnished by the army.[1]

In sympathy for what the families endured on "his" wagon road, Beale felt compelled to assist in some way. He offered the emigrants the opportunity to join his huge convoy and travel under his protection to California.

Beale provided, at his own expense, wagons, mules, and the necessary supplies to complete the journey. The families accepted the generous offer and the combined train rolled out of Albuquerque on March 8, 1859.

During the next ten days, the weather was cold and windy, with temperatures below freezing at night. Road construction slowed but did not stop.

Beale had purchased an ample supply of food for their journey, which would be supplemented with wild game killed by the two Indian hunters he had hired for that purpose. "Delaware Dick" and Dick's friend Little Ax provided a variety of game, including beaver, antelope, and deer, depending on the abundance of each near a campsite.

Occasionally Beale was tempted to do a little hunting himself, almost always accompanied by Absalom. He recorded in his journal on March 14, "I remained behind with my Negro servant, Absalom, to kill ducks which abound here. We killed some sixty to eighty-five canvas back, red-head, mallard, and spring tail." Everyone enjoyed roasted duck that evening.

On April 16, some of the men worked on a hillside, changing the route slightly to offer a "better grade," but mostly they followed Beale's westbound trail of 1857.

With picks and shovels, rakes and ropes, they moved rocks and boulders, leveling here and grading there, often lining the trail with stones to guide future emigrants.

During a morning of misty rain, they worked their way out of a forest and, with the snowcapped San Francisco Mountains to their backs, entered a prairie five miles wide and fifteen miles long. Near the trail they located a new spring. "I determined to improve it," wrote

Beale, "and therefore camped for the day and put all the hands to work to dig it out."

The next morning dawned clear with the temperature mild and pleasant. After breakfast the men continued to work on the spring. At midmorning Beale was startled by his men shouting. They were pointing and waving toward the west.

Two men rode toward them, appearing only as dark spots in the distance. When they came closer Beale could see they were riding camels. One man with a barrel chest was leaning forward, clinging to the neck of a huge white camel. He waved his hat and shouted something to Beale.

Behind them followed more men on camels. Beale counted ten, fifteen, and then twenty. Finally he could see them clearly. Sam Bishop riding Seid, flanked by Hi Jolly and followed by his little army of young men—all were waving as they rushed into the cheering crew of workers.

Bishop had traveled fourteen days since leaving Pah-Ute Creek and covered 290 miles of rugged desert.

There is no record of how many Indians were killed during the camel charge, perhaps none. Bishop planned the charge to shock the Mojave and break through their formation, not necessarily to kill warriors. Even though most men fired their revolvers until they were empty, it is doubtful their shots struck anyone. None of the boys had practice or experience shooting from the back of a fast-running camel.

All the men were given the day to celebrate. Work was halted so they could exchange stories. During this time, it became apparent to Beale that the first camel charge in American history had been successfully conducted by civilians, not by the military. He reported, "Once again, I was proud to be an American. All of Bishop's boys were from so many different ethnic backgrounds."

Beale was also relieved to know that his clerk, F. C. Kerlin, had made it through safely to Los Angeles.

And so, as the hours faded into darkness, the stories of Pah-Ute

Creek, Beaver Lake, and the battles continued. No one gave a thought to the fact that the great adventure at the Colorado might have been the last camel charge in America.

On April 18, Beale recorded in his journal, "Looking down the valley I saw two men approaching rapidly on dromedaries; I recognized at once the white Egyptian dromedary, my old friend from last year [Seid]. As they came nearer I saw that one of the men was S.A. Bishop, esq. And the other, Ali Hadji, who accompanied me on my former expedition."

Beale never forgot that his journals would be read by members of Congress as well as staff at the War Department. He went on to relate some of Bishop's experiences at the river. "[The Indians] immediately attacked him but did not calculate on the character of the men he had or the deadly efficiency of the frontier rifles in the hands of frontier men."[2]

Then Beale explained how he saved the U.S. Mail: "The mail was brought on *my* camels and delivered to the agent, Mr. Smith who was traveling with my party . . . Thus the first mail of the 35th parallel was brought on *my* camels both ways" (italics added).[3]

His last entry in the journal that day: "Little Ax killed two antelope and the Delaware, a deer."

Ed Beale was so pleased to see his camels again that he wrote on April 20, "Our camels with their solemn faces make our camp look like old times again."

Then it was construction work, as usual, with Beale rerouting the road occasionally to keep it close to valuable water sources.

Soon signs of Indians were everywhere: tracks in the dirt and smoke signals rising from nearby hills. A mule was stolen one night and another killed by arrows. The next night two more were stampeded from the herd.

Beale had been pushed to his limits and his temper flared. He ordered a few men to lie in ambush near the dead mule while the train rolled on. At dawn several Indians appeared, ready to butcher the mule and carry it off.

Beale recorded, "Our party fell upon them and killed four, returning to camp bringing bows, arrows, and scalps as vouchers."[4]

On April 30, 1859, the road crew crossed through the mountains on the east side of the Colorado River.

Not knowing the result of the conflict between Major Hoffman and the Mojave, Beale planned for combat. All the men were ordered to check their weapons, but he decided to take only a small force on a "reconnaissance" mission.

He recorded that day, "Preparing for a descent on the Mojave. All hands getting ready their arms. I shall take with me 35 men and three days provisions on three camels. The men will go on foot so that we will not be encumbered with mules to guard while we are fighting. As for the camels, they require no guarding as they will feed well, tied to a bush."

The camels by now had a reputation for remaining calm during combat. But they often ate the bush they were tied to.

Meanwhile, Udell discovered the remains of the wagons his party was forced to leave behind the year before. All had been burned and various iron parts lay where they fell during the fire. As depressing as the scene may have been, the emigrants remained composed. They were grateful to have survived.

Within minutes after arriving at the river's edge, Beale's men spotted a few Mojave and had them in their rifle sights when they heard a clear command, "Hold your fire!" Someone noticed white men walking with the Mojave.

The riflemen were surprised and somewhat disappointed. The opportunity for revenge had been snatched away by Major Hoffman's army.

Sam Bishop calculated correctly while he waited at Pah-Ute Creek: Hoffman did not arrive at Beale's Crossing until April 20. By that time Bishop and his boys had already joined Beale near the San Francisco Mountains.

At least Hoffman's idea of impressing the Mojave with the size of his army was successful. Armed men on the steamboat *General Jesup* and hundreds of troops blocking the southern entrance to their nation was enough to convince the Mojave chiefs to surrender without a fight.

A meeting to discuss the surrender terms was held on April 23, 1859, with Captain Henry S. Burton, using the Spanish he learned from his wife, supervising the translation. Spanish was only part of the process. The Mojave understood a few words of the language, but everything had to be translated into Yuma and then back into Mojave by a Yuma Indian.

The terms for peace were fair and simple but it is unlikely that the meaning of Hoffman's demands were completely understood. Perhaps the details made little difference at the moment because both sides were ready for peace. The soldiers wanted to return home and the Mojave would welcome their departure. Of course, things could never be that simple.

The Mojave were told that in the future, they had to offer "no objections or restrictions" to a military post in their territory and "whites traveling through must not be molested."

The Indians were required to provide "hostages," one from each of six tribes along with the chief who was in command at the attack on Hoffman's unit during his January reconnaissance. The Mojave agreed and the hostages were transported to the Fort Yuma prison compound on the *General Jesup*.

A few days later, Major Hoffman, convinced he had settled all the problems in Mojave territory, departed Beale's Crossing with most of his army. He left behind two companies of Sixth Infantry under the command of Captain Lewis Addison Armistead and Captain Richard Brooke Garnett along with Captain Burton and the unit of Third Artillery. They were to build and occupy a fort on a plateau overlooking Beale's Crossing, in the middle of Mojave territory.

At first the new post was called Camp Colorado, but soon the name was changed to Fort Mojave.

In the beginning, spirits were high and the men set about assembling their fort using materials available in the area: cottonwood, willow, mesquite trees, mud, stones, and reeds from the river's edge. They purchased corn, pumpkins, and grain from the Mojave, but soon food and other supplies ran short.

An odd event occurred either during Major Hoffman's short stay along the river or in the early days of his unit's departure for Los Angeles. Most of the food hidden by Bishop's men at Pah-Ute Creek disappeared. Suspicion fell on some of Hoffman's soldiers, who were accused of digging up the cache and stealing food for their own use and/or for trade or selling to other hungry soldiers.

Naturally, Beale and Bishop were furious when they learned of the theft. They depended on the food being available for the work crews, who still had two hundred miles of construction to complete through the Mojave Desert to Los Angeles.

In a letter written on May 13, 1859, Ed Beale blasted Major Hoffman, reminding him that an "important public work is greatly delayed" by the disappearance of the supplies. And, if Hoffman was not going to be moved by that detail, Beale reminded him that the work on the wagon road was being done in a way that was "agreeable to the instructions of the Secretary of War."

The mention of Hoffman's overall commander, the secretary of war, captured the major's attention. Investigations, a hearing, letters, and finally military court-martials followed. Beale was eventually reimbursed for part of the loss he'd sustained at Pah-Ute Creek.

Meanwhile, as the debates over Beale's lost supplies got under way, Hi Jolly and Greek George returned with the twenty camels to Tejon Ranch.

Thanks to Beale's compassion and generosity, the emigrants who joined his train in New Mexico made it safely into California.

After a short vacation with his family, Sam Bishop joined Ed Beale for a journey east along the wagon trail. Only a few camels traveled with them this time.

This was Beale's fourth journey cross-country along the thirty-fifth parallel, but it was Bishop's first trip east since his emigration to California ten years earlier.

Accompanying them would be Absalom Reading, hunters Delaware Dick and Little Ax, clerk Frederick E. Kerlin, and forty to fifty men who wanted to work their way east, and home.

Beale and his team crossed the Colorado on June 29, 1859, and began to put some finishing touches on the wagon trail. Most of the road was now ready for emigrant wagons, but Beale would reroute it slightly to make it pass near springs or simply to improve "accessibility."

They arrived at Albuquerque on July 30, proving they could make the trip from the Colorado in only one month.

Sam Bishop, the camels, and a few men returned by the road to Tejon Ranch while Beale and the others continued east. Again, Beale presented a journal recounting his voyage to the secretary of war.

Sam Bishop, at Tejon, reverted to ranching, never again to ride camels in combat. His charge at Beale's Crossing was the last.

While Beale and his team were working their way east, things did not remain peaceful along the Colorado.

Apparently not understanding how long they were to be held as hostages, the Mojave at Fort Yuma broke out of prison and attempted to return to their villages. One was quickly killed by guards; the others evaded capture for a few minutes. Five more Mojave were shot dead, but four escaped and disappeared into the desert.

Major Armistead's men were still busy at Fort Mojave erecting shelters of logs and sticks to protect themselves from the scorching summer sun when they received news of the prison break at Yuma.

Trouble continued through July 1859 as various groups of Mojave warriors raided outposts and security details. In early August, Armistead, with a force of twenty-five soldiers and twenty-five more "in reserve," engaged the warriors in a battle several miles south of the new fort.

The victory went to Armistead's riflemen, who suffered a few minor wounds but none of whom was killed. It was, however, a major defeat for the Mojave, who lost more than fifty killed and at least that many seriously wounded.

Over the next few weeks Armistead continued an aggressive campaign to show the Indians the strength of the U.S. Army. Lodges were burned and crops destroyed. On August 31, the Mojave finally gave in, agreeing to live in peace. They, as an organized tribe, would never fight the white man again.

Far from the Colorado River in Arlington, Virginia, Colonel Robert E. Lee was on leave from the Texas Second Cavalry and enjoying a visit with his family. He suddenly found himself back on active duty.

Lee was advised that the country had an emergency close by and was given a temporary command of a detachment of U.S. Marines. They were ordered to march to Harpers Ferry, where, on Saturday night, October 16, 1859, abolitionist John Brown, his sons, and several followers seized an arsenal containing one hundred thousand rifles.

With these weapons Brown planned to arm slaves, who, according to his dream, would revolt and follow him to freedom.

The plan did not go well for Brown. Lee and the marines quickly defeated him and his men. Brown stood trial for treason, not against the United States, but against the Commonwealth of Virginia, and was hanged for the crime on December 2, 1859.

At the same time, back in California, the camels on Beale's Tejon Ranch were moved to a new home. Their lives drastically changed.

CHAPTER 36

Camels vs. Mules

The superiority of the camel for military purposes in the
badly watered sections of the country seems to me to be
established.

Lieutenant Edward L. Hartz, 1859 Report from Big Bend
Country, Texas

The Chihuahuan Desert, one of the three great warm deserts of the
United States, covers a vast area in southern New Mexico, southeastern
Arizona, and West Texas. It is higher in elevation than the Mojave or
Sonoran deserts; consequently, it has a slightly milder climate (though
soldiers stationed there during the mid-1850s might not have agreed.
To them, if the temperature was over 105 degrees, it was hot!).

The Chihuahuan was the hunting ground for the Apache, Kiowa,
and Comanche, who traveled ancient trails, crossing the desolate country and the Rio Grande into Mexico to raid ranches and villages and
steal cattle, horses, women, and weapons.

White emigrants came to the Pecos River Valley of Texas in the
mid-1800s, and Indian attacks on them became so frequent that the
U.S. Army was forced to take action.

In August 1855, Camp Lancaster was established as one of a series
of forts erected on the West Texas frontier. Originally the camp was
nothing more than portable shelters of canvas, offering little protection
from the weather and none during Indian attacks.

But by 1857, Lancaster, then officially a fort, possessed permanent buildings of adobe and stone. It also acquired a new army lieutenant from Pottsville, Pennsylvania, West Point graduate Edward L. Hartz.

West Point, at the time, offered very little education on "modern" military tactics for fighting Indians. The school's focus was on history, engineering, physics, languages, and math. Tactics for the "wild frontier" were left to the imagination of each officer. And so it would be for Lieutenant Hartz, who had a number of ideas on how to deal with the "Indian problem."

Though Hartz was not remembered as an especially bright student at West Point, he did have a reputation for finding unusual solutions to problems. Today we would say he seldom "went by the book."

Chasing Indians on foot or riding mules, the Texas Rangers already knew, was useless and dangerous. Indian ponies outran everything and warriors disappeared into the canyons and hills. Lieutenant Hartz believed the Indians must be lured into traps, not chased through the country, which had been their home for centuries.

He devised a plan that was used several times in the West and reenacted by Hollywood actors in films one hundred years later.

The first attempt to put the plan into practice came on a warm June morning in 1857. Hartz rode out of Fort Lancaster with only a few soldiers, who were being sent to guard what appeared to be a convoy of supply wagons. He planned for the wagons to be a tempting target for any Indian war party.

On June 24, the lieutenant noticed that he and his men were being followed by Indian scouts who had been waiting for the convoy to reach a distance from the fort where it would be difficult, perhaps impossible, for army reinforcements to arrive in time if an attack came. At forty-five miles from Fort Lancaster, the convoy reached such a point.

The scouts were joined by a raiding party of over fifty warriors. The combined force rode directly toward the convoy. Then, with yells, they started their charge and rode into a trap.

The covered wagons were not loaded with supplies; what they contained instead was four companies of infantry. The soldiers waited until the Indians were in close range, then tossed off the canvas and began firing their rifles. Twelve warriors were killed instantly. Several others, wounded, fell from their ponies during the retreat.

This tactic would be tried many times from Texas to Arizona over the next three decades.

Hartz wrote to his father expressing sadness that it was necessary to kill so many people in the effort to bring peace to West Texas, but at the same time confessed joy in the "excitement, adventure, and constant novelty of active campaigning as compared to office and garrison duty."[1]

In early 1859, while Major Hoffman and Sam Bishop were facing problems with the Mojave along the Colorado River, the U.S. Army headquarters in Texas had a new project in mind, one that required the service of an officer of unusual abilities and Indian-fighting experience. Lieutenant Ed Hartz was selected to undertake the mission.

North of San Antonio, at Camp Verde, the army camels had enjoyed a somewhat easy life for two years. They and their offspring were the animals that Ed Beale had not chosen to use when he passed through with his thirty-fifth parallel road-building crew in 1857. The Texas camels, as they had become known in some parts, were used for a number of minor experiments, hauling supplies between nearby towns. But now the army had decided to test these camels in addressing the Indian problem in West Texas.

The time had come to confirm the dependability and durability of the camels in military actions. By army thinking, this should be done in one of the most arid and rugged parts of the country: the Texas Big Bend section of the Chihuahuan Desert.

On April 26, 1859, the U.S. quartermaster general sent a lengthy letter of instruction to his officers in San Antonio regarding a new expedition the War Department wanted to undertake. Apparently, the army brass in Washington had studied the reports of both Edward Beale and Major Henry C. Wayne and concluded that they needed to take the camel experiment a step further. Camels were to be tested against army mules to decide which was superior for military transportation of supplies and troops in the desert.

A number of factors played a part in the quartermaster's decision at that particular time. First, of course, was convenience: camels were already in Texas and a desert was nearby.

Next, the army's role in the Mormon conflict was winding down. All-out war had been avoided and the War Department could now focus its efforts on preventing Indian raids on emigrants and settlers in the West. The needs of officers like Lieutenant Hartz were finally going to receive some attention.

The army seldom begins an experiment with only one objective. True, they needed to know how well camels would perform in the Texas desert, but there was to be another purpose for the new experiment, soon to be called "the Expedition for Topographical Reconnaissance." The army believed they needed to build a new fort along the Rio Grande in the Big Bend section of Texas.

To accomplish this, they had to have good maps and trails to support a fort. Trails existed, but they were the ones used by Indians to raid Mexico. Few white men had traveled those routes, and no maps that were suitable for military use were available at the time.

Lieutenant Edward L. Hartz, acting quartermaster of the Eighth Infantry in San Antonio, was advised in the April 26 letter from Washington that twenty-four camels, twenty-four mules, and "a conductor and six drivers" would be detailed to him for a trial of the camels' "capabilities and usefulness as a means of transportation for military purposes."[2]

The letter formally stated that the "camels must not lack for anything which may tend to their thorough efficiency." It even speculated on the amount of weight the camels were to carry and when the baggage should be lightened.

Mules were to be "adjuncts" and have their "efficiency compared with that of camels."

Hartz was also ordered to be fair and good to the civilian camel drivers. Specifically, the letter read, "Let the camel drivers be treated kindly." (Neither the quartermaster's letter nor Hartz's report indicated if the drivers were to be American or "Arab.")

Lieutenant Hartz was not a mapmaker but a tough Indian fighter who was the perfect choice to command an army escort for the twenty-five-year-old topographical engineer Lieutenant William H. Echols, who had already proven his efficiency in drawing accurate, detailed maps of part of Texas for the army.

In many ways Echols, a quiet "southern gentleman," was very different in personality and cultural background from the combat-hardened northerner Hartz. Despite their differences, though, the two young officers formed a friendship, based in part on their military assignment, and set about preparing to follow their orders.

Fortunately, they both believed camels to be interesting creatures and recognized the superior qualities mentioned in Beale's and Wayne's reports, which they were given to study before the expedition began.

On May 18, 1859, Lieutenant Ed Hartz began his "diary," which later became his official report to headquarters. He wrote on the cover letter of this report, "The details are written as they appear at the time, without the coloring of afterthought or well-digested considerations."[3]

He first noted that one of the camels arrived at San Antonio with a foot wound (from stepping on a large nail) and would be left behind at Fort Hudson.

Originally, the camels were herded on hillsides where there was an abundance of grass for grazing. But they showed no interest in grass once they discovered the variety of bushes, hackberry, daisies, wild grapevines, thistles, and "many other plants the names of which are not known to me," reported Hartz.

At night the camels were ordered by their keepers to lie down in a circle, four camels tied to one "picket." They remained in this position until released for morning grazing.

Hartz claimed that the camels "afforded no trouble as compared to mules which were wild and unbroken. The mules were not only difficult to manage, but were even dangerous."

The expedition drew food rations for eighteen days and loaded the camels, five hundred pounds on the males, three to four hundred pounds on the females (in addition to their sixty-pound saddles). Of course, their loads would diminish as the trip progressed.

From the beginning they experienced problems with loose packs falling from the camels. This problem was partially blamed on the inexperience of the packers, but the design of the saddle had much to do with it.

On May 24, 1859, the expedition crossed the San Pedro River and entered what Hartz called "a dense jungle" (actually, a wooded area with vines and thick underbrush). Here, the trail was broken with large rocks and washed-out ravines.

The next day, Hartz recorded a description of the territory and made an observation regarding the foot of the camel: "Traversing for several miles a succession of steep hillsides and rocky ravines; ascending and descending the mesas, encountering the ledges or shelves of limestone, the outcropping of which constitutes a series of regular stratifications rising like terraces, one above another, often several feet in height; the sharp and angular fragments so thickly strewn over the service, and from which I anticipated much injury to the feet of the camel, produced no apparent effect."

This report is contrary to many others that were made in different parts of the country that claimed that sharp stones caused the camel to experience foot problems. In some cases this undoubtedly was true, but it did not appear to be a problem on the Hartz expedition. He went on to observe, "Mules and horses, unshod, cannot tread for any considerable time over such a surface without becoming lame. In this fact we find an advantage in the camel over mules and horses."

For the next eighteen miles, the camel packs continued to be a problem, but supplying food for the animals was not. They ate "almost every bush and herb in the immediate vicinity of the camp."

On May 27, following a "general westerly direction," the expedition entered a desolate area of narrow canyons, which Hartz labeled "this miserable country."

That day they covered twenty-five miles between the Pecos and San Pedro rivers without finding water. Then, on the following day, they resorted to emergency supplies.

The days were hot, with temperatures above one hundred degrees and high humidity, but the camels with their loads showed no signs of fatigue. The horses and mules, though, were "suffering."

Scouting parties sent to find water returned with reports that the Pecos River was near, but that hills, several hundred feet high, had to be crossed to get there. The expedition finally reached the river, where the men, mules, and horses "went wild and uncontrollable," but the camels, having traveled two and a half days and seventy-five miles with no water, "took turns peacefully drinking."

Then it was time to cross the river, which did not please the camels at all. But it turned out that it was not the water but the steep, slippery banks that alarmed them. The men solved this problem by throwing a little water in their faces and slowly leading them down the inclines into the river. Then, holding their heads high, the camels swam across with no difficulty.

A similar problem occurred on a slippery rock trail. One of the male camels stumbled and fell. He suffered no injury and, once relieved of his five-hundred-pound pack, continued up the hill. The men learned that the smaller females, carrying lighter loads of three hundred pounds, climbed without difficulty.

In early June, the expedition measured the angle of different hills they climbed and found that camels carrying four to six hundred pounds could climb a twenty-three-degree slope "with the greatest ease whereas mules pulling a loaded wagon would find difficulty going over anything above 8 degrees."

The expedition marched into Fort Lancaster on June 6 and reported that the normal walking pace of the camel had been about three miles per hour, the same as an average infantryman.

They rested at the fort several days, during which time Lieutenant Hartz expressed concern that the male camels held "belligerent feelings towards each other." He recommended special care and attention be given the males to be sure they were separated from one another as often as possible.

On June 15, Lieutenant Hartz was joined by Lieutenant William Echols to officially begin a "reconnaissance." Since they planned to cover over twenty-four miles a day, the camels' packs were lightened to about 250 pounds.

Once they got under way, they covered thirty miles a day, often marching into the evening. Then they discovered something no one had reported before: that camels can see in the dark at least as well as men and horses.

But after a few days in the intense heat, the horses and mules began to "show signs of failing" even though they had been given five quarts of water a day.

On June 23, after covering thirty-six miles without water, a female camel was bitten by a rattlesnake while grazing near the camp. The wound was immediately cut and liquid ammonia, one of the accepted treatments for snakebite at the time, was rubbed into it.

The men guessed that the animal would be dead by dawn, for they were certain the venom had entered its bloodstream and was working its way to the heart. But around midnight, Lieutenant Hartz examined the wound and found something strange. There was no swelling around the puncture marks and the camel was up and moving about, using her leg in a normal way. The wound area had practically healed.

The camel's rapid recovery remained a puzzle to all the men. Apparently, her body had rejected the poison, leading Hartz to speculate in his report that "maybe camels are immune to American rattlesnake bites." (This is a theory that to this day has never been proven or disproven.)

On June 26, one horse died during the night from exhaustion and lack of water. The remaining horses and mules were nearly exhausted, but the camels, Echols reported, appeared "strong and vigorous."

Echols's report for the twenty-sixth went on to read, "It is doubtful by any other means of transportation than the camel the journey could have been performed over an entirely unknown country . . . The superiority of the camel for military purposes in the badly watered sections of the country, seems to me to be established."[4]

The expedition reached Fort Davis on June 26 and rested four days. On June 30, they were joined by Company C, Eighth Infantry, which would march with the expedition.

They set out in a heavy rain on July 1, retracing the trail covered a few days earlier. They now had fifty men and enough food for twenty-three days.

On July 13, Hartz noted, while watching the camels' pace, that they "appeared to have acquired, by practice, a greater facility in crossing mountains with their ability to surmount almost any obstacle that might be encountered." In other words, the camels were learning as they journeyed and remembered what they learned.

They came to "Dog Canyon" on July 14, where the terrain was even worse. They described the area as "rocky, rugged country with small mesas, deep slopes, and thickets of vegetation in the valleys."

Although Lieutenant Hartz made no mention of encountering wild animals in his report, mountain lions are abundant in the Big Bend country and so are black bears and javelinas. Mostly, the men remained alert for Comanche attacks, though the true enemy was the heat, humidity, and rugged country through which they traveled.

In some places, men dismounted and led their horses because the trail was narrow and dangerous along hillsides. Even the mules stumbled from time to time, but the camels continued on as if they had been raised in the Big Bend and not thousands of miles away.

By the time they reached the Rio Grande on July 17, more horses and mules had to be abandoned. The government had now lost four horses and an equal number of mules. The number of camels remained as before, and Hartz recorded, "The patience, endurance, and steadiness of the camels during this march is beyond praise."

Lieutenant Echols completed his drawings and data gathering at the river and the expedition started for home. The next day another horse died from the intense heat.

On July 22, they followed the old "Comanche trail" for a few miles but then turned northeast through a prairie for a "shortcut"; at least that is how Echols described it. Apparently, no one thought to consider why the Comanche had avoided the area for hundreds of years, following, instead, another route.

Within ten miles, traveling into the prairie, they learned they had entered a very dangerous area for infantry and animals. The surface of the land was covered with an extremely dense growth of maguay (also called soap weed). The blades of this particular plant are thin and narrow, one or two feet in length, pointing up and out and tipped with a tough, sharp thorn two inches long. They can inflict a severe and painful wound, which can quickly become infected.

But luckily for the expedition, the camels had apparently encountered this plant before and found it not to be very tasty, so they flattened it with their wide front feet. The maguay may have been the only plant in all of Texas that the camels did not like. The camels that day instantly placed their feet against the blade sides and crushed the leaves, thus providing a path for the infantry and horses to follow. The men traveled twenty-one miles through the maguay and camped that night, finally out of the prairie and safe from the horrible plants.

During the last days of July, they traveled on, enduring the unbearable heat over rocky beds of dry streams, rolling country, marching on trails that followed dangerous ledges, without losing a man. Though the camels were praised for their endurance, the same must be said for Company C of the Eighth Infantry, whose men covered the entire distance with nothing but the water they could carry with them.

On July 27, a heavy rain finally brought relief to the expedition, but on the twenty-eighth one of the male camels suffered a leg wound so severe that it could not continue. Lieutenant Hartz left a squad of men to care and "hand water" the camel until he reached Fort Stockton and could send relief troops to bring the animal in. After marching another two and a half days without water, they reached Fort Stockton. Hartz's first action was to "dispatch a party to bring in the camel abandoned."

On August 7, 1859, the expedition reached Camp Hudson and learned that the camel with the nail wound in his foot (the one they were forced to leave the first day) had died of tetanus.

That day Lieutenant Hartz reported, "I am now encamped with the troops, awaiting further orders."

His report would eventually be read by the quartermaster general, who was impressed with the performance of the camels. He turned the report over to both the secretary of war and Congress.

The camels had proven they could often carry up to five hundred pounds over twenty miles a day through the difficult Big Bend with little or no water. The only serious problem the expedition had encountered was with the saddles, and the army set about redesigning those.

Hartz and Echols returned to their headquarters for "desk jobs." In less than a year, the army ordered Lieutenant Echols into the Big Bend Country once more, again with camels.

A year after that expedition was complete, the Civil War separated Hartz and Echols forever.

CHAPTER 37

Camels Return to the Army

Death rides a fast camel.

Old Saudi Arabian Proverb

As 1859 came to a close, the U.S. Army in California decided it was time to take back their camels.

Samuel Bishop, at the request of his partner, Ed Beale, and complying with army demands, rounded up most of the camels that were roaming their huge ranch and turned them over to Lieutenant Henry B. Davidson of the First Dragoons at nearby Fort Tejon.

At the fort, through the month of November, the camels enjoyed oats and hay, consuming large quantities of the food usually reserved for horses and mules. Contrary to some historical reports, the camels and mules got along fine together. There was no panic on the part of the mules. In fact, they behaved like friends. But the camels needed their own space for grazing and simply were consuming too much food at the army's expense, so the army leased twelve acres of grazing land located about seven miles away, just for the camels.

By March 1860, the camels were enjoying a life of retirement under the care of Hi Jolly (Hadji Ali) and Greek George (Yiorgos Caralambo), who were hired by the army to continue what they had been doing on Bishop's ranch. Meanwhile, Bishop's men located the rest of the camels, which had wandered away during a heavy rainstorm, about seventy-five miles from the ranch. They appeared very content to once again be part of the herd.

By mid-1860, the army experiment with camels, at least in California, seemed to be drawing to a close, and the army was puzzled about what to do with those they currently possessed. They had proven their worth on Beale's expedition and wagon road construction and had exhibited an ability to perform in combat conditions under command of Sam Bishop.

Now the War Department, indeed all of Washington, seemed preoccupied with the possibility of a civil war. It would be mostly up to the military in California to find a use for the camels until the War Department issued new directions.

Captain Winfield S. Hancock, the army's assistant quartermaster in Los Angeles, with all good and practical intentions, suggested that the camels be tested as a possible means of delivering dispatches between his headquarters and fellow officers (and friends) Captain Lewis A. Armistead and Captain Richard B. Garnett at the new Fort Mojave on the Colorado River.

Captain Hancock had two goals in mind. First, he wished to cut the expense of the current messenger service, which employed a two-mule buckboard. Second, he hoped to save time. Hancock was aware of the camels' ability to travel great distances, often at speeds faster than a mule or horse, but no one really knew how far they could travel at full speed. Not even Hi Jolly could provide an answer.

In mid-September 1860, Hi Jolly, seated on an army camel, took off like a Pony Express rider, pushing the animal at the maximum speed for 130 miles. The camel died of exhaustion about sixteen miles east of present-day Barstow.

Hi Jolly convinced the army staff that the camel might have been ill and was given another camel to try again. Perhaps he had dreams of becoming an army mail carrier along the Mojave trail he knew so well. That would have secured a future for both himself and his beloved camels, or he might have driven himself and the camels to prove that they could outperform the alternatives. He, an Arab, was capable of being an equal to any "Anglo" in the army. Whatever his motivation, the results were tragic. The second camel died too, a few miles short of Barstow.

What Hi Jolly (and certainly the army) did not know is that camels can run full speed up to about seventy miles. As with horses and people, the distance varies with the animal.

Hi Jolly had orders to deliver the mail to Fort Mojave. Tossing the pouches over his shoulder, he continued on foot, covering the remaining 170 miles in two weeks. Dehydrated and suffering from scrapes, bruises, and blistered feet, he staggered into the Colorado River garrison with the pouches still tied to his back. The dispatches were in perfect condition.

The idea of a camel mail express was a failure, but Hi Jolly remained in his post as camel herder for the army. Greek George, though, was "relieved of duty" (i.e., fired) and went to work as a ranch hand. Some say whiskey was his enemy; others blamed his inability to read or write in English.

Perhaps if the camel express had been designed like the Pony Express, which was operating in the north with horses, the outcome might have been different.

The Pony Express started in April 1860, shortly after the camels in California were returned to the army. It was a fast, successful mail service from St. Joseph, Missouri, to Sacramento, California. Mail was carried by (mostly) teenage riders on horseback in relays across the prairies, deserts, and mountains through the Northwest.

A total of 190 Pony Express stations were placed at intervals along the 1,900-mile route. The rider changed to a fresh horse at each station. Their mail pouch could carry twenty pounds of mail plus twenty pounds of supplies, which included a water sack, a horn to alert the next station to prepare a fresh horse, a revolver, and a Bible. In addition, the rider was given a choice of carrying a second revolver or a rifle.

The Pony Express delivered the mail between Missouri and Sacramento in about ten days, but in October 1861, a little more than a year after the service began, the business would no longer exist. A new technological innovation, the telegraph, replaced it.

Although the Pony Express was no more, once again the rugged individualism of Americans had been demonstrated through the skill, bravery, and enduring determination of young men who left their mark on our history.

The military in California owned fast, strong camels, but they lacked the manpower and money, even if they had the imagination, to embark on anything like the Pony Express system.

The use of army camels in California, however, was not yet over. Soon a few would be put to another test, and this time their performance would exceed expectations.

CHAPTER 38

Into the Perilous Big Bend (Again)

The camels have performed most admirably today. No such march as this could be made with any security without them.

Lieutenant William Echols, Report, July 1, 1860

While the military in California puzzled over what to do with their camels, the army in Texas made good use of the animals in two important expeditions. The first was the Hartz-Echols journey into the Big Bend Country to test camels against army mules.

By early 1860, the army had another expedition planned for the Big Bend, but meanwhile camels continued to haul supplies between their base at Camp Verde and military installations in San Antonio. Camel drivers were afforded good treatment, which included being quartered and fed well. Likewise, the army had standing orders stating that camels were not to be mistreated and never overloaded.

The camels had proven their superiority during that test with mules in mid to late 1859. Now the army was ready to use the animals for a very practical program in Big Bend.

The Big Bend is named for the vast curve in the earth formed by the Rio Grande as it cuts its way through remote southwest Texas. Thanks to the Hartz expedition, the army now knew what to expect in this part of the Chihuahuan Desert, though few, if any, understood the forces that had created this vast geological formation.

Lieutenant Hartz encountered the results of 500 million years of violent collision of tectonic plates, uplifted, twisted by cataclysmic change, and finally torn apart by volcanic eruptions, followed by tidal waves and floods.

This produced deep and winding canyons with wash deposits of sand and gravel and overlooked by towering mesas and sharp mountain peaks.

Where there is soil in the region, it is usually dark, calcareous clay supporting such plant life as juniper, grass, and mesquite.

The Big Bend was the perfect place for the army to test just about anything. If it survived several days in this environment, it would do well anywhere else in the United States. And no doubt only the army would dream of building something in a place where no one else really wanted to go.

Lieutenant Edward L. Hartz had completed his assignment in 1859 and, though he disliked garrison duty, was returned to the San Antonio quartermaster office. Now it would be Lieutenant William H. Echols's turn to lead a new expedition. And the army did not select a mild time of the year for this trip. As before, Echols would be required to move through the desert during the extremely hot days of summer. This time he would have to resume the reconnaissance of the area between the El Paso Road, the Pecos River, and the Rio Grande as the possible site for an army post.

Echols was a natural-born engineer. Creating things, modifying existing equipment, and drawing detailed maps were his obsessions, and he was good at all three.

As we mentioned earlier, the major problem during the first expedition Echols had participated in had not been the camels but their packs and saddles, which the army had copied from those used in the Middle East for centuries.

Hartz and Echols at first blamed the man doing the packing, but this, they subsequently learned, was only part of the problem. A pack and saddle that would not slip and slide off the camel needed to be designed. This was a challenge because the camels' hump changes in size over the course of a month depending on how much fatty tissue the animal is storing.

Echols's diary does not elaborate on the details of his design of a new saddle, but he did record that he made special hoops of iron for water barrels, which prevented them from shifting. This innovation also allowed for a larger barrel to be carried. Echols's other innovations practically eliminated the slipping and shifting altogether.[1]

His convoy left Camp Hudson with thirty-one infantrymen (they would walk during the entire expedition) under the command of Lieutenant James H. Holman, several "camel herders and attendants," fifteen pack mules, and twenty camels. Only one male camel was selected this time. Even though the males are stronger and can carry more supplies, Echols did not wish to deal with their "belligerent" attitude toward one another.

The new water barrels the camels carried for men and mules had a total capacity of five hundred gallons, which Echols calculated would last twenty days.

The first night they camped at Devil's River, and Echols recorded his findings with pride. Thus far, not a single pack had fallen, thanks to his "improvements." Then he went on to describe his new invention for measuring distance. He stated, "I have succeeded in contriving, consisting of shafts, two light wheels on an axle three and a half feet long, a chest on springs, answering for a seat for a driver, all very light, and, attaching the odometer, and the machine is complete."[2]

Up to this time, odometers were usually attached to a wagon wheel and distance measured by the number of wheel rotations. But wagons were too large to be used on this expedition, so Echols invented a much smaller version.

Realizing his expedition would be studied by future generations and being a good topographical engineer, Echols recognized the importance of his maps and measurements.

Unfortunately, the rough territory the expedition and his invention would be traveling through would soon begin to destroy both men and equipment.

The second day of the expedition, June 25, Echols took a shortcut through a rough canyon during which the "odometer [was] upset, breaking one of the shafts, which, however, was soon repaired by a rope."

On the twenty-sixth, the camels complained in their grumbling fashion to such a degree that the herders let them take the lead. They, with humans and mules following, took the expedition directly to a water hole two miles from the trail. To the amusement of the soldiers, the camels proved what the herders already knew. Camels don't need maps to find water.

At the water hole the men drank and filled the twenty-gallon water kegs. They would again be empty in two days.

The expedition began to encounter problems on June 29. They crossed the Pecos River and were ascending the side of a mountain several hundred feet above when Echols's new odometer "machine" turned over and began making somersaults, with the mule that had been pulling it, down the side of the rocky slope. The animal, though scratched in several places, was not seriously injured, but the machine suffered damage and could no longer be pulled by a mule. As usual in the military, when machines fail, soldiers have to take over their jobs. Thus men pulled the cart until Echols found the time to repair it.

The next day they encountered more high bluffs and attempted to maneuver around them through rocky canyons. As they began to ascend a mesa, two camels slipped on the smooth stone ledge and fell. Actually, one fell and the rope attaching the two to the train pulled the other one down. An alert Lieutenant Holman leaped forward with his Bowie knife and cut the line before others were pulled off their feet.

The animals were not hurt, but the water kegs they carried were smashed, their valuable contents lost on the cliff.[3]

As the caravan continued up the mesa, the camels resorted to a method they often used when they encountered a dangerous trail. They dropped and walked (or crawled) on their heavily callused knees until they believed the trail to be safe. Then they stood and continued on normally.

The men then entered a canyon described by Echols as "very dry, rough, rocky, and barren. Every blade of grass was dry and dead." Now the mules began to suffer from lack of both water and food. But the camels' performance continued to impress Echols, who wrote, "The camels have performed most admirably today. No such march as this could be made with any security without them."[4]

By July 2, with no water holes in sight, Echols became concerned for his expedition's survival. There was enough water for the men for thirty hours but none for the mules. "Our march today," the lieutenant wrote, "has been rough. I fear for many lives that are now with us to stem."

He expected to abandon most of the mules the next day. In desperation, he selected the strongest mule and sent one man out in search of water with a promise of a big "reward" if he succeeded.

It had been four days since the camels drank any water. They began their grumbling complaints but showed no signs of fatigue.

On July 3, most of the men were ready to give up marching but were reminded of the consequences if they stopped. They were down to one quart of water per man, not even the minimum required for survival. A man walking in any desert in the United States in July requires about one gallon of water a day to survive.

Echols considered permitting the men to divide up and leave the convoy to search for water on their own. He began to believe that the men would "never again meet but by chance."

That night the men used their canteens as pillows to secure the last of their water from desperate comrades.

Part of the supplies, considered unnecessary equipment, was abandoned so as to lighten the loads of both camels and mules, and then the men, still soldiers in the United States Army, marched in "perfect formation" another thirty miles with their one quart of water apiece.

Lieutenant Echols that day described the desert that was about to kill his animals and men as "a region in its original chaotic state, as if the progress of civilization was too rapid for the arrangement of chaos; a picture of barrenness and desolation when the scathing fire of destruction has swept with its rapid flame, mountains, canyons, ravines, precipices, cactus from the limestone cliffs and almost every barrier that one can conceive of, to make an impossibility of progress."[5]

It seemed to everyone, including the officers, that the end was near, but as they crossed over a small hill, they thought they saw water. Was it a mirage, the horrible trick the eye and brain can play on one in the desert?

Fifteen miles away was a ravine where the San Francisco Creek once flowed. Did it contain water now?

Suddenly the camels began to bellow and tug on their ropes. They knew there was water in the distance. The men cheered. Their guess had proven to be true. The camels were never wrong when it came to finding a water source. The creek was not a mirage.

The little unit of the American army had marched over 120 miles in temperatures exceeding one hundred degrees in the shade (of which they had none) through the most rugged part of any desert in the United States on severely rationed quantities of water for five days. More than once they almost broke, but they continued on, walking in formation, and at last made it to the cool, fast-flowing waters of San Francisco Creek.

In the creek's valley was an abundance of good grass for the mules, but four had died during the two-mile dash to water.

The men celebrated, shouting, "Hurrah for the 4th!" It was July 4, 1860, an Independence Day they would never forget.

Lieutenant Echols's "odometer machine" sadly had had to be abandoned somewhere during the last thirty miles of travel. But he needed that instrument for his maps and calculations, so he gave his men a two-day rest at the creek and then sent a squad to retrieve it. Echols worked on his broken invention for hours and managed to repair it.

During the two-day rest, another mule died from exhaustion and Echols recorded that the others were "almost worthless."

On July 9, they continued on toward Fort Davis, covering twenty-five miles.

On July 10, the weather took a sudden turn. It began to rain and continued to do so until the men reached Fort Davis.

While the men enjoyed a few days' rest to recuperate from their journey, Echols managed to obtain a supply of new shoes for everyone, then they were off again on another march.

The weather remained mild for the next few days and they averaged twenty-two miles a day as they crossed relatively flat land. But then the trail become rough as it wound through broken country. Echols recorded, "I cheerfully concur with all who regard this region as impassible."

His odometer suffered from "several falls and broke both of the shafts which have been replaced by saplings." His machine now required three men to pull it.

On July 25, with the remaining mules too weak to carry their 250-pound loads, Echols permitted them to be unpacked and the men were given the opportunity to take turns riding the animals.

Finally they reached the Rio Grande, but the first few places they investigated turned out not to be suitable for a fort, according to Echols. On July 26, however, they entered a valley that he believed to be a perfect location. He described it as "very pretty, plenty of timber, abundance of wood, grass, and building sites, easily accessible from the river."

The place Echols selected was twenty miles below the area where Comanche war parties crossed into Mexico, close enough to be patrolled by dragoons from the new fort.

With its leader satisfied that he had found the perfect location, the expedition set out for home. This time the lieutenant selected what he calculated to be an easier, more direct route north. But once again they encountered rugged, barren land.

A few days into the return journey, the camels began to have problems with sore feet. Their soles had been abraded by sharp, ragged rocks unlike those they had traveled over during previous days. Echols devised a simple solution and recorded his idea on July 30: "I would recommend to anyone using the camel over rough country, in case of tender feet, to shoe them with a piece of circular rawhide gathered around the leg by a slipping cord."

That idea worked perfectly and the camels continued on as if they had worn the "shoes" their entire lives.

But on that same day, Echols made a strange entry into his diary, one that still puzzles historians. He recorded, "One of the men left the command a short distance yesterday and has not been seen or heard of since."

What did Echols mean by "a short distance"? Was any effort made to locate the missing man? Was he a member of the army or a civilian camel driver? What was his name?

Perhaps the man deserted. That would not be surprising, considering all the hardship the expedition had endured. It is possible he was a member of Lieutenant James Holman's command and Echols did not have a record of his name.

William Echols was a good, experienced officer, a meticulous engineer. He was known to be compassionate, realistic, and sometimes emotional (as indicated often in his diary entries). Nonetheless, the circumstances regarding the man's disappearance remain a mystery.

On August 4, 1860, the expedition staggered into Fort Stockton. Several camels with "tender feet" could go no farther. The few exhausted mules that remained alive needed new shoes and days of rest. One man suffered from inflammation of the eyes due to prolonged exposure to the sun.

One man had wounded himself in the hand by "accidental discharge of his pistol," and the "lost" man was never found.

Lieutenant Holman reported to Echols that his troops could "no longer serve as escorts." They were exhausted and some were near death. It would be weeks before Holman could march his men in "the field" again.

Despite the cost in materials, animals, and men, Second Lieutenant William H. Echols of the United States Army Topographical Engineers had accomplished his mission. He located a perfect spot for an army post along the Rio Grande in Big Bend Country and proved that men could march, despite the difficulties, to its location.

But 1860 was coming to a close and with it the War Department's interest in evaluating camels in Texas. Despite Lieutenant Echols's efforts and the sacrifices of the men in completing an almost impossible assignment, no fort would be erected at that "pretty" location along the Rio Grande. The coming Civil War shifted attention elsewhere.

Today the strong and determined can reach Lieutenant Echols's pretty spot on the Rio Grande by traveling only on foot . . . or, perhaps, by camel.

CHAPTER 39

Into the Valley of Death

(Or, Where Is Nevada?)

The camel and his driver—each has his own plan.

North African proverb

Since their territory had been granted statehood in 1850, the people of California were content with the belief that their boundary with Nevada was the Sierra Nevada Mountain chain, which extends from Lake Tahoe in the north to Mexico in the south.

The mountains and some distance east, most believed, belonged to California. But how far east? For many years, the exact boundary was not important. Then gold was discovered in the rugged terrain east of the mountains and boomtowns sprang up as thousands of prospectors moved in to seek their fortunes. It became necessary to establish local governments in order to handle civil disputes and maintain some semblance of law and order. But which law—the state of California's, the U.S. government's, or local regulations that were enforced with guns?

In 1860, as the army in California tried to decide what to do with their camels and the army in Texas put camels to good use exploring the Big Bend area, President Buchanan appointed the man who was the first to be publicly associated with camels in the United States, Edward F. Beale, the new United States surveyor general for California.

Ed Beale certainly knew the state well, and with his ranch in the good hands of his friend Samuel Bishop, he would be free to devote his energies to problems related to boundary disputes. Beale was based in San Francisco with the new boundary commissioner, former army officer Sylvester Mowry, who was also appointed by President Buchanan.

Beale, of course, was well known in California. The governor of the state had even appointed him to the rank of general of the militia, but Mowry was mostly a familiar name in the territory of Arizona, where he had many supporters (and a few enemies).

As an army officer stationed at Fort Yuma in 1855, Lieutenant Mowry explored the Arizona wilderness and became convinced that precious metals were in abundance and lay waiting in the desert near Tucson. He resigned his army commission in 1858 and purchased an old Mexican mine, changing the name to Mowry Mine in 1859.

Tubac, with a population of over four hundred, was the center of commerce in what would later become the state of Arizona, but at the time all of that part of the country was in New Mexico Territory.

In March 1859, the *Weekly Arizonian* made its debut in Tubac and promoted the idea that Arizona should be a separate territory. Sylvester Mowry became wealthy with his mine operations and was elected as a representative to Washington, where he promoted the idea of Arizona separating from New Mexico Territory. He quickly made influential friends, including the president. Although he failed to convince Congress that Arizona was ready to break from New Mexico, President Buchanan rewarded him with appointment to the position of California boundary commissioner, answering to Ed Beale, the surveyor general.

Mowry did not believe in slavery but was a strong supporter of states' rights. In order to promote his ideas, he purchased the Tubac newspaper and moved it to Tucson, which had already become a hotbed of pro- and antislavery advocates. Sylvester Mowry's San Francisco appointment may have come just in the nick of time.[1]

In October 1860, Mowry arrived in California and began to work at once to establish the boundary between Nevada and California. His first plan would be to determine the exact point where the thirty-fifth parallel crossed the Colorado River. He believed it to be a little south of Beale's Crossing, and in this he was correct, according to Lieutenant Joseph Christmas Ives, who traveled from Fort Mojave to make the calculations.

The thirty-fifth parallel crossing of the river became the starting point of an oblique line traveling at an angle north—the actual boundary of California and Nevada.

Now someone was going to have to travel that line and survey every foot of it. This was not expected to be an easy task, as it would take one through some of the most forbidding terrain in North America.

Mowry consulted with Ed Beale, who had more experience than anyone in crossing the Southwest. What would be the best mode of transportation for a boundary expedition? Naturally, Beale suggested Mowry use camels.

Neither of the two had traveled the desert along the proposed boundary route, but there were a few Americans who had. The "49ers," the prospectors and some of the emigrants who came west in 1849 to search for gold, survived that part of the desert they called "the valley of death." The area, which was believed to be "lower than the sea," became known as Death Valley because of its horrible heat, lack of water and vegetation for animals, and the large number of people who died trying to cross through it.

Army headquarters in California wasn't too excited about turning their camels back over to Beale and another civilian-led expedition. It had been difficult in the past to get civilians (mostly Ed Beale) to return the animals. But the army did want to find a practical use for the camels and reluctantly agreed to furnish four for the Boundary Commission's use, providing, of course, that they be returned in good condition.

At Beale's recommendation, Hi Jolly would join the expedition to care for the camels. He was the most qualified for the job and the American members of the expedition had no experience with the animals.

Things were off to a bad start before the expedition got under way. Someone placed the male camels in a small corral with two females. The males began to fight and Seid, the large white favorite of Ed Beale, was killed by Tuilu.

Beale was saddened when he received the news of Seid's death. He had ridden the animal many times since 1857 and had a fondness for him. Likewise, Sam Bishop expressed sadness and anger. Seid had carried him safely through the Mojave warriors only a year before.[2]

Now only three camels made the march to Fort Mojave to await the Boundary Commission team's arrival.

Mowry chose as the expedition leader forty-two-year-old medical doctor J.R.N. Owen, an adventurer who had attempted to bring some civilization to the Wild West.[3]

Dr. Owen, a native of Virginia and son of a preacher, came to California with an interesting education and experience. He attended the University of Alabama, fought in the Seminole Wars at age eighteen, graduated as a medical doctor from Transylvania University in Lexington, Kentucky, and served as a hospital "steward" during the Mexican War.

The 1849 Gold Rush lured the doctor to California, but he had little luck prospecting. He invested in mining prospects in the Coso Mountains and settled in that area, offering his services as a physician while pursuing his other love, prospecting.

Dr. Owen gained a reputation as a fine marksman, or so reported the San Francisco Bulletin on September 13, 1860: "With no other firearm than a Colt's Navy revolver, he shot an antelope last week at a distance of 150 paces."

Sylvester Mowry had a number of reasons for choosing Dr. Owen to lead the survey expedition. Both men were educated (Mowry graduated from West Point) and both had military experience. Both had an interest in mining and both were southern sympathizers. And the advantage of having a medical doctor on the expedition was obvious.

But there was yet another reason Mowry needed Dr. Owen; he believed he could trust Owen in regard to their mutual interest—prospecting. What a great opportunity the expedition provided to prospect for gold and silver at the government's expense! Because of his position, Mowry himself could not go with the expedition. If he did so, and they discovered precious metals, it could prove embarrassing to him.

Other members of the expedition were the respected topographer Aaron Van Dorn, whose job was to draw maps of the new region and write a detailed account of the trip, and James Macleod, an astronomer who would determine latitude using sextant and compass, and elevation by means of barometric readings.

With the exception of Hi Jolly, who cared for the camels and mules (also on loan from the army), the list of the other members of the fourteen-man expedition reads like a list of employees of a mining company, which most of them were. They included J. H. Lillard, "silver hunter," James Hitchens, prospector, Federico Biesta, assayer, and Joel Brooks, a less-than-qualified trail guide and noted gunfighter who claimed to have traveled that part of the desert before.

On January 11, 1861, the survey expedition set out from Los Angeles on the Mojave Road (aka Beale's trail) for Fort Mojave. Their bad luck continued. Heavy rains closed off Cajon Pass, so they traveled south and crossed the summit from another direction.

They reached Fort Mojave safely, organized the packing of the camels, and then proceeded south to meet Lieutenant Joseph C. Ives, who had succeeded in using his astronomical skills to locate the exact point where the thirty-fifth parallel crossed the Colorado. That position on the west bank marked the southernmost tip of Nevada.

On the cold morning of February 9, 1861, Dr. Owen led his expedition northwest along the oblique line established by Lieutenant Ives's calculations. After traveling a short distance, they began to experience delays because of the poor condition of some of the pack mules. The camels patiently waited for the mules to catch up.

The cold winds that had lashed the group in the Colorado valley became warmer as they moved northward.

There were other winds far away in the east, the winds of war. The United States had begun to split apart. The expedition was unaware that South Carolina had seceded from the Union in December.

In February, as the expedition marched along the borderline, Florida, Mississippi, Alabama, Georgia, Texas, and Louisiana voted for secession. As the Confederate states in the South began to organize, they elected former U.S. secretary of war Jefferson Davis to be their president. Davis was the man who had believed so strongly in the camel experiment for the U.S. Army. Now the camels in the Southwest had lost a very important friend.

February 11, 1861. Two days into their journey and the boundary expedition was already in trouble. Low on water and food for the mules, the party turned away from their oblique boundary line somewhere along the eastern base of the San Bernardino Mountains between modern-day Nipton, California and Primm, Nevada.[4]

With the mountains on the west, they moved through Sandy Valley, Nevada, and into the Amargosa Desert, crossing over the "Old Spanish Trail." They continued on, following what they thought was the boundary line, but soon were forced, for the second time, to search for water and food for the mules (the camels fed themselves, as usual, on a variety of plants and cacti that the mules would not touch). They turned west, finding water at the Resting Springs range, east of Tecopa and Shoshone.

The mules continued to suffer, not only from lack of food and water but from walking through some areas where the desert crust gave way and their feet sank inches below the surface. The feet of the camels, on the other hand, were perfect for walking on the sandy terrain.

Soon the party discarded less critical equipment, giving the mules a better chance of survival. But they carefully packed and unpacked their special instruments, such as the sextant and the "Green Mountain Barometer," invented in the 1840s by James Green.

Green's invention was surprisingly accurate, becoming the Smithsonian Institution's standard instrument for determining elevations at various points in America. It was about to aid the expedition in making a startling discovery.[5]

The expedition reached Travertine Springs (a little east of today's Furnace Creek Inn) and camped there. The weather was pleasant, as it usually is in that part of the desert until May introduces six months of energy-sapping heat, the sun destroying anything not prepared to live there.

Surveyor Aaron Van Dorn had a theory that the valley to their west was lower than the level of the sea, so to prove it, he took a barometer reading on a small mesa. Later he reported, "It was nine o'clock when the barometer was suspended . . . it was found to read 30.038. Its temperature being 75 degrees and that of the atmosphere 67 degrees, with the sky perfectly calm and clear. This reading indicated that we were already near the level of the sea while the bottom of the valley was still several hundred feet below us."[6]

Actually, their camp was about three hundred feet above sea level, but the expedition moved down the hill for another check. Van Dorn, accompanied by James Macleod, rode onto the flatland.

Van Dorn's report reads, "We dismounted and walked out about a hundred yards, where we suspended the barometer . . . assuming it to read just 30.000, at the sea line with both thermometers at fifty degrees would give the depression to be—377 and 1/3 feet."[7]

So far the expedition had accomplished little in establishing an accurate Nevada-California boundary, but they were the first to prove Death Valley was situated at the lowest elevation in the United States.

They spent a few days at Travertine Springs and then headed north along "the valley of death" to Cow Creek. With no maps except the ones they drew as they traveled, they started northwest. They were now moving parallel to the true oblique boundary line but off course, fifteen miles to the west.

Though the men (and mules) were suffering from the rough terrain and dry climate, which burned eyes and cracked lips and exposed skin, they did locate springs. Southern California had had torrential storms that winter that covered the mountaintops with snow.

But earlier travelers had not been so lucky. Bones, both animal and human, were found by the expedition in several locations. Mostly, these were the unburied remains of early prospectors and emigrants who were unprepared to challenge the valley of death. And here and there they found the remains of pots, digging tools, and abandoned wagons.

The expedition soon turned southwest, crossed dry Salt Creek, cut across the northern tip of Tuckie Mountain, crossed miles of sand dunes, and then cut south. Now their food and water supply was running low. The expedition suddenly ended their survey, turning their attention to . . . prospecting for gold and silver.

As they passed along the sloping north ridge of Tuckie Mountain, the exhausted mules began to die, two one day and two more the next.

Desperately short of water, they detoured south into Emigrant Canyon and accidentally found a spring. After a rest the party split up, a few men continuing up the canyon into Jayhawker Canyon, where they found another spring. The mules that remained were practically useless and the slopes of the canyon walls were too steep for the camels to climb, so more equipment was discarded.

They turned south and continued several miles through Wild Rose Canyon. By now they were completely lost. Survival took priority over prospecting. They did not know that Abraham Lincoln had been sworn into office on March 4 (before they measured the altitude of Death Valley) and that four more states, Virginia, North Carolina, Tennessee, and Arkansas, had voted for secession and joined the Confederacy.

Dr. Owen's orders from Commissioner Mowry stated, in part, "examine the general character of the country and report upon the same."

The expedition had a lot to report even if they seemed to have forgotten the boundary project. Wandering through Panamount Valley, they apparently found no evidence of precious metals but somehow managed to locate an active waterfall and a large spring called Darwin Falls.

The camels knew at once that the water was safe to drink, and for the first time in over a week they drank an estimated ten gallons each.

Now the men had water, but food was down to a few rations. Owen left the party for a few days and traveled to the Coso mining district, where he tried to buy food. The Coso area had no extra food to sell, and according to reports, mining camps within one hundred miles were likewise short of supplies.

Owen returned to his men. During a meeting, they decided it was time to give up the expedition, cross the mountains, and return to civilization. The camels seemed to be the only living creatures capable of making the return trip. Leaving the rest of their equipment behind, the men took turns riding the camels, but mostly following them out of the valley of death.

They traveled, limping, staggering, half carrying one another 170 miles west, to the safety of Visalia, California.

At Visalia, Dr. Owen and Van Dorn wrote their reports to Commissioner Mowry. Hi Jolly and the camels returned to Los Angeles and waited for the army to decide their fate.

The reports reached Mowry in mid-April. By then the United States was in turmoil. Confederate forces had shelled Fort Sumter on April 12, 1861. The United States was now engaged in a civil war.

The border dispute between Nevada and California continued into modern times. In 1985, Congress got involved and put an end to the problem—so they thought. In early 2010, the National Geodetic Survey stated that the established boundary might be off to the east 1,807 feet of where it should be.

CHAPTER 40

The Camel Experiment Comes to an End

> But the times change and we change with them . . . was
> it all a last night's dream?
>
> *Edward F. Beale, April 30, 1887*

As the Civil War began, most U.S. Army camels were in two locations, California and Texas.

The army in Texas had made good use of the camels. A few were scattered about at different army posts, but the majority were still based at Camp Verde.

In California, it was a different story. Those that were originally brought to the state by Lieutenant Edward Beale and held at his ranch were returned to the army at Fort Tejon during November 1859. In the fields assigned to them for grazing, they enjoyed a work-free life until September 1860. But in early 1861, as the Civil War began in the East, they were transferred to the control of Captain Winfield Scott Hancock of the quartermaster's department at the Los Angeles Depot. There, they were reunited with the three camels returning from service with Dr. J.R.N. Owen's boundary expedition. The camels were all placed in corrals with government mules and they quickly became friends and got along well together.

At the beginning of the war, the army deserted many of the posts in the western territory as troops were relocated to the battlefronts in the East. The First Dragoons rode out of Fort Tejon for duty at San Bernardino, there to guard against any trouble from southern sympathizers in the area. For a while Fort Tejon was closed.

By the time the camels arrived in Los Angeles, Fort Mojave had also been abandoned. But the southern garrison at Fort Yuma on the Colorado River remained at full staff.

In early 1862, military leaders believed that Confederate troops near Tucson were about to march on Fort Yuma. The commanding officer at Fort Yuma received the following message from his headquarters: "Qui vive! [stay alert.] If necessary defend your post to the last extremity, then, if you are obligated to give way . . . destroy it and fight your way across the desert."

Many of the messages to Yuma were written in French or Greek, which, of course, West Point graduates could read, but most rebels could not.

In Los Angeles, the quartermaster unit and the camels were moved to Camp Latham (now Culver City) and then to Drum Barracks. Here the camels witnessed a number of changes in their management.

Captain Hancock was relocated to San Francisco but then accepted a position in Ohio, was promoted to general, and moved to western Virginia.

First Lieutenant David J. Williamson then had responsibility for the camels. He wisely hired Hi Jolly and Greek George as "caretakers."

Fort Mojave reopened, manned by California Volunteers. This seemed like a good place to move the camels, but there was not enough forage to support them. A herd of thirty to forty camels would clean out every cactus and bush within a year.

So as the army pondered the problem of how to make use of the camels, federal surveyor general Edward F. Beale once again entered the picture. He suggested that the camels be returned to him, or his department of the government, for use in surveying wilderness areas of Nevada, which was about to become a state.

Some high-ranking military officers agreed with Beale's suggestion, but some were reminded of the difficult time the army had had getting their camels back once before, and Beale's political enemies were at it again, accusing him of "misusing government funds." The camel-surveying idea was scrapped.

In September 1863, the quartermaster general authorized the Department of the Pacific to sell the California camels at auction at the Benicia Depot near San Francisco. The cheapest way of getting the animals there was to march them. Once they arrived, not at all tired from the trip, they were corralled behind newly constructed stone buildings.

Since no one had indicated any interest in the camels in Los Angeles, the military believed they could get the best price at San Francisco, where some businessmen had been importing Siberian (two-hump) camels since 1860.

On February 26, 1864, Samuel Leneghan bought, at government auction, thirty-seven army camels for a total price of $1,945 ($52.56 each).[1]

The army experiment with camels, at least in California, was over.

Leneghan hired Hi Jolly to care for his new camel herd, sold a few to ranchers near Sacramento, at least one to a California zoo, and in early 1865 moved the rest to a mining district in Nevada. There, the Bactrians (two-hump) imported by those businessmen were being used to haul salt to Virginia City from salt marshes near Fort Churchill. (Salt was necessary at the time for ore processing.)

But soon salt was discovered closer to Virginia City, so the camels were put to work hauling firewood between mining camps.

Marius and Louis Chevalier, having served with the French army in North Africa, knew the value of camels and how to best use them. They purchased some of the unwanted animals for their ranch along the Carson River.[2]

Leneghan was unsuccessful in Nevada, so he, his herd of remaining camels, and Hi Jolly began a long desert journey to Fort Yuma. Mining camps between Yuma and Tucson were in need of pack animals possessing the camels' qualities.

Samuel Leneghan died soon after his arrival in Yuma. Most of the camels were then purchased by miners, and Hi Jolly ended up with a few. He began a freight business, hauling water and supplies in and out of Yuma, but was not very successful.

Those who had invested in the Bactrians used them in Utah and British Columbia, but eventually, they too were reported to have been marched to Yuma.

With all the movement, some camels in Nevada (both the Bactrians and the army's dromedaries) managed to wander away. Still others were released to survive on their own. Enjoying their freedom, camels began to appear in towns, not in search of food but driven by curiosity and, apparently, a need to be near humans. People at first had no objection to the visits by the strange creatures, but frightened horses objected, and this prompted the state of Nevada to take action to put a stop to the visitors. On February 9, 1875, a law known as Chapter XII was passed and would eventually bring the use of camels in the state to an end.

"Chapter XII—An act to prohibit camels and dromedaries from running at large on or about the public highways of the State of Nevada." This law was passed long before the invention of automobiles. The mode of comfortable transportation was, of course, horse-drawn wagons and carriages, and if any horses became frightened while at work, serious accidents could, and did, occur.

So the California army camels' journey had taken them from Fort Tejon to Los Angeles to San Francisco to northern Nevada and, finally, to Fort Yuma, Arizona.

Before they made that trip, at least a dozen were reported to have been purchased from Samuel Leneghan by Ed Beale and moved back to the Tejon Ranch. (It is possible that Beale did not buy the camels, but that those that had been at the Tejon Ranch had been "overlooked" and never returned to the army in 1859. In 1862, a few camels were at the ranch, and the true version of this story will no doubt never be known.)

Life for the army camels in Texas during the Civil War was very different from what it had been before.

The elite United States Second Cavalry originally sent to Texas to protect emigrants from Indians split apart, much the same as the military throughout America was doing at the time.

On February 4, 1861, Lieutenant Colonel Robert E. Lee, a familiar officer about Texas for years, was ordered to Washington and offered command of the Union Army. He declined, resigned his commission, and joined the Confederate army to fight for the State of Virginia. Colonel A. S. Johnston, who had led the army in the Utah War, did the same.

Lieutenant John Bell Hood, unhappy with the "neutrality" of his native state of Kentucky, also resigned his commission, declared himself a Texan, and joined the Confederate army. And U.S. Army Engineer Lieutenant William H. Echols, soon after completing the expedition into the Big Bend, resigned and joined the rebels, but his associate in the camel experiment, Lieutenant Edward L. Hartz, remained with the Union.

On the last day of February 1861, Confederate troops marched into the large quartermaster headquarters in San Antonio and demanded that the Union soldiers there surrender. Greatly outnumbered, the latter complied without a fight.

Lieutenant Edward Hartz, serving as assistant quartermaster since the camel expedition, surrendered his office and staff but successfully hid the Eighth Infantry regimental flag ("colors"). It was a tattered old standard that had survived the Mexican War with burns and bullet holes, but it had led the regiment into several battles. Hartz was not about to let it be captured by the Confederates. He knew his own trunk, desk, and personal property would be searched for loot, so he and his staff corporal, John C. Hesse, devised a simple but bold plan.

Knowing a corporal would normally not have much of value to steal, Hesse volunteered to hide the flag by wrapping it around his body beneath his uniform shirt.

Lieutenant Hartz and his staff were "paroled" and permitted to travel to Washington after they signed an "oath" to never "take up arms against the Confederate States of America." Once in Washington, Hartz presented the regimental flag to the War Department. Later, he was promoted to captain and, keeping his word as an officer and gentleman, remained in Washington for the duration of the war.

After taking over all Union positions in San Antonio, the rebel army marched toward Camp Verde, arriving on March 1, 1861. The garrison there appeared to be in no mood to surrender without a fight. Lieutenant Hill, the Union officer in command, stated that he had orders to defend his post (and the herd of camels) "to the last man." Actually, this was a bluff to gain the best terms. Lieutenant Hill had orders to evacuate to the north or, as a last resort, surrender.

The Confederate commander made Lieutenant Hill an offer he couldn't refuse. All Union officers and men might leave unharmed as prisoners but retain a horse, personal possessions, and weapons (unloaded). Hill agreed to the terms and he and his men were taken to San Antonio.

At 2 P.M. that day, the rebels took possession "of the fort, the stores, ammunition, twelve mules, eighty camels, and two Egyptian camel drivers, for all of which I had to give a receipt."[3]

The camels were certainly a curiosity to the Confederate army, but for the first few months of the war, they had no idea what to do with them. Some of the animals, which were not corralled, wandered off to freedom on the Texas range.

From time to time, troops brought camels to San Antonio to entertain children and to "please the ladies" with rides.

Due to Union seaport blockades, the Confederates put the camels to work hauling cotton bales to Mexico, exchanging the cotton for badly needed supplies such as salt, which they carried to various towns in South Texas. During those journeys, some camels drifted off, some simply disappearing, others captured by ranchers.

A few camels were taken by rebel soldiers into Arkansas and Missouri. Most were "recaptured" by Union forces and sold to farmers, it is believed, in Iowa. But at least one camel ended up with Confederate general Sterling Price, hero of the Mexican War, former governor of Missouri, and, in 1862, commander of Confederate Missouri troops.

At the close of the Civil War, army posts including Camp Verde were taken back by Union forces, and soon the quartermaster general ordered the camels to be sold to the highest bidder, as he had done with the California camels.

There were over sixty camels remaining at Camp Verde at the time. Buyers from small, traveling circuses and zoos purchased a few, as did a number of ranch owners, but Colonel Bethel Coopwood and his partners were the highest bidders for most of the herd, paying thirty-one dollars per head.

The Coopwood family, Confederate sympathizers, had made their home in Hermanos, Mexico, until the war was over. Ringling Brothers Circus management learned of Coopwood's camels, traveled to San Antonio, and purchased five of the animals.

The U.S. Post Office contracted with Coopwood to carry mail into Mexico and the camels were put to work again. But profits fell sharply as Mexican bandits robbed the camel caravans on a routine basis.

Coopwood gave up his business in Mexico and moved his camels to a farm in Travis County, Texas, where he practiced law and bred the animals in an attempt to build up the herd again.

An unknown number of camels had been released to survive on their own in the deserts of California, Nevada, Arizona, and Texas in the late 1800s. For a work animal or "beast of burden," perhaps this was a fair and humane way to be disposed of. At least their owners thought so.

The camels were capable of finding water in remote areas and could survive on the plants in the southwest they found so tasty.

But from another perspective, it was a sad, yet necessary move. Camels are herd animals, preferring to be with other camels, and like horses, they have become conditioned over hundreds, perhaps thousands, of years to serve man as a work animal and companion.

Some camels did not, at first, understand the meaning of their new freedom and continued to stay near their last home until they were finally driven off.

A few animals were killed and eaten by Indians who discovered they were easy to approach. Others were killed by hunters or frontiers-men who shot them as they did deer or elk.

But man and nature did not destroy all the camels in America's Southwest. Long forgotten by the army, the camels did not disappear.

In 1913, a work crew for the Santa Fe Railroad reported seeing a camel in the desert near Wickenberg, Arizona. Then some were spotted in 1930 near Palm Springs, California; at Ajo, Arizona, in 1931; and at the Salton Sea in 1941.

Could these camels have been the descendants of the army herd that was released in the late 1860s, grandchildren of those who traveled with Lieutenant Ed Beale or fought with Sam Bishop, those who listened to the calming words in Arabic from Hi Jolly?

There are still vast territories in our Southwest that are seldom, if ever, visited by man. A camel might survive in those dry areas with very little difficulty.

Were those reports of camel sightings a prank or the result of an overactive imagination? Maybe. But a herd of camels was photographed in a desolate section of West Texas between U.S. Route 287 and the BNSF Wichita railroad tracks. The date? September 17, 2003. It seems the camels are still with us.

But what became of General Sterling Price's camel?

During the spring of 1863, General Grant's Union Army was on the offensive, driving southern forces from Tennessee. General Price, or "Old Pap" as his soldiers called him, crossed the Mississippi River with his army to reinforce Confederate general P.G.T. Beauregard at Corinth. General Price brought his pet camel with him.

Somehow, during the horrible days of battle at either Iuka or Corinth, the camel was assigned to the care of Colonel William H. Moore of Mississippi's "Bloody 43rd" Infantry Regiment. The camel was quickly accepted as the regiment's mascot. Then on retreat, the 43rd desperately needed something to serve as a symbol of strength and endurance. Word of the camel's assignment spread rapidly, and with a few chuckles here and there, the morale of the men improved.

General Price returned to Missouri as the 43rd continued its retreat toward Vicksburg. Colonel Moore was killed, but the men still had that camel to lift their spirits.

It was another long walk for the camel. He had journeyed all the way to Texas from Smyrna on a sailing ship, traveled through the rugged desert of the Big Bend with Lieutenant Hartz, and then again with Lieutenant Echols.

From Texas to Missouri and now to Mississippi to meet his fate . . . killed by a shot from a Union sniper.

The men of the Bloody 43rd knew their camel by only one name: Old Douglas.

CONCLUSION

Old timers down in Arizona tell you that it's true/That you can see Hi Jolly's ghost a-riding still/When the desert moon is bright, he comes ridin' into sight/Drivin' four and twenty camels over the hill.

"Hi Jolly, the Camel Driver"
(Lyrics by Randy Sparks, New Christy Minstrels, 1962)

The Civil War put an end to the army camel experiment. The original, influential supporters of the idea, Secretary of War Jefferson Davis and his replacement, John Floyd, both joined the Confederacy and their attention was mostly devoted to battles in the South and East, not in the desert.

The camels, by performance, had proven themselves to be superior to horses and mules in the desert, but dreams of a U.S. camel cavalry, a true camel corps, faded as the dedicated men involved in the evaluation were divided by the Civil War. Major George Crossman remained with the Union, and Major Henry Wayne joined the Confederacy. Edward Beale and Lieutenant Ed Hartz supported the Union, while Colonel William Loring and Lieutenant Echols fought for the Confederacy.

After the war, Americans set about rebuilding and reuniting and the camel program was never resurrected. Our history is often that way. We survive by creating, building, and moving on while memories fade. Perhaps it is our way of healing wounds.

Stories surfaced from time to time, telling of army personnel abusing camels. This is highly unlikely. Abusing government property was (and is) a serious crime. Officers responsible for the property would never tolerate such behavior. Others say that soldiers resented or even hated camels because "they spit" and "smell bad." That may be true in some cases, but working with an ill-tempered mule is no fun either. And so the acceptance, or not, of the camels by soldiers had nothing to do with the program's coming to an end.

Was Ed Beale's wagon road along the thirty-fifth parallel a waste of time and taxpayers' money? Not at all.

The country was soon joined by telegraph and a railroad from east to west, but military and emigrant wagons depended on Beale's road from 1860 through the early 1900s.

Traces of the trail can still be found in parts of New Mexico, Arizona, and as the Mojave Trail through the tip of Southern Nevada and California to Barstow.

A major highway constructed of asphalt and concrete connected Chicago to Los Angeles in 1926. It followed closely the old trail Ed Beale created in 1857.

This new highway was called the Mother Road, sometimes the Will Rogers Highway, but is mostly remembered as Route 66.

By the late 1960s, Route 66 had been replaced by Interstate 40, also following the thirty-fifth parallel. We can thank Edward Beale, some dedicated American laborers, and, of course, the camels for being the first to connect east to west with a functional road.

At the beginning of the Civil War, Edward F. Beale, former U.S. Navy lieutenant, general in the California Militia, superintendent of Indian Affairs for California, superintendent of the thirty-fifth parallel wagon road construction, and surveyor general of California and Nevada, asked President Lincoln for a Union Army command. Lincoln convinced Beale he could best serve the country by remaining as surveyor general and do everything possible to keep California in the Union.

After the war, Beale "retired" to his sprawling Tejon Ranch. In 1871, with a desire to return to the East, he and his wife, Mary, purchased the Decatur House in Washington, and beginning in 1872, they divided their time between Washington and the ranch.

In Washington, the Beale family became important leaders in the social and political world. Beale was a close friend of President U.S. Grant, who appointed him minister to the court of Austria-Hungary in 1876, where the frontier American hero would use his charm to calm some hard feelings that existed between that country and the United States.

Ed Beale's son, Truxtun, born in California in 1856, began his diplomatic career by serving as secretary to his father in Vienna.

On April 22, 1893, explorer Edward Fitzgerald Beale died at De-catur House at the age of seventy-one. His widow, Mary Edward, blind for the last ten years of her life, died there in 1902 at age seventy-five.

Truxtun inherited both Decatur House and the Tejon Ranch, and was later appointed minister to Persia by President Harrison. Beale Air Force Base was named in Ed Beale's honor.

As the Civil War raged in many parts of the country, Fort Tejon was abandoned and the "keys" were turned over to Samuel Addison Bishop, who had leased the land to the United States for "military purposes as long as it should be deemed necessary." In 1861, Bishop found himself the proprietor of a village complete with homes, storage, office buildings, a jail, and a hospital—only he had no one to occupy the complex.

He believed that a new county should be created from sections of Los Angeles, Santa Barbara, and Tulare counties and donated "old Fort Tejon" with all of its buildings to that new county, which was given the name of Kern in 1865.

While the state legislature worked on creating Kern County, Sam Bishop embarked on a number of projects.

In 1861, new boomtowns grew in population and wealth as rich deposits of gold and silver were discovered along the California-Nevada border. This was especially true of Aurora, Nevada (originally believed to be in California).

The northern Owens Valley of California was unsettled at the time, and Bishop, with experience in ranching, recognized a new business opportunity. The population of Aurora had swollen to almost ten thousand and more prospectors were in the hills. They needed beef, and Bishop planned to supply that need.

Only two years after his battle with the Mojave at the Colorado River, Samuel Bishop was on the move. He and his family, along with several trusted men, drove six hundred head of cattle and fifty horses from the Tejon Ranch to the Owens Valley, arriving in August 1861.

Bishop established a homestead, which he named San Francis Ranch in honor of his wife, and began selling beef to the miners and businesses in Aurora. By 1862, a frontier settlement developed about two miles from San Francis Ranch named Bishop Creek. Today, the town is known as Bishop, California.

With a successful beef business well under way, Bishop and his family visited the "Atlantic States." He returned to California, excited by new ideas.

The Bishops moved to San Jose and in 1867 started the San Jose–Santa Clara horse-car railroad. Within two years, he sold the company, the new owners substituting electricity for horses.

In 1870, Bishop was president of the San Jose Savings Bank and then became involved in the lumber business. In 1876, he purchased the Stayton mines and invested in a successful wine company. Despite all these activities, he still had time to obtain a high position in the Masons. But in 1893, Bishop met with an "unfortunate accident," as one local paper called it.

He had swallowed a pine-nut kernel, which became lodged in his appendix, causing a severe infection. Three local doctors and one summoned from San Francisco removed the nut and the appendix but had no way, at that period of time, to stop the spread of infection.

In the early morning hours of June 3, 1893, Samuel A. Bishop, frontiersman, gold prospector, Indian fighter, rancher, and businessman, died at the age of sixty-seven. He was buried at Oak Hill Cemetery. His widow, Francis Ella Young, died in 1923 at the age of eighty-three.

One of the pallbearers for Samuel Bishop was Lewis Amiss Spitzer, who, at age nineteen, had been the only member of Bishop's party to be wounded by a Mojave arrow at Beale's Crossing in 1859.

An interesting historical side note is the so-called Bishop Stone. In May 1973, historian Dennis Casebier and his brother Cecil were examining what they believed to be the remains of Bishop's fort at Pah-Ute Creek when they discovered a large black stone inscribed *S. A. Bishop*.

In 1859, Sam Bishop had kept his men busy constructing a small fortress to protect themselves while he waited for a reply to his request for military support from Major Hoffman. One of Bishop's men chiseled his leader's name into the stone either then or after Bishop and his twenty-man "army" departed with the camels to meet Ed Beale. The stone sat on the edge of the cliff, overlooking Pah-Ute Creek, for almost 120 years. Perhaps the stone was intended to mark the location of hidden supplies.

Casebier returned to Pah-Ute Creek almost a year later and was shocked to see that vandals had rolled the Bishop Stone off the cliff. It lay, broken, in the creek bed.

With the help of Casebier and a few friends and the Bureau of Land Management, U.S. Department of the Interior, the stone was lifted by helicopter and finally found a safe home. The Bishop Stone is now on public display at the Mojave River Valley Museum in Barstow, California.

Through his service with the army as a camel driver, Yiorgos Caralambo, better known as Greek George, met Major Henry Hancock, a wealthy Los Angeles landowner. Major Hancock hired him and let him build an adobe house in the northwest part of his ranch. The area is now known as West Hollywood.

In 1867, Greek George became a naturalized U.S. citizen and changed his name to George Allen. He had long before lost contact with his pal Hi Jolly, but continued to work on the ranch caring for the major's cattle and horses. George Allen, aka Greek George, died in 1913 at the age of eighty-four and is buried in Founders Memorial Park in Whittier, California.

Hi Jolly (aka Filippou Teodora, aka Hadji Ali) was alone with his camels at Fort Yuma at the end of the Civil War.

He first tried the freight business from the Colorado River to Tucson and mining camps in between. This was unsuccessful. In 1868, he landed a job as "pack master" for the army at Fort McDowell.

Over the next ten years, his jobs alternated between working for the army and prospecting. Then the army hired him as a full-time scout during the "Apache Wars." When these were over, he rounded up a few of his freed camels and tried the freight business again, this time between Yuma and Tucson.

In Tucson, sometime in early 1880, Hi Jolly fell in love and, using the name Philip Tedro, married Gertrude (also spelled Gertrudis) Serna, and fathered two daughters, Amelia and Herminia.

For a while they lived as a happy family, Hi Jolly finding steady work making saddles. But then the restless spirit that haunts most adventurers pushed him into prospecting for gold once more. He drifted into Tyson's Wells near modern-day Quartzsite, Arizona.

Tyson's Wells was a stagecoach stop in 1866 and still had a little pastureland and good water. It seemed like an ideal campground, so Hi Jolly purchased a few burros and a mule and began to prospect in the surrounding hills. He soon became famous in southern Arizona, not from the gold he found (which varied from very little to none) but for his storytelling.

Other prospectors, businessmen, politicians, writers, and cowboys visited his camp to enjoy fascinating tales of his days with Lieutenant Beale and the army camels, of fighting Mojaves with Sam Bishop, and tracking Apaches for the army.

By 1898, Hi Jolly's health had deteriorated. Some of his friends managed to get him medical treatment at hospitals in Tucson and Phoenix, but there was nothing that medicine could do to reverse the aging process.

With the help of influential friends, he appealed to the government for an army "pension" he should have been entitled to. In 1901, statements on his behalf were submitted to the U.S. Commission of Pensions by the territorial delegate to Congress, the governor of Arizona Territory, businessmen, and his last commanding officer from Fort McDowell, Colonel George A. Sanford, all praising Hi Jolly's service to his country.

The government, however, rejected his pension claim with the excuse that there was "no written contract on record" between the army and Hi Jolly.

On a windy day in mid-December 1902, Hi Jolly was sitting in a Quartzsite cantina talking with an old Texas friend when he overheard some local cowboys telling the bartenders they had seen a camel that morning along the Wickenburg trail.

In his book, *Texas Camel Tales,* author Chris Emmett tells what happened next.

Hi Jolly inquired of the cowboys the exact location of the camel they had seen. He listened carefully, then with his old tattered hat pulled down to protect his face from blowing sand, he started out the door. That was the last time he was seen alive.

The next day, December 16, 1902, the cowboys were riding along the Wickenburg trail searching for strays. They had ridden about two miles from town when they saw what appeared to be the body of a man, partially covered with sand, lying along the side of the trail next to a pile of earth.

The cowboys dismounted and walked slowly toward the figure. Then they realized that what they had taken to be a mound of dirt was a dead camel. Hi Jolly was lying next to his old friend, his arms wrapped around the camel's neck. They apparently had died together during the night.

Hadji Ali, or Philip Tedro, or Hi Jolly, as history would remember him, died at the age of seventy-three and was buried in a simple grave in the Quartzsite cemetery.

Ten years later, in 1912, Arizona was admitted into the Union as a state.

Hi Jolly's friends passed on and his grave was almost forgotten until 1934. Then the Arizona Highway Department—in fact, the entire state government, including the governor—supported the idea of a monument at Hi Jolly's graveside.

A pyramid-shaped tomb, constructed of natural stone, ten feet in height and crowned with a copper silhouette of a camel, was dedicated in 1935. Known as "the Last Camp of Hi Jolly," it is today one of the most visited historical monuments in the Southwest.

But there is more to the story. In April 1934, about the time Arizona decided to erect a monument to Hi Jolly, the *Oakland Tribune* ran an article with the headline "Topsy, the last American Camel That Trekked Across the Desert of Arizona and California, Died Today at Griffith Park Zoo."

The article went on to say that the army camel was believed to be eighty years old. She had outlived all her human friends from the camel experiment by decades.

At the base of Hi Jolly's pyramid tomb is a vault containing his last possessions (a few coins and letters) and the ashes of a friend, Topsy, the army camel.

The Other Characters

What became of the characters in this story? Some disappeared from recorded history and nothing could be learned of their lives after 1859. Others are listed here, somewhat in the order of their appearance. A few became famous nationally, most did not. Still, they each played a part in the growth of America.

Brevet Major William H. Emory of the Topographical Engineering Corps gave us the first accurate maps of the route from Fort Leavenworth to San Diego. Fought at the Battle of San Pasqual and later participated in the Mexican boundary survey. Famous for his accurate maps but also for descriptive notes on plants, animals, and Indians of the Southwest. Served with the Union during the Civil War and died in Washington, D.C., in 1887 at age seventy-six.

Jean Baptiste Charbonneau Son of Sacagawea, served as a guide for General Stephen Kearny during the Mexican War, was already a famous mountain man, but from 1848 through the Gold Rush days became a miner in California. In 1866, he left for Montana with plans to prospect but died on May 16, 1866 at age sixty-one of pneumonia. He is the only child depicted on a U.S. coin, as a baby on the back of his mother (Sacagawea dollar coin).

General Stephen W. Kearny After the Mexican War, he was promoted to major general and, for a while, remained in Mexico as governor of Mexico City. In 1848, he contracted yellow fever, returned to the United States and died in St. Louis in October 1848 at age fifty-four. He is credited for starting the army dragoons, later called cavalry.

James Ohio Pattie Mountain man and adventurer, he managed to escape the Mojave only to be arrested by Mexican officials. Released from jail in San Diego and sailed home to Augusta, Kentucky, where it is said he died of cholera in 1833. He was thirty-one.

Jedediah Strong Smith Adventurer and explorer credited for being the first white man to travel into what is now Nevada, Utah, and Oregon. Somewhere south of present-day Ulysses, Kansas, according to biographer Dale L. Morgan, Smith, riding alone, encountered fifteen to twenty Comanche. In the ensuing fight, Smith was wounded but managed to fire his rifle and kill the chief. Warriors then killed Smith with lances. He was thirty-two.

Major Richard Hanson Weightman Killed famous explorer F. X. Aubry with a Bowie knife; later became a colonel in the Confederate army and was killed at the Battle of Wilson Creek (Missouri) on August 10, 1861.

Colonel Philip St. George Cooke Famous for leading the Mormon Battalion during the Mexican War, he stayed with the Union during the Civil War but resigned his commission as general in 1862 at age fifty-three.

William Walker Famous American filibuster planned to return to Nicaragua and resume his revolution in South America but was captured by the British in Honduras while attempting to march overland into Nicaragua. Was executed by firing squad on September 12, 1860, at age thirty-six.

Josiah Harlan Prince of Ghor, unsuccessfully attempted to sell Afghanistan camels to the U.S. War Department. With a deep hatred for slavery, he raised his own regiment to fight for the Union. After the Civil War, he married and moved to San Francisco, worked as a doctor, and died of

TB in 1871 at age seventy-two. Rudyard Kipling's story "The Man Who Would Be King" is said to be based in part on Josiah Harlan's life.

Major George Hampton Crossman (or Crosman) Credited for being the first to promote the idea of using camels in the U.S. Army, remained with the Union during the Civil War and was promoted to colonel. He died in 1882.

John B. Floyd Resigned as secretary of war in December, 1860 and, like Jefferson Davis, joined the Confederate states. Promoted to major general and died in 1863 of "natural causes" at age fifty-seven.

Major Henry Constantine Wayne Organized the first camel-buying expedition and got the "experiment" under way only to be ordered back to Washington before his work was complete. Resigned his commission in 1861 and became a general in the Confederate army. But he refused to enter combat against his fellow West Point graduates. Served as inspector general until the end of the war and then entered the timber business. Died in Savannah, Georgia, at age seventy-two.

Gwinn Harris Heap Edward Beale's cousin, joined the camel program as a key member of the buying expedition. Volunteered for the Secret Service during the Civil War, later served as consul in Tunis, then Constantinople. Died in Turkey, March 6, 1887, at age seventy.

Lieutenant David D. Porter Redesigned the sailing ship *Supply* to carry camels from the Middle East to Texas. Remained with the U.S. Navy and promoted to admiral during the Civil War. Led a fleet of warships up the Mississippi and became part of the siege of Vicksburg. Died in 1891 at the age of seventy-seven. His wife is buried next to him at Arlington National Cemetery.

Captain Innes N. Palmer After Major Wayne's departure from Camp Verde, Texas, he was responsible for the army camels. Remained with the

Union during the Civil War and was promoted to lieutenant colonel for gallant action at the Battle of Bull Run. Later promoted to colonel. Served at an outpost in Wyoming, returned in 1879, and died of "natural causes" a few years later. Buried at Arlington National Cemetery.

Captain Lorenzo Sitgreaves Led the 1851 expedition into the western territories to explore the Zuni and Colorado rivers. Spent the Civil War years in Washington. Died in 1888 at age seventy-eight.

Colonel William Wing Loring ("Old One Wing") After meeting Ed Beale and riding a camel in 1857, he was ordered to the Mormon War front but arrived as the conflict was ending. Resigned his commission in 1861 and, in spite of having only one arm, rose to the rank of general in the Confederate army. After the war, the U.S. government sent him to Egypt to assist in training that country's new army. Returned to New York and died of pneumonia in 1886 at age sixty-eight.

Lieutenant Amiel Whipple First to complete the exploration of the thirty-fifth parallel to the Pacific Ocean and accepted as a friend by the Mojave. During the Civil War, he led the III Corps into combat at Chancellorsville, was wounded by a sniper, taken to Washington, and promoted to major general a few hours before he died at age forty-six.

Captain John W. T. Gardiner With the First Dragoons at Fort Tejon from 1855 to 1858. Wrote the wonderful description of Samuel Bishop (see Chapter 10). Promoted to major in 1861 and served as a recruiter in Maine. Promoted to lieutenant colonel in 1865 and died in Gardiner, Maine, in 1879 at age sixty-two.

Peachy Gilmer Breckenridge Placed in charge of the camels by Ed Beale during the first expedition. Peachy left his name on Inscription Rock at El Morro in 1857, 1858, and 1859 as he crossed the country during those years. Joined the Confederate army as a captain. Killed in action at Kennons Landing, Virginia, in 1864 at age twenty-six.

Olive Oatman After her release by the Mojave at Fort Yuma, she was reunited with her brother, Lorenzo, who, unknown to the attackers, had survived the massacre and never gave up looking for his sisters. In 1865, Olive married John B. Fairchild and they moved to Texas. She died in 1903 at age sixty-five. The town of Oatman, Arizona, was named in her memory.

Lieutenant Charles E. Thorburn After the first camel expedition with Ed Beale, Thorburn resigned his U.S. Navy commission to become a lieutenant in the Confederate navy; later promoted to colonel. Lived in New York after the war and died in October 1895.

May Humphreys Stacey With Beale's expedition as a nineteen-year-old. He joined the Union Army as a lieutenant at the outbreak of the Civil War. Wounded at Gaines Mill and carried the bullet in his side the rest of his life. Promoted to colonel and fought at the Second Battle of Bull Run and Fredericksburg. After the war, he, his wife, and children journeyed to Nevada then Arizona, where he was assigned to various outposts. They lived on the frontier for the next twelve years. Transferred to New York and died there of "bad health" in 1886 at the age of forty-nine.

L. J. Rose After surviving the Mojave massacre along the Colorado River in 1858, Rose eventually made it to the San Gabriel Valley with his family. He started Sunny Slope Winery and a ranch known as Rosemead, where he raised champion horses. Later became a state senator but lost most of his property through bad investments. In 1899, at age seventy-two, Rose committed suicide by taking sixty-seven morphine pills.

Ed Jones and his horse, Picayune Brother-in-law of L. J. Rose made it to California with his horse and lived on the Rose ranch still with the arrow point in his back. He died at age sixty-six.

Ed Akey Fought his way through the Mojave at Beale's Crossing and rescued his friend Lee Griffin. Akey returned to Keosauqua, Iowa, and died at age eighty-five.

Lee Griffin Recovered from his Mojave arrow wounds and became a "Confederate Bush Wacker" during the Civil War. Griffin was captured, escaped, and, armed with two Colt Navy Revolvers, refused to surrender when cornered by Union forces. "Shot to death while firing both pistols at Union soldiers." Died at age thirty-six.

Billy Stidger After the Mojave battle at Beale's Crossing, returned to Iowa and enlisted as a private in the 15th Iowa Infantry. Wounded at Shiloh and again at Corinth. Died peacefully at Red Oak, Iowa, in 1880 at age fifty-nine.

Sally Fox-Brown First to give the warning of an Indian attack at Beale's Crossing. Survived her arrow wound and walked back to Albuquerque, assisted by the Smith brothers' wagon train, members of which then carried Sally and her family safely to California. Sally lived on a farm with her uncle Josiah Allison at Vacaville, and in late 1859 or early 1860, they planted the nuts Sally found while in New Mexico. Sally became a schoolteacher in San Francisco while her black walnut "nut tree" continued to grow, becoming a landmark for early travelers. The tree lived longer than Sally, dying in 1952. Today, the Nut Tree Plaza is a sprawling complex of shops and restaurants on Nut Tree Road, near Interstate 80 (Vacaville, California).

Captain George Alonzo Johnson Owner of the *General Jesup* side-wheeler on the Colorado River at age twenty-four. Proved the army could reach Mormon territory by steamship. Continued in the business until retiring in 1877. Died in San Diego in 1903 at age sixty-eight.

Lieutenant Joseph Christmas Ives Crossed the country with Whipple along the thirty-fifth parallel. Ordered by the army to take the steamship *Ex-*

plorer up the Colorado to supply Fort Mojave. Traveled cross-country from the river, making extensive notes on the Grand Canyon. Later assisted the California Boundary Commission but resigned his commission and joined the Confederate army as a captain. Served as an aide to President Davis. Worked as a merchant in Detroit after the war and began to "drink heavily," dying of "alcohol indulgence" in 1870 at age thirty-nine. Remembered for his beautiful descriptions of the Colorado, Grand Canyon, the desert, and the Indians he encountered.

Jesse Chisholm Guided Beale on the second expedition and had a famous western trail named for him (Chisholm Trail). Died of food poisoning in Oklahoma in 1868 at the age of sixty.

Black Beaver ("The Delaware") and Little Ax Trail guides and hunters hired by Ed Beale for his 1858 and 1859 expeditions. Both died peacefully in Oklahoma in 1880.

Captain Henry Burton Learned Spanish from his wife, Maria Ruiz, and served as translator for Major Hoffman during the Colorado expedition. Burton was promoted to general during the Civil War and died of "Malarial Fever" in 1869. His widow, then age thirty-seven, had a literary career, publishing two novels in English and becoming the first Latina in the United States to do so. She died in 1895 at age sixty-three.

Major W. W. Mackall General Clark's adjutant in 1859. Resigned his commission and appointed colonel in the Confederate army. After the war, became a farmer in Virginia and died in 1891 at the age of seventy-five.

Thomas L. Kane Successfully negotiated a peace between Mormon leader Brigham Young and the U.S. government in 1859. At the start of the Civil War, Kane organized a Union regiment of mounded riflemen. Its members decorated their caps with the tail of a deer, thus becoming known as the "Pennsylvania Bucktails." Wounded twice, he was promoted to major general for bravery at Gettysburg. He died in 1883 of pneumonia at age sixty-one.

Colonel Edmund Alexander Replaced by Colonel A. S. Johnston during the Mormon War, went on to serve in the Union Army during the Civil War. Died in 1888 at age eighty-five.

Major William Hoffman Commanded the Colorado expedition against the Mojave, later promoted to lieutenant colonel. Sent to San Antonio, where, at the start of the Civil War, he was taken prisoner by the Confederates. Exchanged as a POW in 1862. Later promoted to "Commissary General of Prisons" with the rank of major general. Retired in 1870 with over forty years of military service.

Lewis Amiss Spitzer Wounded by a Mojave arrow at Beaver Lake while serving with Sam Bishop. Later worked in mining, married Elizabeth H. Easterday, and raised nine children. Became a farmer in Santa Clara County, California, and served as county assessor. Reunited with Sam Bishop. Died at his office of natural causes in 1912 at age seventy-two.

Captain Winfield Scott Hancock The first to send supply wagons over the Mojave Road to Fort Mojave, proving the route very useful. Promoted to major general during the Civil War, assigned the Cemetery Ridge position at the Battle of Gettysburg, and credited for stopping Pickett's Charge. Suffered a serious thigh wound during the battle. Lost a very close race for the office of president to James Garfield. Hancock died in 1886 at age sixty-two.

Major Lewis Addison Armistead As a captain, assigned to command the new Fort Mojave and finally defeated the Mojave nation. Resigned his commission and joined the Confederates. Promoted to general. Killed at Gettysburg leading his unit during Pickett's Charge on July 3, 1863. He was forty-six.

Captain Richard Brooke Garnett Assigned to Fort Mojave with Captain Armistead. Resigned his commission, becoming a general in the Confederate army, and killed during Pickett's Charge at Gettysburg in 1863. He was forty-six.

General Albert Sidney Johnston Led U.S. troops during the Mormon War. Resigned his commission and joined the Confederate army as a general. Wounded at Shiloh on April 6, 1862, and bled to death on the field of battle at age fifty-nine. The highest-ranking officer killed in the Civil War.

Alfred Cumming Sent to Utah to replace Brigham Young as governor. Served four years in that position then returned to Washington. Died at his home in Augusta, Georgia, in 1873 at age seventy-one.

Captain Stewart Van Vliet Sent ahead of Colonel Johnston's army to meet with Brigham Young. Spent most of the Civil War in New York as quartermaster, later promoted to major general, and moved to Washington, where he died in 1917 at the age of eighty-six. Buried at Arlington National Cemetery.

Brigham Young President and leader of the LDS (Mormons) from 1846 until his death in 1877 at age seventy-six. It is believed he died from a ruptured appendix infection or cholera. Successfully led the Mormons through difficult changes from 1859 to 1877.

Frederick E. Kerlin Brave clerk and friend of Ed Beale sent ahead of the road-building expedition with a message for Sam Bishop to bring supplies to the Colorado River. Left Tejon Ranch in April 1863 carrying money for either Beale or Bishop and was killed by a steam boiler explosion while aboard the SS *Ada Hancock* in San Pedro Bay, port of Los Angeles at 5 P.M. on April 27, 1863. Twenty-six others died in the explosion.

Captain Edward L. Hartz Indian fighter, leader of the first camel expedition into the Big Bend area of Texas; remained with the Union and was promoted to captain and based in Washington during the Civil War. Assigned to the 27th Infantry at Fort Reno, Dakota Territory, after the war and later Company I at Fort C. F. Smith in Montana. He was involved in the Hayfield Fight with Lakota Indians in March 1868. Like so many frontier officers, Captain Hartz developed a fondness for alcohol, and died of "unknown causes" on November 11, 1868, at Fort Sully, Dakota Territory at age thirty-six. He had lost contact with fellow officer Lieutenant Echols after the outbreak of the Civil War.

Lieutenant William H. Echols Rode with Lieutenant Hartz on the first camel expedition into Big Bend, Texas, and in 1860 led a second expedition with camels to the Rio Grande. Resigned his commission and entered the Confederate engineering corps and was soon promoted to major. Known as one of America's leading cartographers; his maps are sought today by collectors. After the war, he worked as a civil engineer and director of the Huntsville Nation Bank. Died at his home in Alabama in 1905 at age seventy-five.

Lieutenant James H. Holman He and his men provided the escort for Lieutenant Echols during the 1860 Big Bend expedition. In April 1861, Lieutenant Holman resigned his commission and enlisted in the infantry of the Confederate states. He was promoted to lieutenant colonel and survived the war.

Major James Henry Carleton After his investigation into the Mountain Meadows massacre, Carleton was appointed colonel, First Infantry, California Volunteers, at the start of the Civil War. Eventually promoted to the rank of general. Marched 2,350 men from California to El Paso and became military commander of the Department of New Mexico, securing the territory from Confederates. Ordered to subdue the Indians, especially the Navajo. Remained in Texas as commander of the Fourth Cavalry and died in San Antonio of pneumonia on January 7, 1873, at age fifty-nine.

Captain Reuben P. Campbell Second Dragoon officer assisted Major Carleton in the investigation at Mountain Meadows, which left him emotionally and physically ill for months. He requested "sick leave" to recover. Resigned his commission and joined the Confederate army. Campbell was killed at the Battle of Gaines Mill, Virginia, in 1862 at age forty-four.

Dr. J.R.N. Owen Frontier doctor and gold prospector known for the failed California Boundary Expedition. Returned to the South at the start of the Civil War and served at a Confederate hospital in Raleigh, North Carolina. After the war, Dr. Owen moved west again and set up a medical practice near Ely, Nevada. Later he moved to Eureka, Nevada, and practiced medicine there until age eighty-one. His health failed and he died in May 1900 at age eighty-two.

Sylvester Mowry Resigned his position as California boundary commissioner at the outbreak of the Civil War and returned to Arizona Territory only to be arrested by Union soldiers and charged with treason, accused of selling lead to the Confederates. He was placed in the Yuma jail but soon released for lack of evidence. Meanwhile, the Union seized his newspaper and mining operations. After the war, Congress awarded Mowry forty thousand dollars for his losses, but he had traveled to England, where he died in poverty of an "unknown illness" in 1871. He was thirty-nine.

Acknowledgments

The Gold Rush of 1849 in California perhaps started it all, the beginning of the *Wild West*. Emigrants rode or walked through the wilderness to reach the land of sunshine and riches. Soon settlers followed, creating homesteads, farms, and villages along the way, and from those, determined Americans began the legends, the exciting stories of heroes and villains, of events rewarding but often tragic.

Some stories were true, maybe slightly altered over the years like all human communication. Some were based on a shred of truth, while other stories were fiction.

The story of the camel in our Southwest became a victim of legends. The army experiment, in concept and execution, was bizarre for the 1850s when the majority of people had never seen even a picture of a camel.

And so, as I began to study what I thought to be a simple story, I discovered something far more complex, riddled with false legends, and the experiment itself influenced by external events, the Mormon War being only one.

I particularly wish to thank author and historian Dennis G. Casebier for his suggestions and valuable information. Mr. Casebier has studied the history of the Mojave Desert, especially the Mojave Road, for more than four decades and is the author of numerous books and articles on the subject.

Special thanks to Tim Grandi and Linda Heimerman for their computer and typing expertise, converting my almost illegible writings into a manuscript. And thanks to Master Sergeant Ed Hines, USMC (Retired) for his map designs.

Once again I owe a large debt of gratitude to my agent, Agnes Birnbaum of Bleecker Street Associates, New York. Her marketing skills, patience, guidance, and understanding kept my spirits high and the project on track.

And, of course, my appreciation goes to the wonderful people of Berkley Publishing Group, especially Natalee Rosenstein, senior executive editor and vice president, Michelle Vega, editor, and Robin Barletta, editorial assistant, for having faith in this story and doing what they do so well. They are a pleasure to work with.

With all my heart I thank my wife, Chieko, my best critic and cheering section, my companion in visiting museums and libraries, big and small. You explored with me unmarked desert trails in search of Beaver Lake in 115-degree heat and listened to my versions of the camel story until late hours. You have my gratitude and a hug. You deserve much more.

In researching and writing the complex history that is contained in this book, I depended on numerous works (most of which are listed in the bibliography section) but also on knowledge from individuals and organizations. The completion of of this book would have been impossible without their contributions. I express my sincere appreciation to the following:

Mojave Museum of History and Arts, Kingman, Arizona; Kay Ellerman, librarian.

Arizona Historical Society, Tucson, Arizona; Jill McCleary, librarian; Loraine Jones and Robert Orser.

Hampton Sides, author and historian.

Laws Railroad Museum

Bishop Museum and Historical Society, Bishop, California; Mary Arlen.

Huntington Library, San Marino, California; Jean-Robert Durbin, Alan Jutzi, Peter Blodgett, and Katrina Denman.

Dan Messersmith, Mojave County historian, Kingman, Arizona.

Main Street Murals, Barstow, California; Jane and Davis Brockhurst.

Robert "Bullet Bob" Smith, rail historian, Texas.

Willa Lucas, historian, Oatman, Arizona; Jackee Ramons, historian, Oatman, Arizona.

Herb Cartwright of the Abell-Hanger Foundation, Midland, Texas.

Archives of the Big Bend/Bryan Wildenthal Memorial Library, Saul
    Ross State University, Alpine, Texas; Jerri Garza, archivist.

The White House Historical Association (the Decatur House),
    Washington, D.C.; Hillary Crehan, right and reproduction
    coordinator; Ian Campbell.

Chamber of Commerce and Historical Society, Quartzsite, Arizona.

San Jose Historical Society.

Santa Clara Valley Historical Society.

Vacaville Museum, Vacaville, California.

Los Angeles County Museum of Natural History.

Seaver Center for Western History, Los Angeles.

U.S. Department of Transportation, Federal Highway
    Administration.

U.S. Archives, Washington, D.C.

Old Army-Navy Records Branch.

U.S. Department of the Interior, Bureau of Land Management.

Mojave Desert Heritage and Cultural Research Association.

South Dakota State Historical Society.

U.S. Naval Historical Center.

Madison County Public Library (Archives), Huntsville, Alabama.

Mojave River Valley Museum, Barstow, California; Robert Hillburn,
    president.

Wayne McMaster, historian, Sons of Confederate Veterans,
    Vicksburg, Mississippi.

Fort Tejon State Historical Park, Lebec, California; Sean Malis, state
    park interpreter.

Permian Basin Petroleum Museum, Library and Hall of Fame of
    Midland, Texas; Lislie Meyer, director of archives.

Rose Tompkins, author and historian.

Kern County Museum, Bakersfield, California.

Maggie Rapp, Alls Welcome Camels, Colorado.

Ashley Adair, reference, the Dolph Briscoe Center for American
    History, University of Texas, Austin.

Notes

Chapter 1

1. Colonel R. S. Bevier, *History of the First and Second Missouri Confederate Brigades, 1861–1865* (St. Louis: Bryan, Brand and Company, 1879).
2. Ibid.
3. Ibid.
4. J. W. Cook, *Confederate Veteran Magazine* 11:494 (1893).

Chapter 2

1. James B. Allen and Glen M. Leonard, *The Story of the Latter-Day Saints* (Salt Lake City: Deseret Book Company, 1976).
2. Ibid.
3. *Warsaw Signal* (Carthage, Ill.), June 9, 1844.
4. Allen and Leonard, *The Story of the Latter-Day Saints*.
5. Officers in the Mormon Battalion were issued sabers. Firearms were mostly Model 1816 smoothbore flintlock muskets and a few Harpers Ferry Model 1803 rifles plus bayonets, extra flints, and tools necessary to maintain the weapons.
6. N. B. Riketts, *The Mormon Battalion; U.S. Army of the West, 1846–1848* (Logan, Utah: State University Press, 1996).

Chapter 3

1. Douglas A. Watson and William Heath Davis, "60 Years in California: The History of San Diego," California Historical Society, 1929.
2. Some historians report that the Native American Indian who volunteered to accompany Lieutenant Beale and Kit Carson to San Diego was a "Delaware Scout." Others say he was a "Delaware Servant." The Delaware were Christian Indians forced from their homes in the New Jersey area. They first migrated to Pennsylvania and Ohio; then some moved (or were forced) farther west. Ed Beale had Delaware servants several years later, but it is doubtful he had one on ship.
   Lieutenant Emory, in his "notes," does not indicate who the "Servant" worked for. Author and historian Hampton Sides in his book *Blood and Thunder* (New York: Doubleday,

2006) states that the man was a Diegueno guide named Chemuclah. The home of the Dieguenos was the San Diego area.

3. William Hemsley Emory, lieutenant (brevet major), Corps of Topographical Engineers, "Notes of a Military Reconnaissance from Fort Leavenworth in Missouri to San Diego in California," 1849.
4. Watson and Davis, "60 Years in California."
5. For the best biography of Kit Carson, read Sides's *Blood and Thunder.*
6. Gerald Thompson, *Edward F. Beale and the American West* (Albuquerque: University of New Mexico Press, 1983).

Chapter 4

1. The creation of the Mojave nation as taught in their native history. Furnished by the Fort Mojave Indian tribe, Mojave National Preserve.
2. Ibid.
3. Lorraine M. Sherer, *Bitterness Road: The Mojave, 1604–1860, with Comments by Francis Stillman, a Mojave Elder,* completed and edited by Sylvia Brakke Vane and Lowell John Bean (Menlo Park, Calif.: Ballena Press, 1994).
4. Ibid.
5. Ibid.
6. Winfred Blevins, *Give Your Heart to the Hawks: A Tribute to the Mountain Men* (New York: Forge, 1973).
7. Ibid.
8. The creation of the Mojave nation.
9. Dale L. Morgan, *Jedediah Smith and the Opening of the American West* (Lincoln: Bison Books, 1964).
10. The creation of the Mojave nation.

Chapter 5

1. In 1850, the construction of a railroad began, crossing the Isthmus of Panama. It was completed in 1855. At that time Panama was Colombia territory. In 1869, the United States Central Pacific and Union Pacific completed the rail linking the United States east to west, resulting in the Panama railroad going broke. In 1879, it was sold to the French, who were attempting to dig the "Panama Canal."
2. A number of similar expeditions taking different routes west began about the same time, all concerned with finding the best direction for a rail line.
3. Captain Lorenzo Sitgreaves, "Report on an Expedition down the Zuni and Colorado Rivers in 1851," 1853, Library of Congress.
4. Ibid.
5. Lorraine M. Sherer, *Bitterness Road: The Mojave, 1604–1860, with Comments by Francis Stillman, a Mojave Elder,* completed and edited by Sylvia Brakke Vane and Lowell John Bean (Menlo Park, Calif.: Ballena Press, 1994). Some historians believe that Yuma, not Mojave, attacked Sitgreaves's expedition. Even Native Americans do not all agree on who

was responsible. Dr. S. W. Woodhouse, the medical doctor with Sitgreaves's expedition, reported in his journal "from Texas to San Diego in 1851" that they were attacked by Yuma, not Mojave, and that the man killed was a soldier named Jones. The journal reads: "Jones was brought in in a terrible condition, his head being clubbed all over and an arrow wound in the elbow. He was almost pulseless." The doctor goes on to report that Jones died the next day and "we buried him in the sand."

Chapter 6

1. H. S. Foote, *Pen Pictures from the Gardens of the World, or Santa Clara County, California* (Chicago; Lewis Publishing Company, 1888).
2. Ibid.
3. Ibid.
4. Annie R. Mitchell, "Major James D. Savage and the Tularenos," *California Historical Quarterly* 28:4 (December 1949).
5. John W. Bingaman, *Pathways: A Story of Trails and Men* (Lodi, Calif.: End-Kean Publishing, 1968). Apparently no one knows the exact number of Native American women James D. Savage married. Reports say between five and eight.
6. It is believed by some historians that the Indian raids along the Merced River were conducted by "outlaw" Piutes (who had crossed the mountains from the east), not the Yo-Semites.
7. Mitchell, "Major James D. Savage and the Tularenos."
8. *Mariposa Daily Herald*, September 4, 1852.
9. Samuel Dickson, *Tales of San Francisco* (Palo Alto: Stanford University Press, 1953).
10. *Mariposa Daily Herald*, September 4, 1852.
11. Ibid.

Chapter 7

1. Jackson survived two famous duels; ironically, one was with his friend Thomas Hart Benton. In 1813, Benton and Jackson had a "falling out," and on September 4, at Nashville's Talbot Tavern, the two, along with several men, ended up in a brawl. They fought one another with pistols, fists, knives, and cane swords. Jackson received an almost fatal wound. He recovered and with Benton at his side went on to lead American forces to victory over the invading British at the Battle of New Orleans.
2. The journal of Gwinn Harris Heap, along with numerous drawings, is titled *Central Route to the Pacific from the Valley of the Mississippi to California*, U.S. Government Printing Office, 1854.
3. James B. Allen and Glen M. Leonard, *The Story of the Latter-Day Saints* (Salt Lake City: Deseret Book Company, 1976).
4. "Mormon Murders Identified!," *New York Times*, May 1, 1857; reprint of a letter sent to the widow of Captain Gunnison, signed by Judge W. W. Drummond.
5. Ibid.
6. Ibid.

7. With the hard work of many Las Vegas historical groups, the "Old Mormon Fort" has been partially restored at its original site and is now a state historical park, listed with the U.S. National Register of Historic Places. The fort can be visited at the Las Vegas Boulevard and East Washington Street intersection.

Chapter 8

1. Details of the Whipple expedition are furnished in his "Report of Expeditions and Surveys to Ascertain the Most Practical and Economical Route for a Railroad from the Mississippi River to the Pacific Ocean." House Exec. Doc. 91, 33rd Congress, 2nd Session, 1869, Vol. III, Itinerary 121.
2. Lorraine M. Sherer, *Bitterness Road: The Mojave, 1604–1860, with Comments by Francis Stillman, a Mojave Elder,* completed and edited by Sylvia Brakke Vane and Lowell John Bean (Menlo Park, Calif.: Ballena Press, 1994). The trade route is now the Mojave Road.
3. Ibid.
4. Whipple's expedition report. Also, Lieutenant Joseph Christmas Ives's "Report upon the Colorado River," Section 68: "Mojave Valley—Establishment of Treaty": "When Lieutenant Whipple passed through the valley, one of the five Chiefs whose name was Cairook, and a sub-chief called Ireteba joined him as a guide and accompanied him through the country west of the Colorado as far as the Mormon Road (Spanish Trail) that leads to Los Angeles."
5. *St. Louis Republican,* June 17, 1848.
6. Ibid, February 1852.

Chapter 9

1. Catamount: slang at the time derived from "cat of the mountains," referring to the bobcat, the wildcat, but usually the larger, more dangerous mountain lion.
2. Mississippi Department of Archives and History, "The James Bowie Sand Bar Fight Historical Marker."
3. Evelyn Brogan, *James Bowie, Hero of the Alamo* (Berkley Heights, N.J.: Gaines Enslow Publishing, 1922).
4. Greg Walters, *Battle Blades: A Professional Guide to Combat Fighting Knives* (Boulder: Paladin Books, 1993).
5. R. L. Wilson, *Colt, An American Legend* (New York and London: Abbeville Publishers, 1985).

Chapter 10

1. Edward Beale resigned his commission as a lieutenant in the U.S. Navy in 1851, though, as was customary at the time, he retained the title. This often confused some historians, who had the opinion that the title "General" came from the U.S. Army. Beale earned the lieutenant rank in the navy and was given the honorary position of general in California

as a leader of a militia, not the U.S. Army. He never actually led military units in California any more than Kentucky colonels lead military units today. The positions, both in Kentucky and California, are honorary, bestowed by the governor of the state.

2. Judy Barras, *Their Places Shall Know Them No More* (Bakersfield: Sierra Printers, 1984).

3. It was legal for fifteen-year-olds to marry in California in the mid-1800s. Today, if the bride is under eighteen, a parent or legal guardian must appear with the couple. In Bishop's case, the bride's parents did join the ceremony.

4. California State Historical Society, Fort Tejon Archives.

Chapter 11

1. Ben Macintyre, *The Man Who Would Be King: The First American in Afghanistan* (New York: Farrar, Straus and Giroux, 2004). The title of "prince of Ghor" is in perpetuity. Harlan's heirs pass on the title from one generation to the next.

2. William Walker, *The War in Nicaragua* (New York: S. H. Goetzel, 1860).

3. On May 14, 1856, less then a month after Charles Webber's death, the first shipment of camels arrived at Texas.

4. George Hampton Crossman's name is often spelled "Crosman."

5. Jane Curtis and Will and Frank Lieberman, *The World of George Perkins Marsh* (Vermont: Countryman Press, 1982).

6. Walter L. Fleming, "Jefferson Davis' Camel Experiment," *Popular Science Monthly*, February 1909.

Chapter 12

1. "Southern Field and Fireside" (Augusta, Ga.), November 19, 1859.

2. George P. Marsh, *The Camel* (Boston; Gould and Lincoln Company, 1856).

3. *Boston Courier*, November 1, 1859.

Chapter 13

1. Gwinn Harris Heap, Lieutenant David D. Porter, and Lieutenant Edward Beale were family related.

2. The Camel File, "The Purchase of Camels for the Purpose of Military Transportation," Senate Exec. Doc. 62, 34th Congress, 3rd Session, 1857,Library of Congress. Also, Charles C. Carroll *The Government Importation of Camels*, Bureau of Animal Industries, 1930.

3. Ibid.

4. *Harper's Weekly* 6:308 (November 22, 1862).

Chapter 14

1. In the story of Hadji Ali, it should be noted that both Greeks and Arabs in the United States claim him as their own. They both have that right, for the man was born of a Greek

mother and an Arab father, raised as a Christian (Greek Orthodox), in early years, then converted to Islam before age twenty-five.

Much credit must go to the following: Professor Paul Nabhan, University of Arizona, for his excellent work "The Camel Whisperers," appearing originally in the 2008 issue of *Arab-American;* and to Steve Frangos of the *Greek-American Review* for his 2006 article "Philip Tedro: A Greek Legend of the American West."

Hadji Ali's name will change from Filippou Teodora to Philip Tedro to Hi Jolly.

2. Charles C. Carroll, *The Government Importation of Camels,* Bureau of Animal Industries, 1930.
3. Ibid.
4. Ibid.
5. Indianola is now an unincorporated fishing village, the city itself considered a ghost town. In 1875, a powerful hurricane almost destroyed the entire town of over five thousand people. Another hurricane struck in 1886, followed by a fire. The city essentially disappeared.
6. Steven Dean Paster, *Go West, Greek George,* 1984.
7. For more information on camel drivers, see Nabhan, "The Camel Whisperers." It is believed that a Syrian Arab, Plutorio Elias, came with the second shipment with plans to be a camel driver. Soon after his arrival in Texas, he separated from the army and traveled to Mexico, settling in the Sonora area, where he married a Yaqui woman.

    Legend has it that in 1877 Elias fathered Plutarco Elías Calles, who became president of Mexico in 1924.

    In spite of name similarities, some historians doubt the story. Calles's son-in-law claimed that the president was the son of a Mexican lady, Maria de Jesus Campuizano, and an Arab named Plutarco Elías, and was raised by a maternal uncle named Calles.

Chapter 15

1. "The Purchase of Camels for the Purpose of Military Transportation," Senate Exec. Doc. 62, 34th Congress, 3rd Session, 1857, Library of Congress. Also, "The Camel File," U.S. Archives.
2. Ibid.
3. Ibid.
4. Ibid.
5. Ibid.

Chapter 16

1. Norman F. Furness, *The Mormon Conflict: 1850–1859* (New Haven: Yale University Press, 1960).
2. *New York Times,* May 1, 1857.
3. *Fayetteville Observer,* July 2, 1857.
4. Did Beale's assignment to construct a wagon road and test camels in the process really catch him by surprise? Some historians believe it did. But we must consider the fact that

Beale's cousin Gwinn Harris Heap had been working in Washington's naval offices since his return from the Middle East camel-buying trip. Beale was truly the best qualified for the assignment, and no doubt Heap reminded key officials of that fact. He had time to get a letter off to his cousin in California. But Beale was a great actor when he wanted to be and was surely at his best in front of Floyd.

5. Daniel H. Ludlow, ed., *Church History: Selections from the Encyclopedia of Mormonism* (Salt Lake City: Deseret Book Company, 1992).

Chapter 17

1. Daniel H. Ludlow, ed., *Church History: Selections from the Encyclopedia of Mormonism* (Salt Lake City: Deseret Book Company 1992).
2. Dragoons vs. cavalry. By mid-1857, some army officers began to call their mounted riflemen cavalry instead of dragoons. The word *dragoons* officially left the U.S. military vocabulary in 1861 at the start of the Civil War.
3. May Humphreys Stacey, Journal; *Uncle Sam's Camels* (Cambridge: Harvard University Press, 1929).
4. Odie B. Faulk, *U.S. Camel Corps: An Army Experiment* (New York: Oxford University Press, 1976).
5. Some of the "Turks" Heap and Porter hired soon became disillusioned and elected to return home. By contract, the navy gave them free passage. The story of one "Turk" who disappeared from army employment is controversial. Elías Calles managed to cross the border into Sonora, Mexico, where he reportedly married Maria de Jesus Campuizano and, in 1877, fathered a son, Plutarco Elías. Maria died at a young age and Elías Calles became an alcoholic. Plutarco grew up in poverty but earned a number of political positions. He was elected president of Mexico in 1924. Some historians believe that Elías Calles was not a Turk, but was Lebanese. Whatever the truth, Calles never returned to Camp Verde and the U.S. Army.
6. Based on the U.S. Army investigative report on the Mountain Meadows Massacre by Major James Henry Carleton, Government Printing Office, 1859, published 1902, Library of Congress.

Chapter 18

1. Edward Beale, Journal, 1857, "Wagon Road. Fort Defiance to the Colorado River," House Ex. Doc. #124, Serial 959, 35th Congress, 1st Session, 1857–1858.
2. May Humphreys Stacey, Journal, 1857. Lewis B. Lesley, *Uncle Sam's Camels;* Stacey's Journal supplemented by the report of Edward Fitzgerald Beale (1857–1858) (Cambridge: Harvard University Press, 1929).
3. Beale's Journal.
4. "Buffalo Soldiers," a name applied to African American troops by Native American Indians, was not entirely based on skin or hair color. The troopers, many having served in "colored regiments" during the Civil War, were mostly large in stature and aggressive in combat, a point that gained them respect with the Indians. Often the troops wore coats

or robes made from buffalo skins in the winter that, combined with their hair and skin color, made the men, in the Indians' eyes, resemble buffalo.

5. Today, a fandango is usually thought of as a particular dance; to the early Spanish people of America's Southwest, it was a dance place (or "hall"), a ball or party involving music and dancing. American frontiersmen picked up the name and applied it to most any event that resembled a dance party.

Chapter 19

1. May Humphreys Stacey, Journal, August 11, 1857.
2. Edward Beale, Journal, August 12, 1857.
3. Ibid.
4. Brevet Major J. H. Carleton, "Special Report on the Mountain Meadows Massacre," May 25, 1859, U.S. Government Printing Office, 1902, Library of Congress.
5. Beale's Journal, August 20, 1857.
6. El Morro, New Mexico, became a national park in 1933, but was actually established as an important landmark by President Theodore Roosevelt in 1906 to protect Inscription Rock.
7. Major Carleton's Mountain Meadows report.

Chapter 20

1. Today, Fort Defiance is part of the Navajo nation, having been finally returned to the Native Americans after a long, bitter struggle. The fort was located near the border of Arizona and New Mexico, about twenty-five miles northwest of Gallup.
2. Edward Beale, Journal, August 25, 1857.
3. Beale's Journal, 1857.
4. Ibid.
5. Jacob's Well is located forty miles east of Holbrook just inside the Arizona border with New Mexico. The well was apparently filled in recent years, leaving only a slight depression in the earth. Traces of Beale's wagon road are still visible to the south. Jacob's Well is on Navajo nation land.

Chapter 21

1. Robert H. Biggs, "The Mountain Meadows Massacre: An Analytical Narrative Based on Participant Confessions," *Utah Historical Quarterly* 74 (2006). Also, Brevet Major James Henry Carleton, U.S. Army, *Special Report on the Mountain Meadows Massacre,* May 25, 1859, U.S. Archives.
2. Ibid.
3. Major Carleton's report.
4. Testimony at Lee's trial by Deputy Marshal Ragus. Also, Major Carleton's report. Also, a survivor of the massacre, Sara Francis Baker Mitchell, three years old at the time, and the story given by an Indian boy named Albert who accompanied Lee during the mas-

sacre and remarked at the scene, "It be a shame to kill the girls because they were so pretty. The older girl [Ruth Dunlap, age eighteen] dropped to her knees and pleaded with Lee to spare her. The younger girl [Rachael Dunlap, age sixteen] did not seem to understand what was about to happen. They both were brutally mistreated before being murdered." Testimony at Lee's trial by "Albert, a Pah-Ute Indian" (some say he was a member of the Snake tribe).

5. Major Carleton's report.

6. Ibid.

7. There are many papers and books published on the massacre and just as many theories regarding its cause. Major Carleton's report was the first to reach the public in mid-1859. Controversy continues regarding the involvement of Brigham Young (most believe he had no prior knowledge of the Iron Brigade's intentions), the amount of Indian participation, the sexual molestation of women, and the distribution of goods taken from the emigrants. In 1867, C. V. Waite published *An Authentic History of Brigham Young*, which touched on the Meadows Massacre.

Mormon scholar Juanita Brooks published a comprehensive book titled *The Mountain Meadows Massacre.*

See also Will Bagley, *Blood of the Prophets: Brigham Young and the Massacre at Mountain Meadows*, 2002, and Ronald W. Walker, Richard E. Turley, and Glen M. Leonard (2008).

In 2007, Christopher Cain released a film titled *September Dawn*, giving us a Hollywood version of the story.

8. Cosnino Indians were a tribe similar in some ways to the Pueblo. After many generations of wars, they fled their beautiful cave structures and retreated to the nearby San Francisco Mountains (west of present-day Winslow).

Chapter 22

1. May Stacey, Journal, 1857, compiled by Rose Ann Tompkins, Arizona Historical Society, Kingman, Ariz., 1989.

2. Ibid.

3. Old Ab's name appears in a number of Edward Beale's writings, but his life after 1859 remains a mystery. It is the author's opinion that Reading did not remain in California but returned east with Beale and, perhaps, worked at the Decatur House in Washington for the Beale family. To date, no records have been found in this regard. Old Ab was a "free" man. Beale had a deep hatred for slavery.

4. Stacey's Journal.

5. Edward Beale's Journal, 1857.

6. Ibid.

7. Ibid; the convoy at this point extended almost a mile.

8. Ibid.

9. Ibid.

Chapter 23

1. Edward Beale, Journal, September 27, 1857, House Exec. Doc. 124, 35th Congress, 1st Session, 1858, Library of Congress.
2. May Stacey, Journal, September 27, 1857.
3. Stacey's Journal, September 28, 1857.
4. Beale's Journal.
5. Ibid.
6. Ibid.
7. Stacey's Journal, October 11, 1857.
8. Ibid.
9. Beale's Journal.

Chapter 24

1. Beale's Crossing is no longer used for commercial traffic. Its appearance was altered somewhat by river currents after the completion of Hoover Dam in the 1930s. It is located on Mojave nation land near the original site of Fort Mojave.
2. Edward Beale, Journal, October 18, 1857.
3. May Stacey, Journal, October 21, 1857.
4. Ibid.
5. Beale's Journal, October 22, 1857. Letter to Secretary of War Floyd, Camel File, U.S. Archives.
6. Interview with Dennis Casebier in 2010. Dennis has devoted over forty years to exploring and writing about the Mojave Trail. A few of his many books on the subject are *Fort Pah-Ute California* (1974), *Tales of the Mojave Road* (2006; several series), and *The Mojave Road Guide* (1999).
7. Norman F. Furness, *The Utah Conflict, 1850–1859* (New Haven: Yale University Press, 1960).
8. Ibid.
9. Leonard J. Arrington, *Brigham Young—American Moses* (Chicago: University of Chicago Press, 1986).
10. Most of Colonel Johnston's wagons and supplies were furnished by civilian contractors. The U.S. government never paid for their losses; however, the owners were given a "mail delivery" contract. They soon began the successful but short-lived Pony Express.

Chapter 25

1. Edward Beale, Eastbound Journal, January 23, 1858, House Exec. Doc. 124, 35th Congress, 1st Session, 1859, Serial 959, Library of Congress.
2. Ibid.
3. Lieutenant Joseph Christmas Ives, "Report upon the Colorado River of the West Explored in 1857 and 1858," U.S. Army Corps of Topography Engineers, Library of Congress.
4. Ibid.

5. Ibid, Chapter 4, "Mojave Valley to the Mouth of Black Canyon."
6. Beale's eastbound journal, 1858.
7. Beale failed to mention the one soldier who vanished during the first westbound expedition. But he no doubt figured that the missing soldier was part of the *military escort* and not a member of the expedition.

Chapter 26

1. Camel Files, National Archives.
2. Kansas finally entered the Union as a "free state" on January 20, 1861.
3. J. W. Cheney, "The Story of an Emigrant Train," *Annals of Iowa* 12:2–3D Series (July 1915).
4. Ibid.
5. Ibid.

Chapter 27

1. J. W. Cheney, "The Story of an Emigrant Train," *Annals of Iowa* 12:2–3D Series (July 1915).
   Also, John Udell, Journal, Ashtabula Press, 1868; L. J. Rose Jr. of Sunny-Slope, Journal, Huntington Library, Calif., 1959, compiled by Rose Ann Tompkins, 1989.
2. Ibid. The "Missouri Preacher" carried a single-shot Kentucky-style percussion rifle. His name is not given in any of the journals.
3. Ibid.
4. Ibid.
5. From President James Buchanan's "Proclamation on the Rebellion In Utah," April 6, 1858.

Chapter 28

1. John Udell, Journal, August 13, 1858.
2. Leonard John Rose, Journal.
3. Ibid.
4. Ibid.

Chapter 29

1. Lorraine M. Sherer, *Bitterness Road: The Mojave, 1604–1860* (Menlo Park, Calif.: Ballena Press 1994). Mormon scouts arrived at Mojave villages, after a journey from their fort at Las Vegas and/or from the San Bernardino, California, area when they were ordered by Brigham Young to abandon their home and move to central Utah to prepare for war with the United States.
2. L. J. Rose, Journal, *1st Attempt—Westbound*, 1858.
3. Ibid.

4. Ibid; J. W. Cheney, "The Story of an Emigrant Train," *Annals of Iowa* 12:23D (August 15, 1915).
5. Ibid; no first name was given for "Young."
6. The story of Sally Fox and her survival is told in another chapter.
7. L. J. Rose's Journal, *1st Attempt—Westbound*, 1858; Cheney, *Annals of Iowa;* John Udell, Journal, *1st Attempt—Westbound*, 1858. Udell reports in his journal that the Bentner family consisted of the parents and five children. However, the Rose journal lists only three children and gives their exact ages. Most historians agree with the Rose report, since the Rose family was in charge of the entire wagon train and were present at the Beales Crossing battle. Udell was eighteen miles away and received the news from Rose a few days after the murders.

   Who committed the crimes? Every member of the Rose party blamed the Mojave. Some historians believe "other" tribes were involved, and the Mojave warriors only assisted them. This theory seems highly unlikely, as Mojave were seen crossing the river at that area and proceeding directly toward the first camp.

   The full names of the Bentners remain a mystery. Most reports simply call them the "Dutch family" or the "German family."
8. L. J. Rose's Journal, *1st Attempt—Westbound*, 1858.
9. Ibid.
10. Ibid.
11. Ibid.
12. Ibid. They knew certain rifle shots hit warriors but could only guess the number killed.
13. Ibid. Rose Jr. later describes his grandfather as "a wise old owl, however, a self-willed, headstrong individual with a volatile temper, a person hard to get along with . . . and very lame."

Chapter 30

1. J. W. Cheney, "The Story of an Emigrant Train," *Annals of Iowa* 12:2–3D Series (July 1915). Also, Leonard John Rose, Journal, *1st Attempt—Eastbound*, 1858, Huntington Library, Calif., compiled by Rose Ann Tompkins, 1989.
2. Ibid.
3. Ibid.
4. Ibid.

Chapter 31

1. Edward Beale and Dr. William P. Floyd maintained journals, describing key events during this expedition. When they arrived in Albuquerque, they were joined by John Udell, who also wrote a journal. Camels are not mentioned in any of these journals until April 18, 1859, when the party was joined by Sam Bishop, who brought camels with him. If Beale employed camels earlier in the expedition, there would have been some mention of them, especially by Udell, who had never seen a camel before April 18, 1859.
2. Hatch's Ranch is often confused with the town of Hatch, located in the southern part of

New Mexico. The ranch and nearby Fort Union are now historic parks. The town of Hatch is famous for its chili peppers.

3. Edward F. Beale, *Wagon Road Journal,* House Exec. Document 42, 36th Congress, 1st Session, Serial 1048, 1848. Also, the Journal of Dr. William P. Floyd, Huntington Library, Calif.; compiled by Rose Ann Tompkins, 1989.

4. "Survey of the Wagon Road from Fort Smith," *Chronicles of Oklahoma* 12:1 (March 1934).

5. Beale, *Wagon Road Journal.*

6. Lorraine M. Sherer, *Bitterness Road: The Mojave, 1604–1860,*(Menlo Park, Calif.: Ballena Press, 1994).

7. Ibid.

8. *Southern Vineyard* (Los Angeles), February 1859.

Chapter 32

1. National Archives Record group RG-94 (Records of the Adjutant General's Office) and RG-393 (Department of California Letters). Also, Casebier, Dennis G., *Fort Pah-Ute California* (Norco, Calif.: Tales of the Mojave Road Publishing, 1974). Historian and author Casebier has accumulated a vast collection of documents related to the Beale-Bishop expeditions and the "Colorado Expedition," 1859.

2. Bishop took twenty camels with him to the Colorado River. Sam Bishop's great-grandson Richard William Bishop printed a "Family History Research and Report" in November 1962, stating that "20 camels" were used. Foote, Horace S., *Pen-Pictures from the Garden of the World* (Chicago: Lewis Publishing, 1888): "Samuel A. Bishop used 20 camels to attack the Mojave." *San Jose Mercury News,* June 4, 1893, "On the Death of S. A. Bishop": "Bishop employed 20 camels at the Colorado River to fight the Indians."

3. A handwritten letter by Lewis Amiss Spitzer, transcribed by Nick Brisbois, 1992.

4. Letter from Charles H. Graves of the Central Mail Route Party to the Los Angeles *Southern Vineyard,* April 12, 1859.

5. Estimate of combined Mojave force on hand at Beale's Crossing in late March 1859 as "1,200-1,500": report by W. W. Hudson to Los Angeles *Southern Vineyard,* May 3, 1859; "600–700" estimated by Sam Bishop in a letter to Major Hoffman, March 24, 1859 (that is the number of warriors confronting Bishop; how many were in reserve and hidden in the underbrush is not known); "1,500–2,000" estimated by Lewis A. Spitzer in a letter to the *Inyo Register,* December 24, 1903. (Spitzer was wounded at the Colorado by a Mojave arrow.)

6. Bishop's letter from Merl Springs was published in the *Southern Vineyard* (Los Angeles), March 29, 1859.

Chapter 33

1. Los Angeles *Southern Vineyard,* March 29, 1859.

2. Historian and author Dennis G. Casebier has studied the Pah-Ute spring for years and written extensively on the subject. One of his best-known works is *Fort Pah-Ute California,* published in 1974 by Tales of the Mojave Road Publishing Company.

3. Beaver Lake was about one hundred miles south of modern-day Las Vegas, Nevada, less than an hour by car from the town of Searchlight, at the southern tip of the state. It sat in the flat (or river-bottom) lands almost two miles west of the Colorado River. Today, the lake is dry, surrounded by a tangle of brush, arrow weed, willow, and mesquite. In recent years, tamarisk trees have moved in.

4. Los Angeles *Southern Vineyard*. Reports in March through April 1859.

5. W. W. Hudson report to the *Southern Vineyard*, appearing in the May 3, 1859, edition.

6. Bishop's letter to Hoffman, March 24, 1859, U.S. Archives.

7. Lewis Spitzer and Sam Bishop became friends in the San Jose area and remained so until Bishop's death in 1893. Spitzer served as one of Bishop's pallbearers. In 1903, at age sixty-two, Spitzer submitted a letter to the *Inyo Register*. This report is confusing, full of historical errors, and it rambles from point to disjointed point. Yet there are some details about events during March and April 1859 that correspond with other reports. To add to this puzzle, in 1992 a handwritten letter believed to have been written by Spitzer was discovered by Nick Brisbois. This letter and the 1903 *Inyo Register* article are very similar. Both the 1903 and 1992 letters prove Spitzer was at Pah-Ute Spring with Bishop and wounded at Beaver Lake. Beyond those facts, other information is questionable.

8. W. W. Hudson, letter to the *Southern Vineyard* (Los Angeles), May 3, 1859. Scalping not only proved one had made a kill, but many western tribes believed a man's soul was in his hair, so to take his hair was to take his soul. This prospect terrified most members of western tribes and the act sometimes frightened warriors into withdrawing from a battle. And such was Bishop's intent: to frighten Mojave warriors into withdrawing, thus eliminating the necessity of killing so many. The idea was ineffective at Beaver Lake.

Chapter 34

1. Letter from Lewis A. Spitzer to the *Inyo Register*, December 24, 1903.

2. Los Angeles *Southern Vineyard*, March 29, 1859. A copy of Bishop's letter was apparently delivered to the paper by W. W. Hudson or Charles H. Graves when they returned to the city from Pah-Ute Creek.

3. Dennis G. Casebier, *Fort Pah-Ute California* (Norco, Calif.: Tales of the Mojave Road Publishing, 1974). Also, Casebier, *Tales of the Mojave Road: The Military*, same publisher, 2006.

4. Los Angeles *Southern Vineyard*. Letter from W. W. Hudson published May 3, 1859. Percussion revolvers of the late 1850s could accidentally discharge as a result of a number of causes, including faulty or worn percussion caps or the hammer unintentionally striking a cap, causing the gunpowder to ignite. Did Renfroe intentionally shoot himself in the leg to avoid the dangerous trip back to Pah-Ute Creek? Very unlikely. Renfroe knew that a leg wound in the desert, where medical facilities were in short supply, was serious. The wound might easily become infected, causing the loss of the leg, even death.

5. Major Hoffman's brevet rank for heroic action during the Mexican War was lieutenant colonel. Many called him by that rank. His "regimental" rank, however, was major. Letter on File, National Archives, RG-94. Records of the Adjutant General's Office and RG-393, Records of the U.S. Army, Department of California, 1859.

6. Casebier, *Fort Pah-Ute California*.
7. Los Angeles *Southern Vineyard*, Los Angeles, May 3, 1859.

Chapter 35

1. John Udell, Journal, March 6, 1859, Ashtabula Press, 1868.
2. Edward F. Beale, *Wagon Road, Fort Smith to the Colorado River*, House Exec. Doc. 42, 36th Congress, 1st Session, Serial 1048, 1860, Library of Congress.
3. Ibid. It is interesting that Beale often refers to the army camels as "my camels." They were, indeed, in his care, but he also developed a personal affection for the animals.
4. Ibid.

Chapter 36

1. Lieutenant Edward L. Hartz, letter to his father in Pottsville, Pa., October 1857. U.S. Archives.
2. Major D. H. Venton, quartermaster, and Major General T. S. Jesup, quartermaster general, letter to Quartermaster's Office, Headquarters, Department of Texas, San Antonio, Tex., April 26, 1859, Clifford B. Casey Collection, File 383. "The Camel Reports: Archives of the Big Bend," Bryan Wildenthal Memorial Library, Sul Ross State University, Alpine, Tex.
3. Lieutenant Hartz's diary (report) dated September 1859. Report of the Secretary of War, Senate Exec. Doc. 2, 36th Congress, 1st Session, Serial 1024, 1860, Library of Congress. Quotations in this chapter are from this report.
4. Ibid.

Chapter 38

1. Most of the information in this chapter is from Lieutenant William H. Echols's Report to the 36th Congress, 2nd session, Exec. Doc. 1, 1861, Library of Congress, pp. 37–50.
2. Ibid.
3. This event was captured by artist Tom Lovell in a painting titled *Camels in Texas*. On exhibit at the Permian Basin Petroleum Museum Library and Hall of Fame in Midland, Tex. Courtesy of the Abell-Hanger Foundation.
4. Echols's report.
5. Ibid, July 4, 1860.

Chapter 39

1. Douglas McMurtrie, *The Beginning of Printing in Arizona* (Chicago: Black Cat Press, 1937).
2. Ed Beale had no objection when Sylvester Mowry shipped Seid's skeleton to the Smithsonian Museum of Natural History in Washington, D.C., where it remains on display

today (as one of the U.S. Army camels). Beale believed this to be a lasting memorial to his friend.

3. "Report of J.R.N. Owen to the Honorable S. Mowry. The Official Reconnaissance Along the Proposed Boundary Line of the State of California," California State Land Commission, Sacramento, April 15, 1861.

4. So that the reader may follow the expedition's route, modern-day names and places are given.

5. Jean and Le Ray Johnson, "Doctor J.R.N. Owen, Frontier Doctor and Leader of Death Valley Camel Caravan," pamphlet.

6. *Sacramento Union*, June 25 and June 29, 1861. Readings taken on "custom barometer #1356, manufactured by James Green, New York."

7. Van Dorn used a formula for calculations created by mathematician and astronomer Pierre-Simon Laplace, based on his work in fluid mechanics during the mid-1700s.

Chapter 40

1. Camel File, Quartermaster Department, R.G. 92, National Archives. Also, publications of the Fort Tejon Historical Association.

2. Douglas McDonald, *Camels in Nevada* (Las Vegas: Las Vegas Publishing, 1983).

3. R. H. Williams, *With the Border Ruffians: Memories of the Far West, 1852–1868* (Lincoln: Bison Press, 1982).

Bibliography

Books

Allen, James B., and Leonard, Glen M., *The Story of the Latter-Day Saints*. Salt Lake City: Deseret Book Company, 1976.

Arrington, Dr. Leonard J., *Brigham Young—American Moses*. Chicago: University of Chicago Press, 1986.

Barras, Judy, *Their Places Shall Know Them No More*. Bakersfield: Sierra Printers, 1984.

Bevier, R. S., *History of the First and Second Missouri Confederate Brigades 1861–1865*. St. Louis: Bryan Brand and Company, 1879.

Bingaman, John W., *Pathways: A Story of Trails and Men*. Lodi, Calif.: End Kern Publishers, 1968.

Blevins, Winfred, *Give Your Heart to the Hawks: A Tribute to the Mountain Men*. New York: Forge, 1993.

Brogan, Evelyn, *James Bowie, Hero of the Alamo*. Berkley Heights, N.J.: Gaines Enslow Publishing, 1922.

Casebier, Dennis G., *Tales of the Mojave Road: The Military*. Tales of the Mojave Road. Goffs, California.

Casebier, Dennis G., *Mojave Road Guide 22*. Gaffs-Essex, Calif.: Tales of the Mojave Road Publishing, 1999.

Casebier, Dennis G., *Fort Pah-Ute California*. Gaffs-Essex, Calif.: Tales of the Mojave Road Publishing, 2006.

Curtis, Jane and Will, and Lieberman, Frank, *The World of George Perkins Marsh*. Vermont: Countryman Press, 1982.

Dickson, Samuel, *Tales of San Francisco*. Palo Alto: Stanford University Press, 1953.

Emmett, Chris, *Texas Camel Tales*. San Antonio: Naylor, 1932.

Faulk, Odie B., *The U.S. Camel Corps: An Army Experiment*. New York: Oxford University Press, 1976.

Fleek, Sherman L., *The Church and the Utah War, 1857–1858*. Provo, Utah: Brigham Young University Press, 2006.

Foote, Horace S., *Pen Pictures from the Gardens of the World*. Chicago: Lewis Publishing, 1888.

Fowler, Harlan D., *Camels in California*. Palo Alto: Stanford University Press, 1950.

Furness, Norman F., *The Mormon Conflict, 1850–1859*. New Haven: Yale University Press, 1960.

Ludlow, Daniel H., *Church History: Selections from the Encyclopedia of Mormonism*. Salt Lake City: Deseret Book Company, 1992.

Macintyre, Ben, *The Man Who Would Be King: The First American in Afghanistan*. New York: Farrar, Straus and Giroux, 2004.

Marsh, George P., *The Camel*. Boston: Gould and Lincoln Press, 1856.

McDonald, Douglas, *Camels in Nevada*. Las Vegas: Las Vegas Nevada Publishing, 1983.

McMurtie, Douglas, *The Beginning of Printing in Arizona*. Chicago: Black Cat Press, 1937.

Morgan, Dale L., *Jedediah Smith and the Opening of the American West*. Lincoln: Bison Books, 1964.

Riketts, N. M., *The Mormon Battalion; U.S. Army of the West, 1846–1848*. Logan, Utah: State University Press, 1996.

Sherer, Lorraine M., *Bitterness Road: The Mojave, 1604–1860*, completed and edited by Sylvia Brakke Vane and Lowell John Bean. Menlo Park, Calif.: Ballena Press, 1994.

Sides, Hampton, *Blood and Thunder*. New York: Doubleday, 2006.

Stacey, May Humphreys, *Uncle Sam's Camels—His Journal, 1857–1858*, edited by Lewis B Lesley. Cambridge: Harvard University Press, 1929.

Thompson, Gerald, *Edward F. Beale and the American West*. Albuquerque: University of New Mexico Press, 1983.

Walker, William, *The War in Nicaragua*. New York: S. H. Goetzel, 1860.

Walters, Greg, *Battle Blades: A Professional Guide to Combat Fighting Knives*. Boulder: Paladin Books, 1993.

Williams, R. H., *With the Border Ruffians: Memories of the Far West, 1852–1868*. Lincoln: Bison Press, 1982.

Printed News Media Accounts

Boston Courier, Nov. 1, 1859.

Boston Courier, November 1, 1859.

Carroll, Charles C., "The Government Importation of Camels." Bureau of Animal Industries, 1930.

Cheney, J. W., "Story of an Emigrant Train." *Annals of Iowa* 12:23D (July 15, 1915).

Cook, J. W., "Old Douglas," *Confederate Veteran Magazine* 1: 4941 (1893).

Fleming, Walter L., "Jefferson Davis' Camel Experiment," *Popular Science Monthly*, February 1909.

Malis, Sean, and Stammerjohan, "The Camel Experiment in California." Fort Tejon Historical Association, Fort Tejon State Park, California, 2002.

Mariposa Daily Herald, September 4, 1852.

Mercury News, June 4, 1893, "On the Death of S. A. Bishop."

Mitchell, Annie R., "Major James D. Savage and the Tularenos," *California Historical Quarterly* 28:4 (December 1949).

Nabhan, Gary Paul, "Camel Whisperers." *Journal of Arizona History* 49:2 (Summer 2009).

New York Times, May 1, 1857, "Mormon Murders Identified."

Rose, Leonard John, Diary, "1st Attempt Westbound 1858." Written Oct. 28, 1858. Published, Nov. 29, 1859. Missouri Republican. Huntington Library.

Sacramento Union, June 25 and June 29, 1861, "Valley of Death."

Southern Field and Fireside, Augusta, Ga., November 19, 1859.

Southern Field and Fireside (Augusta, Ga.), November 19, 1859.

Southern Vineyard (Los Angeles), February 1859; also March 29, April 12, May 3, 1859.

St. Louis Republican, June 17, 1848.

Udell, John, Diary: *1st Attempt—Westbound, 1858.* Ashtabula,Ohio: Ashtabula Press, 1868.

Warsaw Signal (Carthage, Ill.), June 9, 1844.

Pamphlets, Military and Government Reports

Beale, Edward D., Journal: *Wagon Road Fort Defiance to the Colorado River.* House Exec. Doc. 124, 35th Congress, 1st Session, Serial 959, 1857–1858, Library of Congress.

Briggs, Robert H., "The Mountain Meadows Massacre: An Analytical Narrative Based on Participant Confessions." *Utah Historical Quarterly* 74 (2006).

Carleton, Major J. H., "Special Report on the Mountain Meadows Massacre," May 25, 1859. U.S. Government Printing Office, 1902, Library of Congress.

Echols, Lieutenant William. "Report of Topographical Survey of Big Bend." House Exec. Doc. 1, 36th Congress, 2nd Session,1861, Library of Congress.

Emory, Lieutenant William Hemsley, Corps of Topographical Engineers, "Notes of a Military Reconnaissance from Fort Leavenworth to San Diego" (1849). Library of Congress, 1854.

Hartz, Lieutenant Edward L., "Report on the Use of Camels in the Big Bend, Texas." House Exec. Doc. 2, 36th Congress, 1st Session, 1861, Library of Congress.

Heap, Gwinn Harris, Journal: *Central Route to the Pacific from the Valley of the Mississippi to California.* U.S. Government Printing Office, Library of Congress, 1854.

Ives, Lieutenant Joseph Christmas, "Report upon the Colorado River of the West, 1857–1858."

Johnson, LeRoy and Jean, *Dr. J.R.N. Owen, Frontier Doctor and Leader of Death Valley's Camel Caravan.* Death Valley, Calif.: Death Valley 49'ers, Inc. 1996.

Paster, Steven Dean, *Go West, Greek George,* 1984.

"Report of Dr. J.R.N. Owen to Honorable S. Mowry of 'A Reconnaissance Along the Proposed Boundary Line of the State of California,'" California Land Commission, Sacramento, Calif., April 15, 1861.

Sitgreaves, Captain Lorenzo, "Report of an Expedition down the Zuni and Colorado Rivers." Senate Exec. Doc., 33rd Congress, 1st Session, 1854, Library of Congress.

Watson, Douglas A., and Davis, William Heath, "60 years in California: The History of San Diego." California Historical Society, 1929.

Wayne, Major Henry C., "The Purchase of Camels for the Purpose of Military Transportation." Senate Doc. 62, 34th Congress, 3rd Session, 1857, Library of Congress.

Whipple, Lieutenant Amiel Weeks, "Report of Explorations and Surveys to Ascertain the Most Practical and Economic Route for a Rail Road from the Mississippi River to the Pacific Ocean 1853–1854." House Exec. Doc. 91, 33rd Congress, 2nd Session, 1856, Library of Congress.